ELAINE STRITCH

THE END OF PRETEND

JOHN BELL

PAGE PUBLISHING, INC.
New York, NY

First originally published by Page Publishing, Inc. 2019

Cover Photo Credit: Katie Osgood

ISBN 978-1-64462-716-7 (Paperback)
ISBN 978-1-64462-717-4 (Digital)

Printed in the United States of America

Because nothing comes from nothing—nothing ever could—I dedicate this book to my wife, Andra, and the memory of my mother, Nancy, both of whom are proof that I must have, at some point, done something good.

AUTHOR'S NOTE

This book chronicles my six-year rather odd and wonderful relationship with Elaine Stritch. Beginning with an interview I conducted with her at the Carlyle Hotel in New York in 2009 and spanning her remaining years in New York and her final fourteen months in Birmingham, Michigan, I fell into a habit of visiting with her every couple of months.

When I first broached with her the idea of writing a book, she told me she wouldn't sit and answer a list of predetermined questions. If I wanted to get to know her and gather her stories, I'd have to visit frequently enough to get them from her in normal conversation. So that's what I did.

Throughout her life, Elaine Stritch collected people. Sometimes she collected them because she knew they could be useful to her. Sometimes she collected them because she was genuinely attracted to some quality or lack of pretension they possessed. The more I got to know Elaine, the more convinced I became that she collected people because she was on a quest in search of real relationships—something beyond the adoration of an audience.

For whatever reason Elaine collected me, I feel fortunate to have been invited in. This book is a work of nonfiction based upon conversations, notes, recordings, interviews, and transcripts. I have rendered my encounters with Elaine as I remember them. I have verified facts where possible or, in some cases, left Elaine's recollection untouched, accurate or not.

In every instance, I have tried to be as honest as possible because the one thing I learned from Elaine was that she had no patience for anything but the honest-to-God truth. But because the truth can hurt, I have omitted or changed the names of some of the people in Elaine's life—her caretakers, family members, and friends—in deference to their privacy or dignity.

PRELUDE

Wearing a T-shirt emblazoned with "Detroit Athletic Club" and a pair of white short shorts, sneakers, and a white walking hat, Elaine Stritch and I made our way carefully down the elegant steps of her new home in the Dakota, the upscale condominium complex in Birmingham, Michigan. After nearly sixty years in New York City, this brassiest of Broadway babies had come home. Well, not exactly. Having grown up in one of the nicer neighborhoods in the now less-than-appealing city of Detroit, Elaine Stritch, a theatrical legend accustomed to residential life in the toniest hotels in London and New York's Upper East Side, chose a posh suburb dotted with furriers, small boutiques, and trendy establishments of haute cuisine. And why not? Working steadily on stage and in film and television, she had earned a respectable fortune, certainly enough to maintain her standard of lifestyle and befitting her cult celebrity status. Walking with her cane, this eighty-seven-year-old woman, who had just survived a year in New York in which she had fallen on Madison Avenue, lying bleeding in the curb with a cut on her eye as taxicabs roared by and later broke her hip and had a hip replacement, was surprisingly fleet of foot. A survivor? Yes, just relocated and about to face perhaps the most challenging year of her life.

As we crossed the street, which cut up a slightly sloped hill, and passed the playground in the adjacent park, which had drawn her to this location, Elaine paused momentarily to watch a handful of young kids playing. With an intense gaze, she watched and listened to their laughter and giggles, screams and screeches—the running and halting of little people. Transfixed, I wondered, *What does she see? Her childhood? What does she hear? The music of play? How shocking, culturally, must it be to shift from the landscape of skyscrapers and the constant blur of traffic to the carefree world of a jungle gym and merry-go-round?*

After a moment absorbing, she shook her head as we headed away from the playground and down the dirt path toward the wood's edge. Then out of the blue, a male jogger with a Doberman on a leash jutted from the woods, causing this feisty firebrand who gives the impression that she is afraid of nothing to lurch back whooping and whimpering and cowering behind me to let them pass.

Shaken, we walked ahead in escape, moving on to the shadows of the woods. And again Elaine seemed transfixed and amazed by how quickly her surroundings had been transformed. Even the sounds of the laughing children were muffled by the thick canopy of leaves, a curtain of green soundlessness. When she saw the creek, a broad body of water with a strong current, she delighted in the surprise of the discovery, stopping, staring in wonder at having found herself, just steps from her new home, in such natural and untamed surroundings.

I had pulled a camp stool out of my car hoping she might want to find a cool, shaded spot to sit. She did, and we sat quietly listening to the wind whispering through the trees and watching a flock of ducks coming and going in flight.

I made a few attempts to strike up a conversation while we sat, but Elaine didn't seem to want to talk. We sat in silence, Elaine leaning back good and strong so the Michigan sun could get all the way down to her, giving herself time to become preoccupied by her surroundings: the little bridge over the creek, some large fallen trees, the little minnows and crawfish scampering on the creek bottom. I sat below her on the bank and took off my sandals and dangled my feet in the water.

"Is it cold?" she said.

"Very," I replied. "Would you like to dangle? I can help get you situated."

"No, I'll come back in a month when it warms up," she said. Eventually, some of the ducks worked their way over hoping for some food. They frightened Elaine. "Oh, get away, you twits," she said, causing them to paddle off quickly in response to the unwelcome in her gruff voice.

After a moment, she said, "My father used to live on a farm with a creek on it that he used to fish in as a kid. It had a swimming hole, and he would go skinny-dipping."

"Here in Detroit?" I asked.

"No, he grew up in Springfield, Ohio. That's where he met my mother."

Now it was I who was stopped and transfixed.

"Elaine, I grew up in Springfield, Ohio, on a farm that had a creek running through it," I said, excited and amazed.

"Oh, come on," she challenged.

"No, Elaine, I did."

"My father met my mother in the elevator of the Shawnee Hotel," she said.

"Well, the Shawnee Hotel is about two blocks from St. Raphael's Church, my parish church. I know the area well," I said.

"Oh my god, Daddy was an altar boy at St. Raphael's," she said.

I couldn't speak. Elaine however, not one for sentimentality or coincidence, didn't seem in any way fazed or impressed by this shared history. But as we settled back into the creek and trees, an overwhelming sense of serendipity came over me. Springfield, Ohio? I simply couldn't believe that Elaine's parents met in my hometown, that Elaine's story started where my story started. I sat there thinking about this odd friendship she and I had developed over the past five years, feeling as if I had just stumbled upon some mystical kernel of kismet.

CHAPTER 1

I first saw Elaine Stritch up close and personal in 2007. At the age of eighty-two, she was still startling audiences with her one-woman show *Elaine Stritch at Liberty…at the Carlyle*. My wife, Andra, and I arrived early for a performance, anticipating a large crowd. We walked into the storied Café Carlyle with its white-linen-adorned tablecloths and glowing lamps. It had a clubby feel, with some banquettes in the back and flamboyant midcentury murals by Marcel Vertes lining the walls. In front of the grand piano on the tiny stage was a single stool on a performance space about six feet wide and three feet deep. *That'll never contain Stritch*, I thought.

We sat in the front row, hoping to make a connection with this extraordinary performer. We'd come to see the woman called "audacious, original, brilliant, and uncompromising" (by Sandra Bernhard in *Vanity Fair*) and who, according to *The New York Times*, "set an unmatched standard for solo shows." She was the actress known for the famous scene in the 1970 documentary by D. A. Pennebaker (on the making of the cast album for *Company*) in which she has a near-exhaustion-fueled meltdown trying to perform her signature song "The Ladies Who Lunch" after midnight. "The force of personality on display in her volcanic frustration is the stuff that Broadway legends are made of," said *Variety.com*.

A university theater director and researcher of the work of Stephen Sondheim, I had watched Elaine Stritch, the quintessential Sondheim performer, from afar for many years: first on the *Dick*

Cavett Show when I was fifteen (when Sondheim was still off in my future), then onstage in *Show Boat* in Toronto in 1993, and in the *Company* documentary. Now I wanted to see Stritch up close and personal, to get a clear view of this wildly talented and completely uncommon creature.

The café had filled quickly as curtain time approached. The musicians worked their way onto the stage, and Ms. Stritch's musical director, Rob Bowman, was giving last-minute notes to the band as the standing-room crowd buzzed with anticipation. The clock hit eight, and the lights dimmed. Bowman welcomed the audience and introduced his star. From the shadows of a door at the back of the room came Elaine Stritch, wearing her signature black tights, black shoes, and a white silk-collared shirt. It was a simple, but no doubt carefully chosen, ensemble for the style icon, known for eschewing pants.

Everyone craned and crooked to get a glimpse as they became aware that Stritch had appeared. The audience broke into unbridled applause as she wound her way through the tables and made her way to the stage. Once in the spotlight, she milked the assembled crowd of its rapture, and then broke into a very restrained, ironic, and funny rendition of "There's No Business Like Show Business." From that moment forward, for the next ninety minutes, we were hers and she was ours.

As she went into the second song of the night, I realized something. Every line and every gesture was being delivered to the same spot—the eighth, ninth, and tenth rows, behind us. She was playing to the middle of the room! Most of it was going over our heads. I'd been hoping for the kind of connection you can make with a performer in a smaller setting, a connection I thought she desperately needed from an audience. I saw a vulnerability in her, and I sensed that performing in front of other people was how she made friends, how she felt love, and found the courage to speak truth. But having paid extra money to be a Very Important Person, and sitting within reaching distance of her knees, I was unable to connect and give what I wanted to offer.

No matter, though. I still soaked up the timing, the finesse, the glamour. The original Broadway version had been a raging success, earning her a Tony Award and eventually garnering an HBO recording. Here on her home turf, she perfectly accustomed herself to the environs.

To watch her work was revelatory. Her deadpan delivery of Noel Coward's "Why Do the Wrong People Travel?" a saucy social commentary from *Sail Away*, elevated lyrics of the mundane (canasta, doughnuts, and ketchup) into an arsenal of social disgust that was both funny and frightening. The quiet self-effacement she brought to her interpretation of Richard Rodgers' "Something Good" from *The Sound of Music* transformed a simple and somewhat lackadaisical song into a paean of self-discovery that spoke volumes about Elaine's need to be in front of an audience.

The piquant stories Elaine used to connect the songs were offered as confession with every moment earned and then decorated with that daring, tilted smile. I was struck by her incredible control onstage. Control of anticipation and its fulfillment. Control of the comic setup and its punch line. It was a display of the mastery that one only acquires after a lifetime of experience. And when she finished, the room roared in ovation.

Afterward, she walked to the back of the room and, standing in the doorway through which she had entered, greeted those clamoring for photos and autographs. I stood in line and slowly moved to the front. When I got there, I didn't introduce myself; something told me small talk would be tedious to her. Given that there was so much give-and-take during the performance, that she had cultivated such a raw and urgent relationship with the audience, it seemed natural to reach out to take her hand as I told her how much I enjoyed the show. But before I could utter a word, she withdrew her hand and said, "Don't touch me. I can't afford to get sick—I've got to play this show for the next two weeks, and I need the money." People around us laughed. I didn't. Bemused, I withdrew my hand but caught her eye and held it for a moment or two. She paused and considered me with surprise. "I've had my eye on you, Ms. Stritch," I blurted. "Oh yeah?" she said, her eyes still fixed on me. "Yes, and I really appreciated your work tonight," I added. "Thank you, darling, thank you," she said as she backed away.

I didn't think I would ever have another face-to-face encounter with her, but I was glad I'd come. Seeing her perform up close made me even more curious about this mercurial woman.

* * *

Several months after I'd seen her performance at the Carlyle, and a bit preoccupied by that moment of what I'd come to think of as "knowing eye contact" between us, I finally decided to attempt to make direct contact with Elaine. My impression after having seen the show, and experiencing her in line afterward, was that she was an earthy personality, and perhaps not as inaccessible as one might think.

I am a lifelong theater person. When I was nine years old, I decided I wanted to try out for a local community theater production of *Fiddler on the Roof.* To get ready, I memorized one verse of "If I Were a Rich Man." The day came, and I showed up on time for the audition. When called forward to sing it, I began in earnest, but quickly forgot the words and froze. Horrified, I ran crying from the room and rode my bike all the way home, never telling a soul about the experience. Not an auspicious start!

To this day I don't really know what drew me to acting. My mother was a marvelous singer who could miraculously sing a fourth line of harmony against her Peter, Paul and Mary LPs. And I'd taken piano lessons as a boy. But no one else in my family had shown a particular proclivity for stage performance. It amazes me to this day that acting—and theater in general—became a significant part of my life.

In high school, I fell under the tutelage of an inspiring and influential theater director and his wife, a former professional ballet dancer who choreographed the shows. Their names were Mr. and Mrs. Heman. I look back now and know that something in me recognized that the Hemans knew what they were talking about. Rehearsal was taken seriously. Our development was carefully guided. A sense of standard was set.

Because I could pick up movement quickly and was fairly coordinated, I was always cast in roles that required dancing. I was around Mrs. Heman a lot and discovered quickly that she was a taskmaster. Her rehearsals were grueling; if you weren't putting in the time to practice and improve your dancing, she let you know it. Many of us were reduced to tears.

Some feared Mrs. Heman, but I was drawn to her. *Why was she so demanding? Why did this mean so much to her?* On opening night, on behalf of the cast, I gave her a bouquet of roses. This tough, demanding lady who showed virtually no vulnerability in rehearsal became emotional. Fighting back a tear, she thanked the company and then tore one rose from the bunch. "Whenever I received roses when I danced a ballet," she said, "I always give one rose to my leading man." With that, she handed me the rose and hugged me. I was speechless—embarrassed in front of my classmates, but thrust into an adult reality. The truth was, her ballet career had ended abruptly because of an injury, and what I came to realize was that she was demanding because she was living part of her unfulfilled life through us. From her I learned that this was serious business—an art, craft, and lots of hard work.

After high school, I went on to major in music and musical theater in college and then embarked on a career in musical theater as a performer, director, and conductor. I share this information because I believe it speaks to the attraction I eventually had for Elaine.

* * *

The first number I ever saw Elaine Stritch perform was the title song for the Stephen Sondheim musical *Anyone Can Whistle* on the *Dick Cavett Show.* I was in high school. My theater buddy, Sarah, told me that her mother's cousin, a famous Broadway actress, would be appearing as a guest.

During the hour-long program, Dick Cavett interviewed Elaine Stritch on a variety of topics ranging from her appearance in the London production of the Sondheim's musical *Company* to her working relationship with Noel Coward. Cavett asked her about her courtship with Ben Gazarra and her recent marriage to actor John Bay. He also delved into her diagnosis of diabetes and whether she felt she was an alcoholic. After the interview, this caustic, brassy woman sang Sondheim's "Anyone Can Whistle." *"Not much of a voice,"* I thought, but her commitment to the interpretation of the song's lyric was astonishing. I remember finding her compelling. I was glad I stayed up to watch. Since she was related to my best friend, I may have secretly hoped I might one day get a chance to meet her. Little did I know.

* * *

Over the years I had developed a deep appreciation for Sondheim. Throughout college, every research paper I wrote focused on some aspect of a Sondheim show. I found his writing compelling. His songs conveyed a sense of some personal earthquake brewing just beneath the surface. In this way, Stritch, who embodied these qualities onstage and off, was perfectly suited to his writing. I eventually became a regular contributor and guest editor for *The Sondheim Review*, a quarterly journal devoted to his body of work. And a good deal of my research began to include Elaine Stritch.

The first job I had as a professional director was directing a production of Stephen Sondheim and George Furth's *Company,* the musical that sealed Stritch's place in musical theater history. In preparing to direct that production, I researched her performance in the role of Joanne, including the song "The Ladies Who Lunch." A pirated video recording captured the immense restraint and yet abundant specificity with which she imbued each word. I was captivated by her firm and intense gaze, drawing the audience in with her unflinching disdain for the vacuous ladies who lunch. She was daring and unpredictable, demanding the audience to keep up. Even on the poor quality tape, I was 100 percent engaged, unable to look away from her fascinating performance. I wondered from where this power originated. *How does an actor develop this ability—this commanding presence?* Stritch was a complex performer who demonstrated the power of great acting in a way that I had not experienced from any other actor.

Flash forward to 2008 when I realized I could connect with Elaine through *The Sondheim Review*. *"That's my in,"* I said to myself. *"She obviously loves his work, and I can use my association with the journal to see if I can land an interview."* I sent a letter to her at the Carlyle. I have a basic humility about me that is a point of pride, so on one hand, I adopted the position that I likely wouldn't hear back from her. But in all truthfulness, I thought there was a good chance she would respond. I sensed her ego was big enough to be flattered by the request, and that moment of eye contact with her after *At Liberty* suggested that her unpredictability might extend beyond the stage. I was delighted to receive a phone message from her.

> John Bell, this is Elaine Stritch. I just received your lovely note about my performance, and I have to tell you that it is one of the nicest and most detailed letters I have ever received. I'm just overwhelmed by your comments. And of course I would love to meet you. I have no idea what *The Sondheim Review* is. I've never heard of it, and I'm thinking it can't be anything very important if I've never heard of it, but that doesn't matter. I'd love to meet you. We can meet here at the Carlyle. So call me back. And listen, call me late at night. Like after the news. The eleven o'clock news. I hope that's not too late for you. Call me after the news is over, like when the sports come on, then you can have me. Okay, honey bun? Okay.

That evening, I called her at approximately 11:25 p.m., and she could not have been more charming. She asked about *The Sondheim Review* and what I wanted to interview her about. I told her I wanted to discuss her work with Sondheim, and she said, "Oh my god, what can I tell you? He scares the shit out of me. But let's not get into that now, there's just too much." We set a date to meet in the hotel's lower gallery.

When the day arrived, I drove in to New York City and walked through the warm spring air from the Port Authority lot over to the Upper East Side. The Carlyle lobby was quiet except for the occasional movements of hotel staff refreshing the ubiquitous flower arrangements. I found the desk manager and asked for Ms. Stritch. He dialed her number and handed me the phone receiver. Elaine picked up. I greeted her and told her I was waiting in the lobby. She scolded me for being thirty minutes early (which, most assuredly, I was not).

At her direction, I waited patiently in the hotel's gallery, and about an hour later, Elaine appeared at the top of the stairs that led to the hotel's gallery. Dressed in black tights, black sweater vest over a cream blouse and a black and taupe scarf, she was carrying a paper shopping bag from Harrods. I later found out that it contained a cup of coffee, a bottle of orange juice, and a plastic baggy with prunes, among other items such as a clutch of credit cards and her diabetes kit.

She approached the stairs with hesitation. Along with a nearby waiter, I dispatched myself to help her down the stairs. "Wait a minute!" she snapped at us, angry that we were trying to relieve her of her bag and offer an arm to help her down the stairs.

"You," she said, referring to the waiter, "let go of my arm so I can grab the fucking railing.

"You, are you John?" she said to me. "Grab this bag. No, not like that. Hold it by the bottom."

Somewhat starstruck and not quite understanding that there were liquids inside the bag, I didn't register what she was telling me.

"Put one hand on the bottom so everything doesn't spill all over the fucking place," she barked. The more I fumbled, the testier she got.

Ah, first impressions. For a moment I wondered if she'd abruptly dismiss me before we even got to the interview.

With everyone's eyes on her and seemingly enjoying the attention, Elaine finally made her way down the stairs. After we got settled into our cozy table and ordered soup and sandwiches, I set up my tape recorder, placing it in the center of the table.

"Let's move it over here by me," she said. "No one really cares about what you have to say, do they?"

"Certainly not," I conceded as I slid the recorder over toward her.

Elaine at our first meeting in the Lower
Gallery of the Carlyle Hotel
Credit: Lizzie Sullivan

So I started by thanking her for agreeing to be interviewed for *The Sondheim Review*. I wanted to get that on tape so there would be no question in the future that our conversation was on the record and her comments were intended for publication.

"What's your thing with Steve?" she asked.

"Oh, I'm just a big fan of his work. I contribute regularly to *The Sondheim Review,* so I'm real happy that you've agreed to this interview."

"Sure you are. But what do you like about his work?"

"That's a big question," I said. "I guess I'm drawn to the deeper layers of meaning in his songs, they tend to have a lot of sting in them."

"That's an understatement, but it's a good way to put it," she said.

For the next forty-five minutes or so, I proceeded to ask her my long list of questions. In response, she was everything I had expected and hoped.

She was honest when I asked about whether her drinking had ever interfered with getting roles. "The fact that I was a drinker would get in the way of playing the lead in a show. 'Too much responsibility,' they'd say, which is bullshit."

In response to a question about the meaning of Joanne's line in *Company* "I just did someone a favor." Stritch was quick and blunt in correction. "I think it's 'I just did someone a *big* favor.'"

She was impatient with my assertion that she seemed to have reverence for Sondheim. "I wouldn't choose the word *reverence*," she said. When I offered *appreciation* as a substitute, she raised her voice and said, "I'll say what it is. Don't you put words in my mouth."

I was surprised when she described Sondheim as humble. "Most real artists are humble. I once heard someone define *humility*—and humility is a very, very hard thing to define—as high self-esteem. I think Steve has humility. He's very gentle and caring, and he has humility. That's the highest compliment I can pay him."

As we were conversing, I considered referencing my attendance at her *At Liberty* cabaret. Before I could talk myself out of it, I told her I'd seen the show a few months back and met her briefly afterward.

"Yeah, I remember," she said.

Not really believing, I asked, "You remember?"

"Yeah, you were seated down front with a knockout blonde," she replied, again giving me that sustained gaze.

She was right, and I was shocked. Feeling like we were breaking the ice a bit and having finished my list of questions, I told Elaine that I worked in the performing arts department at a university about an hour from Manhattan in eastern Pennsylvania and asked if she'd ever visited colleges and presented master classes. She said she had and that she enjoyed doing them. So I extended an invitation for her to come to my university. I thought for sure she'd deflect, but to my surprise, she accepted. At this point, I was beginning to feel like we were connecting and that we might even stay in touch.

"But we'll have to wait until later in the summer, because this Carlyle gig has absolutely exhausted me."

I suspected that by putting off any further conversation about a visit for such a long period of time, I'd lose the connection—she'd forget about me or change her mind and simply fail to follow through. Like a fool I said, "Well, I'm afraid that in three or four months, you'll have forgotten about me. I wouldn't expect you to remember this conversation."

With that, Elaine Stritch slammed her hand, palm down, on the table, rattling the tea china and drawing surprised and alarmed looks from everyone in the gallery.

"What the fuck do you mean I won't remember you? Why wouldn't I remember you? Don't you think you're memorable? I remember people if they're interesting enough. I told you to call me in a few months because I find you interesting. Don't insult me."

Frozen in embarrassment, I apologized and told her I would, indeed, be in touch.

"Good. Just don't play games with me and you and I will get along just fine," she said. As she packed up her Harrods bag and her pint of soup to go, I grabbed for the check and said, "Please let me, I'm happy to pick up the tab," to which she replied, "You bet you are." I helped her up the gallery stairs to the elevator, thanked her for the interview, and said my goodbye.

"Oh, did you bring a bio and a head shot that I can use with the interview?" I asked.

"Well, what do you think, darling?" she said as she pulled a one-page typewritten bio and two shots of her in brown fur out of her bag with a flourish.

I told her the photos were fantastic.

"Yeah, I think so too," she agreed.

Her bio had a few things crossed out in ink and new text written in the margins.

"Would you mind retyping that for me and making copies?" she asked.

"Sure."

"And can you make copies of the photos, about ten of each, and send them to me here at the Carlyle?" she asked. Again I said okay, happy to have an assigned duty that would require follow-up.

"Oh, that would be marvelous, darling, and don't forget to call about the master class."

I assured her I wouldn't and made my exit. Walking back to Port Authority, I was a bundle of mixed emotions. I felt excited that I was going to have the chance to meet with Stritch again. But I also had this uneasy feeling that she was perhaps too volatile and unsettling for me, that I might find myself in situations with her that would challenge my natural order. I feared that I'd be walking on eggshells around her, always taking care to navigate the minefield. I remained fascinated by her, though—this complicated individual, this icon. In my heart of hearts, I relished the idea of being able to spend more time with her.

* * *

As promised, approximately five months later, I called Elaine to follow up on the prospect of her coming to campus for a master class. She did, indeed, remember me and called me by name.

"I'm delighted to hear from you, John Bell, but where have you been? What took you so long? I thought you forgot about me."

For the next three months, about once a week or so, I'd set my alarm for 11:00 p.m. to wake up and call Elaine. I'm an early riser, which means an early bedtime, so I was always asleep long before eleven. After the alarm went off, I'd gear up to be coherent—maybe even intelligent—before calling her at 11:25, as requested. We'd chat briefly for about five or ten minutes, always with me trying to nail her down for a date for the campus visit. Each time we penciled in a possible date, she'd qualify it by saying that she shied away from making a commitment so far out in case she might get work. "Everything depends on whether or not I get a job, darling." I'd hang up and then spend the next two hours tossing and turning, trying to go back to sleep, uncertain as to whether was I making any headway.

Finally, we set a date for her to visit campus the coming January.

* * *

With Elaine, details are like shifting sands based upon her recollection and mood. After having agreed on the date and discussing the shape of her visit, I was very careful to send her a written confirmation so that she had something to reference. I also wanted to meet with her again as the date drew near to confirm the itinerary face-to-face. We made a date for early January 2009 at 6:30 p.m.

The day of our date came, and I was instructed to arrive at the Carlyle and stop at the front desk to find out which suite Elaine was in. She and her musical director Rob Bowman were rehearsing for an upcoming trip to Palm Springs to perform with Michael Feinstein.

The desk clerk sent me to the appointed room, and hearing Elaine working on music, I waited outside, not wanting to interrupt. After about twenty minutes, she remembered our appointment and came to the door to see if I'd arrived.

"Well, there you are. What the hell are you doing out *here?*" she said.

"Well, I heard you singing and didn't want to interrupt."

"Look, darling, if we're going to get along, you're going to have to drop this ultrapolite crap. That's not how I roll, dig? Now come on in and meet Rob. Rob, this is John, we're going to his college next week, I told you about him."

Rob and I exchanged greetings.

"We need to work on a few more numbers. Would you mind being my audience?"

Thrilled by the prospect, but trying to play it cool, I said, "I'd be happy to."

Elaine and Rob went back to rehearsing. When she'd forget a line, they'd engage in their usual game of "Don't tell me or I'll kill you" / "Tell me, goddammit! Or you're fired."

"This is why I wanted you to come in and watch," Elaine said. "It makes me *audience nervous*, and audience nervous is what tells me where I know my shit and where I don't."

After finishing her solos, she wanted to work on the two duets she'd do with Michael Feinstein. Rob was playing the piano and singing Michael's parts. At one point, he blew a line himself while they were working on Sondheim's "Old Friends" from *Merrily We Roll Along*, and Elaine, knowing I was a big Sondheim fan, looked at me and said, "You know this, don't you?"

Terrified but delighted by the invitation to take part in this unexpected, intimate exchange, I said, "I do."

She handed me the music and said, "Sing Michael's part."

We dove in, and I held my own, feeling comfortable enough to throw my lyrics at her with a little flirtation. She seemed pleased that I was willing to do more than just sing notes and words. The more playful she got with me, the freer I became with her. I was having fun. Here I was sitting in a posh suite at the Carlyle, against a blazing, nighttime skyline of New York City, performing a duet with Elaine dressed in her usual black tights and white shirt. More thrilling than the anticipation of her upcoming visit to campus, it was a night I knew I would never forget.

After the rehearsal session, Elaine, Rob, and I went down to the gallery for soup and sandwiches. Rob ordered water, Elaine ordered coffee, and I had an iced tea. We talked about the upcoming visit. I told her I wanted it to be an actor's-studio-like forum wherein the students could ask her questions about her career and her craft, and then she could sing a handful of songs as she wished.

She didn't like that structure.

She talked with Rob about trying to work in smallish segments from her *At Liberty* show; she seemed to want to default to something rehearsed.

In retrospect, it's clear to me now that she wanted to be in total control. A Q&A forum would be far too unpredictable for someone like Elaine who demands full control on stage. I knew the event was a singular opportunity, the chance to have a legendary actress come and perform for my students, so I was willing to give her some leeway on this point. We compromised. She agreed that she and Rob would come out and do a bit of dialogue and song, à la a cabaret set, and then we'd allow a little time for Q&A at the end. Afterward, she'd finish with one last song.

With the details set, I told her I'd send the limousine for her at 11:00 a.m. so she could arrive by 2:00 p.m. The "Afternoon with Elaine Stritch," as we agreed to bill it, would begin at three. She'd finish by four thirty, we'd go for a quick bite after the appearance, and then the car would take her and Rob back to the Carlyle. The plan was set. I was glad I'd come in to the city to confirm and reinforce it. I wished Elaine and Rob well in Palm Springs and said goodbye.

* * *

Two days before the day of her visit to campus, I called Elaine at the Carlyle. She answered and said, "What a day this is!"

Thinking she was referring to the clear skies and mild temperatures, I said something weather related and went on to ask how her trip to Palm Springs had gone. She cut me off in short order and said, "Wait a goddamn minute. I think we can both take just a moment to reflect upon history as the country inaugurates its first black president."

I stammered as I realized I was hearing news coverage of President Barack Obama's inauguration playing in the background on her television. I told her she was absolutely right and that the event had slipped my mind, as I was at work in my office.

I asked her how she felt about our new president. "I aaaaaaaaaaaadore him," she said. "I think he's sharp, stylish, and very smart—kind of cute too. Don't you?"

"Sure," I said.

After a few more remarks about the country finally loosening up enough to elect a black commander-in-chief, we moved on to the original intention of my call, which was to confirm the details of her visit, including the pickup time for the car.

She reported that the plan was still fine. The 11:00 a.m. pickup time was fine. But the $6,000 fee ($5,000 for Elaine and $1,000 for

Rob) was not enough to cover her hair and makeup girl Bella Botier. Elaine would have to have her hair and makeup done before the car arrived, and that would cost another $500. And that was cheap, she said, given that Bella would have to come over early in the morning to get Elaine ready.

What that really meant was that Elaine, who was accustomed to not even taking calls at the Carlyle until after two, would have to get up early for this gig and wanted it understood that this was going to be an enormous effort for her.

I agreed to the new terms. I was too far in at this point to quibble, especially on the day the country inaugurated its first African American president.

"Elaine," I said.

"Yes, darling."

"There's one more thing that I think I need to mention."

"What's that?"

"Well, your visit is a big thing for us. I'll have some VIPs in the audience, including the university president, who happens to be a Catholic priest."

"Oh, so you want me to watch my mouth, is that it?"

Bracing myself and glad that she filled in the blank without me having to say it directly, I said, "I hope you understand."

"John, I know how to play to an audience. Relax, it'll be fine."

"I know it will. I just felt I needed to put it out there," I said, relieved. "Goodbye, Elaine. I'll see you next week."

"You bet, darling, it's going to be divine."

* * *

The morning of the event, I received a phone call from the dispatcher at the car service. She reported the driver was at the Carlyle at 11:00 a.m. as directed but was told Ms. Stritch wasn't ready. Apparently Elaine wanted the driver to go to another part of town to pick up Rob Bowman, and would I approve? I did, and hoped that by the time the driver ran this unexpected errand, Elaine would be ready to go and would still arrive on campus on time so the itinerary would hold. It did.

At approximately 1:45 p.m., the limo pulled up in front of the performing arts center, and out Elaine came in a cream felt hat, black Marc Jacobs glasses, cream trousers, and a gorgeous brown-and-cream-colored fur coat.

"You look like a million bucks!" I said as I gave her a hug.

Elaine arriving at DeSales University for
"An Afternoon with Elaine Stritch."
Credit: John Bell

Elaine seemed relaxed and, as I would soon come to observe about her, very eager to enter into a new situation. She enjoyed new experiences and was always taking in much more about the setting and circumstances than one might suspect.

I greeted Rob and brought them both into my office to settle in after the drive.

Elaine had brought a couple of bottles of nonalcoholic beer with her and wanted me to keep them cold in a refrigerator so she could enjoy them on the car ride back to NYC. She noticed the candy bars and Fig Newton cookies we had provided for her hospitality basket and pocketed them all, saying, "Those will be great tonight back in my room at the Carlyle."

I escorted Elaine and Rob to the theater where they would perform so they could run through their numbers. On the way, she stopped and looked at the hallway full of archive photographs from theater productions produced by the college over the years. She was quite taken with them—both the quantity and the quality of the photos. "People here take their work very seriously, I can tell that," she said. "This place is special, I can just feel it. I really can."

On the way to the theater, we stopped in the main stage where a production of *Death of a Salesman* was being loaded in. She wanted to take a moment and watch the students at work. They, of course, knowing she was due, were all agog that Elaine Stritch was in the building and watching as they climbed ladders and painted scenery.

When we got to her stage, she let out a few whoops and hollers to test the acoustics and decide whether she wanted to wear a body microphone. Noting the depth of the three-quarter thrust, she thought it might be best if she did. She and Rob started a little bit of "Fifty Percent," and satisfied, she was ready to leave the space so the gathering crowd of students could be allowed in.

Back in my office, one of our sound design students, a young woman named Beth, was assigned to help Elaine get into the body mic. I stepped outside the office and let the two work it out. From the hallway, I could hear Elaine snapping at Beth about getting the cords up under her bra, in her hair, and under her hat the way she wanted it. Afraid I'd thrown a fawn to a wolf, I knocked on the door and asked if everyone was all right. Elaine shouted back, "We're fine, this young woman is divine." A few minutes later the door opened, and Beth, looking a bit shell-shocked, reported that Elaine was set.

As the three o'clock hour drew near, Rob, Elaine, and I headed backstage to start the show.

I went out and introduced Rob and then Elaine. The crowd roared as she entered and gave her a standing ovation. At this, she looked delighted. She was aware that this audience knew enough about her to know what they were in for. I'd prepped my students well, showing them old clips and providing them with a thorough introduction to who she was and the highlights of her career. It was interesting to see the level of comfort that emerged from Elaine as she realized the next couple of hours would be filled with the type of attention and love that I came to realize she craved.

And she didn't disappoint.

She began with a tender and fragile version of Leslie Bricusse's "I Think I Like You" from the film version of *Dr. Doolittle*. Next she performed Irving Berlin's "There's No Business Like Show Business" from *Annie Get Your Gun* in the rewritten form that was created for *At Liberty*.

She followed that with a potent rendition of Bill Goldenberg and Alan and Marilyn Bergman's "Fifty Percent" from the musical *Ballroom*. The song focuses on having lost a love. As she sang, it was clear that she was tapping into having lost her husband John Bay.

When she finished, she said, "I didn't do that song as well as I can, but I did it well enough. It was scary to do it today because I haven't done it in a long time, and it touches on some real pain for me. But I'm glad I sang it for you."

Then she fielded questions from the students and shared stories from her career. She told the students how important truth was on stage.

"And listen, a lot of people think I'm difficult because I'm direct and I tell it like it is, but the thing you have to know is that telling the truth off stage builds courage for truthfulness on stage—and vice versa. And an audience will always, *always* know when you're not telling the truth."

She told the students their job as actors was to make sure every audience member understood, both in delivery and interpretation, every word they spoke or sang.

She didn't sugarcoat her life in the theater. She said that there are good times and bum times, that the highs would be exhilarating and joyful and that the business could be nasty, tricky, and full of deception.

Acting was like taking a train and singing was like flying, she said, and that even with a voice like hers—admitting that she was "no Renee Fleming"—everyone can fly when they sing.

She talked about the physical high she feels when she gets a good review and shared one of her favorites: Noel Coward wrote, "Elaine Stritch is the most dangerous actress on Broadway…"

"I couldn't have liked it more."

When asked why she decided to go into theater, she quoted her friend Margie Stevens, an actress she met on tour with *Company*, who said, "To get out of the audience."

She went on to say she had to get out of Detroit because "the ceilings weren't high enough." She said she enjoyed the escapism of acting, noting that "it takes a load off your shoulder to be somebody else for a few hours. Pretend is a very good place."

Speaking of her failed attempt at developing a relationship with Marlon Brando, she hinted about the integrity of her virginity by stating, "Not even Marlon Brando could break through all that Catholicism."

She commented on the notion of celebrity and awards shows, claiming, "There are more happy people in summer stock than there ever will be at the Golden Globes, the Emmys, or the Oscars put together."

When asked where she got her talent, she replied, "From my parents, who were both very, very funny. As my father would often say, 'Elaine, you didn't lick it off the ground.'"

She talked about having to play the game with directors. "Even the ones who don't really know what they're doing require that you obey them, especially early on. And it's often best not to ask too many questions. I love the quote from Noel Coward who, when an actor would ask what should motivate his cross from the couch to the bar, would say, 'To pick up your paycheck.'"

After about an hour and a half, she announced she was ready to wrap but asked if there were any requests for one last song. Multiple people shouted, "The Ladies Who Lunch" to which she replied, "Oh my god, you people know how to rob a train, don't you!"

She then turned to Rob and said, "Not too slow." And there, before an audience of two hundred rapt young actors, Elaine Stritch sang her signature song, holding nothing back and ending the visit with yet another roaring ovation. Over the course of the hour and a half, she'd clearly charmed her way into the hearts of everyone in attendance. Even the Irish president was charmed, recognizing Elaine as someone who'd treated his students to a once-in-a-lifetime treat.

Elaine signing autographs after
"An Afternoon with Elaine Stritch"
Credit: John Bell

After spending thirty minutes in the theater lobby signing auto-graphs, Elaine, Rob, my wife Andra, and I headed out to the car.

As I pulled out of the parking lot, I took my eyes off the road for a moment and turned back to Elaine in the back seat. She screamed in terror, "Get your eyes back on the road, my god, what are you trying to do, kill us all?" I quickly turned back around and caught Andra's eye. She looked terrified too. Not of my driving, but of Elaine. I would come to learn that Elaine had a very serious fear of riding in any mechanical object—car, airplane, or elevator—being driven by someone else. With my eyes forward and hands firmly on the steering wheel, the four of us headed out to a nearby restaurant for a quick bite before the limo driver returned to take Rob and Elaine back to New York. When I thanked Elaine and said goodbye, she said, "Call me if you get back to New York." I gave her one of those knowing looks and told her I would.

As Elaine drove away, I was flying high. Her visit could not have gone better. She was every bit the theater legend to which I wanted to treat my students, and she also related to them on a very basic yet inspiring level. Her insight, honesty, and wit challenged our beliefs about acting, shaking us out of complacency.

I also felt that in having executed this event together, she and I had bonded. For the first time, I began to sense the delicate nascence of a relationship.

CHAPTER 2

Marion Elaine Stritch was born in Detroit, Michigan, on February 2, 1925. She was the youngest of three daughters born to George Joseph Stritch and Mildred Jobe Stritch.

Elaine's mother, Mildred (Midge) Jobe, was born in 1893 in Springfield, Ohio, in the southwestern part of the state between Dayton and Columbus. Nicknamed the Champion City, Springfield was a solid Midwestern town building a strong foundation in the manufacturing of automobile, truck, and farm machinery. Midge's father, Louis S. Jobe, was a prominent business owner whose family traced back to English, Welsh, and French roots. He ran one of Springfield's most popular taverns, Papa Jobe's, selling drinks and spirits to Springfield's growing industrial middle class. A smart and successful businessman, he eventually changed the name of his establishment to the Senate Sample Room, catering to the more affluent town fathers who came to enjoy "high-class liquors and cigars." Louis's success catapulted the family into a higher echelon of local prominence, and he and his wife, Sally, were able to provide a very comfortable living to Mildred and her brother Howard. As a teenager, Midge worked as a cashier at the local YWCA and as a saleslady at Kelly's Arcade.

Elaine's father, George Stritch, was born in Springfield in 1892. His father, Henry J. Stritch, emigrated from Ireland and married Ellen B. Martin. Henry was a tailor, earning a meager but steady living, and eventually brought his son George into the family's tailor shop. As members of Springfield's St. Raphael's Catholic Church, the first and most impressive Catholic parish in town, Henry and Ellen raised George, his brother, and two sisters in a strict Catholic faith symbolized in the cathedral's high gothic sandstone structure. George attended mass regularly and served as an altar boy.

As teenagers, George Stritch and Mildred Jobe's paths probably crossed as they attended vaudeville and silent movie showings at the city's Grand (later, the historic Regent) and State theaters. Owned by Gus Sun, a theatrical impresario who commanded a chain of 275 theaters, these theaters gave stage and screen time to an entire era of show business stars. Minnie Palmer and her sons, the future Marx Brothers, played the Sun theaters as did a young Springfield native named Bobby Clark who would go on to a successful career in vaudeville, film, and television. Other luminaries included a very young Bob Hope, W. C. Fields, and one of Springfield's favorite daughters, Lillian Gish, whose earliest silent movies were headlined in her hometown.

But it wasn't until the opening in 1917 of the Shawnee Hotel, on the northeast corner of Main and Limestone streets, that George and Mildred would officially meet.

* * *

The Shawnee Hotel generated a great deal of excitement in town because it was designed by H. Ziegler Dietz in a revolutionary new H design that precluded the necessity for any interior rooms. As a result, every room had a window and, therefore, direct access to natural light. Built in the neoclassical style at a cost of $650,000, the 225-room Shawnee featured modern plumbing in each room as well as fireproofing throughout the hotel. The lavish two-story lobby opened to the Grand Ballroom that then led to numerous meeting rooms. With the Shawnee, Springfield, Ohio, had its first first-class hotel.

The Shawnee Hotel opened on Wednesday evening, January 31, 1917. Springfield's high society were greeted by Burton Westcott of the Westcott Motor Car Company and owner of the Springfield's Westcott House, which had been designed by Frank Lloyd Wright. As guests arrived in gowns and formal suits, they worked their way through the lobby entertained by musicians and vaudeville performers who filled the lobby and mezzanine with music and dancing. Once inside the Grand Ballroom, they were treated to a menu that featured lobster and sirloin steak as well as "Roast Young Ohio Turkey" all served on Syracuse China emblazoned with the new hotel's insignia. On the guest list that evening was Mr. and Mrs. Louis S. and Sally P. Jobe and their children, Howard and Mildred. There is no evidence that George and Ellen Stritch and their four children were in attendance.

But sometime during the spring of 1917, George Stritch and Mildred Jobe met one another in the elevator off the lobby of the Shawnee Hotel. George Stritch and his father, Henry, had been angling for a small stall in the hotel lobby to establish a second family tailor shop. Whatever the reason for being in the elevator for that one serendipitous meeting, George and Midge met, and as George would later tell Elaine, "We fell in love in the elevator of the Shawnee Hotel and were married within three months, both of us ready to get on with life outside of Springfield, Ohio."

By the end of the summer, Mr. and Mrs. George J. Stritch headed north to Toledo for a brief two-year stay before making it to Detroit, Michigan. It was in Toledo, in 1918, that they gave birth to their first child, a daughter named Georgene. Once settled in Detroit where George established himself with the B. F. Goodrich automobile tire company, George and Midge expanded their family with two more daughters, both born in Detroit's Ford Hospital—Sally, named for Midge's mother, was born in 1921, and Marion Elaine, born in 1925.

From left: Georgene, Elaine and Sally Stritch
Credit: Unknown/Provided by Elaine Stritch

* * *

As George Stritch's career developed, he became an executive at B. F. Goodrich and eventually moved the family to 18210 Birchcrest Drive, a modest but attractive home in one of Detroit's better neighborhoods. George, eager to demonstrate his growing success, invited his cousin, Fr. Samuel Alphonsius Stritch, who attended seminary in Cincinnati and later studied in Rome, to the house for dinner. George was proud to host his cousin who had served as the bishop of Toledo and would go on to serve as the archbishop of Chicago before attaining the appointment of cardinal of the Roman Catholic Church. The Catholic streak in the Stritch family ran deep.

In 1928, Midge received news of her father's death. The *Springfield News-Sun* ran a death notice and photo on the front page under the headline "Louis S. Job(e) Succumbs at His Residence" stating that the "well-known retired saloon keeper and businessman of this city died suddenly at his residence. Death was caused by heart disease." In his will, Louis's estimated estate of $100,000 was left to Sally with their children Howard and Mildred each receiving a one-time payment of $5,000. Also listed in the will was a onetime payment of $500 each for his granddaughters Jean (Georgene) and Sally.

From the beginning, Mildred Jobe brought to her union with George Stritch a financial advantage that assisted the young couple in establishing their family, weathering the Great Depression and advancing George's career.

Mildred Stritch had a taste for fine clothing and kept a well-furnished home. A state census showed that, for a period of time during the Stritch girls' childhood, Mildred and George employed a domestic servant to assist with the running of the house. The girls would attend the Convent of the Sacred Heart—or *Sacré Cœur* as alumni of the school refer to it—Detroit's prestigious Catholic school for girls. Georgene was an excellent student, excelling in English and literature while Sally and Elaine were very involved in the arts. Sally held a particular affinity for ballet, and Elaine's theatrical abilities were noted early on leading to featured roles in many of the school's theater productions. "I was always dressing up at home—I loved wearing Daddy's shirts around the house—and playing starring roles in my great invented playlets." Of all the memories she had of her childhood, Elaine's professed love for wearing her father's shirts seems perfectly prophetic given her later inclination toward men's shirt and ties.

The Stritch household was a seemingly happy home. George and Midge would often entertain George's business colleagues, and Elaine would later recall the music and romance of her parents' deep affection for one another. Clearly blessed by God-given talent, Elaine's gifts were shaped by the rich mixture of DNA into which she was born. On her father's side she inherited a full line of Irish blood, and from her mother came Welsh and French lineage. Elaine came to realize the potency of the mix: "From the Irish I got a great sense of humor and a love of song and drink, and from the French I got a sharp sense of style and a taste for the finer things in life." These qualities laminated in Elaine and defined her personal and professional style.

* * *

Elaine knew, early on, that she was destined to be a performer. She was often called upon to entertain guests at her parents' dinner parties, and the nuns at the *Sacré Cœur* noted the ease with which the young and boisterous Elaine could play male roles.

So while not entirely expected, it wasn't a big surprise when, at the age of nineteen, Elaine announced that she wanted to go to New York to study acting at the Dramatic Workshop at the New School of Social Research under the tutelage of Erwin Piscator. Elaine enlisted the aid of Reverend Mother Radamacher at the *Sacré Cœur* who conspired to make arrangements for Elaine to stay at the Convent of the Sacred Heart in New York, positing that her parents would be more likely to back the move if they knew she would be attending school and residing at a convent.

So in 1944, she landed in New York. And as she had in Detroit, Elaine quickly established a good relationship with Reverend Mother Benzinger who helped Elaine navigate the big city, boys, and her studies.

Elaine enjoyed her time at the New School. Fellow students included Bea Arthur and Marlon Brando. She was surprised to learn how much she didn't know about acting, claiming that she was often the least successful in class when presenting scenes and monologues. "I brought *me* to my work when everyone else was bringing technique. I really felt out of water, if you know what I mean. But I picked up quickly and learned that the *me* was truth and truth is crucial for an actor. It didn't take me long to float to the top of the class."

Elaine landed plum roles in productions at the New School starting with the roles of Cow and Tiger in *Bobino* in 1944. After a few years with roles in plays in New York, Philadelphia, and

Connecticut, she made her Broadway debut at the age of twenty-one in *Loco* at the Biltmore Theater. The following year she appeared in her first musical role in the revue *Angel in the Wings*. For the next few years, she continued to land roles in productions in New York, Long Island, and New Haven. But it was in 1950, at the age of twenty-five, that she got her first taste of the theatrical career that would follow.

* * *

From 1950 through 1952, Elaine understudied Ethel Merman in Irving Berlin's original Broadway production *Call Me Madam* at the Imperial Theater in New York. While understudying Merman, she was granted permission to take on a role in the Broadway production *Pal Joey*. When *Call Me Madam* ended its Broadway run, Stritch starred in the national tour.

Two years later, she appeared in a revival of *On Your Toes* on Broadway directed by George Abbott and followed that stint with the role of Grace, the wry diner owner, in the Broadway production of William Inge's *Bus Stop* opposite Kim Stanley, an actress for whom she developed great respect and appreciation. Stritch's work in *Bus Stop* garnered her the first of a string of Tony Award nominations.

At this time in her life, Elaine began a serious relationship with the actor Ben Gazarra. However, since Stritch was gaining notice as a serious actress with strong comedic and musical abilities, it didn't take long for a significant film offer to come her way. In 1957, she was cast in the remake of *A Farewell to Arms* starring Rock Hudson. She was taken with Hudson who was flirtatious with her on and off the set. Thinking it was a relationship she wanted to pursue, she ended her courtship with Gazarra. Elaine was often quoted saying, "And we all know what a bum deal that turned out to be."

Stritch enjoyed working in film but knew her real home was the stage. "My talent was always just a little too big for the camera," she said. So back in New York, Stritch's headlining moment came when she was cast in a musical with book and lyrics by Walter Kerr, the future chief drama critic of *The New York Times*, and his wife Jean Kerr and music by LeRoy Anderson. *Goldilocks* opened at the

Lunt-Fontanne Theater in 1958. The musical was panned. But critics noted Stritch's obvious talent.

After *Goldilocks,* Hollywood came calling again. Stritch was cast as Trixie Norton in the pilot for Jackie Gleason's *The Honeymooners,* a role for which she claims she was fired for "acting too much like Jackie Gleason in drag." Shortly after, Stritch began work on a short-lived television series titled *My Sister Eileen* on the CBS television network.

In 1961, having seen Elaine's performance in *Goldilocks,* Noel Coward contacted Elaine with an offer to play the comic relief role of Mimi Paragon, the recreation cruise director, for his new musical *Sail Away!* Stritch, thrilled by the opportunity to work with Coward and appear in another big Broadway musical, lamented that she might not be able to accept the role due to her commitment with the sitcom *My Sister Eileen.* Stritch reported that Coward's response was, "Elaine, I have seen the sitcom, you'll begin rehearsals with me next month."

Noel Coward's *Sail Away!* opened at the Broadhurst Theater in New York in 1961 to strong notices. In Boston, the romantic female lead was fired, and the comedic and romantic female roles were compressed into one and awarded to Stritch. She became the toast of Broadway and secured her second Tony Award nomination. She reprised her role in *Sail Away!* when Coward took the production to London's Savoy Theater. Stritch was thirty-six and had established herself as a bona fide leading lady both in New York and London.

* * *

In 1962, back in New York, Stritch replaced Uta Hagen in the Broadway production *Who's Afraid of Virginia Woolf.* In 1965, she appeared in the cult film classic *Who Killed Teddy Bear?* portraying a lesbian nightclub owner opposite Juliet Prowse.

Stritch returned to Broadway in 1970 in George Furth and Stephen Sondheim's *Company* starring as the acerbic Joanne and delivering a showstopping rendition of Sondheim's "The Ladies Who Lunch," which would go on to become her signature tune. Her work in *Company* also secured her a third Tony Award nomination. Elaine followed the production on its national tour and headlined its London production. While with *Company* in London, Elaine moved into the Savoy Hotel and began residing in high-end hotels, a pattern that would last the next forty years of her life.

After *Company* ended its run in London, Elaine stayed on, enjoying the city and a lifestyle of luxury and fame to which she had become accustomed. While working there in a production of Tennessee Williams's *Small Craft Warnings*, she met the American actor John Bay. They were married in 1973. A talented mimic and impersonator, Bay brought a marvelous sense of humor to their marriage and provided Elaine with a level of affection and companionship that eluded her for nearly fifty years.

Elaine enjoyed one of her most exciting and productive decades in London. In addition to her marriage, she starred opposite Donald Sinden as an American expatriate mystery writer fond of jousting with her English butler in *Two's Company* from 1975 to 1979. The sitcom was very successful in London and earned Stritch a BAFTA award nomination.

Stritch's film career continued in 1977 when she starred opposite John Gielgud in Alain Resnais's *Providence*. In 1979, Stritch and Bay returned to the United States and purchased a home in Nyack, New York. Elaine continued to commute to London regularly to appear in the sitcom *Nobody's Perfect*, a British version of *Maude*, an American sitcom that starred Bea Arthur, her schoolmate from the New School.

In 1981, John Bay was diagnosed with brain cancer. He died in 1982. Elaine sold the house in Nyack and moved back to New York and began teaching acting at the Stella Adler Conservatory.

Through the eighties, Stritch played roles in regional theater and on television and in films including the ABC sitcom *The Ellen Burstyn Show*, Woody Allen's *September*, Ron Howard's *Cocoon: The Return*, and a recurring role on *The Cosby Show*. In 1990, she earned an Emmy Award for a guest appearance on the legal serial *Law & Order*.

In 1990, Stritch returned to Broadway to star opposite Jason Robards in *Love Letters* on Broadway and in Harold Prince's vaulted revival of *Show Boat* in the role of Parthy. Her Broadway run continued with another Tony Award nominated turn playing the alcohol-soaked Claire in Edward Albee's *A Delicate Balance* in 1996 at the age of seventy-one. And she reunited with Woody Allen on his *Small Time Crooks* in 2000.

In 2001, Elaine began a new pathway in her career. She wrote and starred in her own one-woman autobiographical cabaret show *Elaine Stritch at Liberty.* The show was a revealing and personal reflection of her life in show business accentuated with a string of Broadway show tunes. The show was a smash hit in New York, and she toured it in the US and in London. The production earned Stritch her first and only Tony Award for Best Special Theatrical Event. In 2004, the documentary filmmaker D. A. Pennebaker shot a film version that aired on HBO. The HBO production earned Stritch a second Emmy Award for Outstanding Individual Performance in a Variety or Music Program.

In 2005, Stritch took up residence on the third floor of the ultra-posh Carlyle Hotel on Madison Avenue. Between 2005 and 2013, she presented a number of cabaret acts at the hotel's famed Café Carlyle.

In 2006, Stritch began a string of guest appearances on NBC's *30 Rock* playing Alec Baldwin's acid-tongued mother. This work earned her a third Emmy Award for Outstanding Guest Actress in a Comedy Series.

In 2009, Stritch played Jeannette, the piano player in the Paper Mill Playhouse production *The Full Monty*, and her final Broadway appearance was opposite Bernadette Peters in Trevor Nunn's revival of Stephen Sondheim and Hugh Wheeler's *A Little Night Music* replacing Angela Lansbury in the role of Leanora Armfeldt.

When asked about her career, Stritch acknowledged she hadn't hit Hollywood's A-list. "I wasn't pretty enough for movie contracts. But I always worked, and I could always hold my own on the big screen and on television. But I could always do a whole lot more than that on stage in front of a live audience."

CHAPTER 3

After Elaine's campus visit, I sent flowers to her at the Carlyle. She called to thank me. "I had a great time, John. I think it went well, don't you?"

I assured her I did. "The students are still talking about it," I said.

"Well, good. Now when you coming to New York?"

Elaine always ended our conversations with what felt like an open invitation to advance the relationship. My nature would chalk this up to polite posturing, but with Elaine, she was always ready for the next point of contact. I began considering that perhaps she was challenging me to see just how far I'd go with her. And since she rarely turned down an opportunity to meet, two months after her visit to campus, I called Elaine at the Carlyle and told her I'd be coming to New York and would love to take her to dinner. She was delighted, and we set a date.

I was excited for this next encounter because it would be the first time I visited without an agenda. I wasn't angling for an interview or trying to tie her down for an appearance. It was just me, going to New York, to see her. One on one. Dinner and a visit. I was flattered that she was interested, but, as was always the case when in Elaine's presence, a little nervous.

Arriving at the Carlyle, I called up from the front desk, and she told me to wait in the lobby and that she'd be down in a few minutes. About forty-five minutes later, she emerged from the elevator, singing some great old standard with the elevator man. Apparently, this was a long-running occurrence between the two, bringing them both obvious delight.

Dressed in a white T-shirt and black stirrup pants and sneakers, with a white hat and black Marc Jacobs sunglasses, and carrying a Saks shopping bag with her coffee, juice, pills, and diabetes monitors, we left the Carlyle and started walking.

My job was to carry the bag and give her my arm. I soon learned that with Elaine, you were always assigned a job. Elaine used the people around her to help her accomplish errands. It became part and parcel of being with her. She knew it, and so did those she let in.

Dressed for a dinner date, I was wearing dress shirt, necktie, jacket, and dress shoes, I was not prepared for the thirty-block (about a mile and a half), fast-paced walk Elaine inflicted upon me. I honestly had a hard time keeping up.

After about forty-five minutes, she suggested we go to Sant Ambroeus, one of her favorite neighborhood eateries, for dinner. We settled in, and Elaine ordered a cold nonalcoholic beer. Wanting an alcoholic beer but deciding I didn't want to make an insensitive choice, I ordered an iced tea. Elaine went on to order a scrambled egg and toast, and I ordered a club sandwich. Before the waiter could retreat from the table, Elaine barked that she required a smaller fork as the one on the table was too large for her mouth. "Every time I come in here I have to ask for a smaller fork. What's with you people? Come on and let's get it right!" she shouted as he walked away.

Then before the waiter could even submit the order, she began harping about why the food was taking so long. I tried to divert and change her mood by telling her how much the students at the university had enjoyed her visit and asking her if she felt good about the day. She reported she did but reiterated she didn't feel she performed "Fifty Percent" as well as she could have. "I wasn't inside it while I was singing it," she said. "I can usually get myself inside when I know I'm not there, but that day, I just couldn't get it to take hold. And the more you work to release into it, the more you become obsessed with it, which is always going to kill it," she said.

I told her I thought the rendition was quite moving and asked if, when singing it, she was thinking of John Bay, her husband. She said no. "I don't relive moments from my life in my work. I just play in the words until I find my way to the moment. No, theater isn't therapy, not for me. Although, maybe it should be."

Elaine fielding questions in "An Afternoon with
Elaine Stritch" at DeSales University.
Credit: John Bell

After checking her blood sugar and ordering a cappuccino with two packets of Equal and cinnamon "to go," the waiter brought the check. I told her I'd get it, and she said, "You bet you'll get it, you asked me to dinner, didn't you?"

As we exited, she stopped by the bakery counter, considering a couple of the various chocolate treats. She decided on a few to take back with her, insisting that she'd pay for them. I wouldn't let her. We said goodbye in the lobby, and up she went, shouting at me to let her know when I'd be coming back into the city.

* * *

Always wanting to keep the door open but not wanting to appear too eager, I called Elaine about a month later. "Where have you been?" she asked. "Nowhere, just working at the university," I replied. "Well, I thought you forgot about me," she said. "I've got some breaking news."

With that, I planned a visit and arrived a couple of days later for my second visit with Elaine at the Carlyle. When I called up, she told the desk staff to send me up. This was new, this invitation into her personal quarters. I took it as a sign of growing comfort and fondness. I found my way to room 309, a corner room overlooking the intersection of Madison Avenue and Seventy-Sixth Street.

The Carlyle was built in 1930, just after the great Wall Street crash. Over the ensuing years, it came to define Upper East Side class and attracted the elite from the worlds of finance, fashion, politics, and entertainment. From Truman and Kennedy to Clinton, the Carlyle is known for the care with which it has cultivated its reputation for style and privacy. That Elaine would be attracted to the hotel makes perfect sense.

On the floor outside Elaine's door there was a small cache of trash stacked inside a shipping box with Bays English Muffins printed on the outside. I knocked, and Elaine came to the door and let me in. She greeted me warmly wearing a white T-shirt and no pants.

This was the most casual that I had seen her, and I was flattered that she was comfortable in front of me without being dressed or made up. She offered me a Diet Coke and settled back into her king-size bed.

Elaine's residence at the Carlyle consisted of one large room containing her bed, a closet, a dresser, and a small refrigerator, which she used for her diabetes medicine. There was also a desk, a large flat-screen television, a set of chairs and lamps, and a table as well as an antique washing station that she brought with her from the house in Nyack that she and John Bay purchased in the early 1980s before his death. Off this room was a small anteroom that served as her kitchen with a sink, a microwave oven, and a second refrigerator freezer used to store food. Adjacent to this anteroom was her bathroom. The suite was elegantly appointed in soft, muted, natural colors and plush fabrics. On Elaine's dresser were her Emmy awards draped with necklaces. Her small closet was carefully organized with her hats, furs, and favorite outfits all hanging in dry-cleaning bags. Beside her bed, on the wall, were taped pieces of small paper with the names and phone numbers of all the pertinent and current people in her life. I was surprised to find my name and number there.

Elaine in suite 309 at the Carlyle with her yellow
sticky notes with names and phone numbers of
"important people" to the right of the bed.
Credit: Lizzie Sullivan

The TV was on a news station, and the volume was up rather high, so high that it was difficult to make conversation—for me anyway. As we sat, enjoying our Diet Coke "cocktail" as she called it—Elaine liked the vocabulary and ritual of drinking even in her sobriety—I asked Elaine where she wanted to go. She said she wanted to take another walk, this time through Central Park and, after that, we'd stop wherever to eat.

"Well, what's your breaking news?" I asked.

"My what?" she screeched back at me.

"When I called, you said you had breaking news."

"I don't know what you're talking about," she said. Then after a moment, "Oh, yes, I do. I'm doing *The Full Monty* at the Paper Mill Playhouse," she said.

"In what role?" I asked.

"Well, that's a dumb question. What role do you think, you twit?" she snapped.

"Jeanette the piano player?" I said.

"You got it."

Thinking that a return to the Paper Mill Playhouse (she had appeared at the Playhouse in 1982 in *A Suite for Two Keys*) seemed like a step down for Elaine, I asked her what motivated her to accept the role.

"What do you mean? It's a job, and the Carlyle ain't cheap, darling."

Besides, she said, the role was pretty good, and she was able to get good terms. I asked what terms, and she reported, "Well, not that it's any of your business, but it's a decent weekly salary, a car and driver of course, and a daily masseuse."

I congratulated her and told her I looked forward to seeing the show.

"You'd better," she said.

After finishing our drinks, she told me to divert my eyes while she slipped into a different white T-shirt and her white walking shorts. She asked me to help her with her socks and sneakers. She grabbed her sunshades and her white walking hat and did a quick check of her blood sugar. With her levels in good shape, she elected not to travel with the shopping bag today but rather just a small pouch that contained her diabetes supplies. She checked to make sure I was prepared to pick up the tab for dinner—she wasn't bringing a credit card with her. I was, and so off we went—me and Elaine Stritch wearing a fanny pack.

This time, I had prepared by dressing a bit more casually and in more sensible shoes. I was able to keep up with her as we walked about forty minutes through Central Park. For dinner we stopped again at Sant Ambroeus. She ordered lentil soup and a cappuccino with cinnamon. When the soup came, it was too cold, and she sent it back, snapping at the waiter to "get it right." While waiting for the return of the soup, she checked her sugar levels on her Dexcom monitor. She decided that she needed some insulin, so she hiked up her T-shirt, rolled down the waistband of her shorts, and gave herself a shot of insulin.

The soup returned steaming hot, and she asked for crackers, "something to munch on while I wait for this nuclear bowl of soup to cool down, I mean Jesus Christ," letting the waiter know that he had not yet achieved Goldilocks's preferred level of perfection.

Over dinner, we talked about diabetes. Elaine had battled with it for quite some time. "I was diagnosed in 1979," she said. She said she felt like she had it under control. She revealed her stomach monitor to me. This small device, about the size of a small remote garage door opener, was embedded by injection on the outside of her lower abdomen. The device gets changed by a health care assistant once a week. Elaine was trying to learn how to change it herself but was finding the contraption a bit difficult to handle due to the limited dexterity in her hands and her waning eyesight. She also had trouble remembering the correct sequence of the process of changing the device. But she felt very secure wearing it because it sends an alarm to her wireless monitor if her sugar levels get too high or too low.

I asked her if she and Mary Tyler Moore had ever commiserated over their diabetes diagnoses. She said that they had.

"Well, I don't know if we 'commiserate,'" she said. "But we've shared war stories." She said that Mary's diabetes was a much more serious form than hers and was taking a toll on Mary's eyesight. "Is it taking a toll on your eyesight?" I asked. "No, my eyes are just getting old," she said.

I asked her if she ever worked with Mary—she had not. But she really liked her and respected her work. She said she thought Mary was a great comedienne with excellent timing and smart instincts. And Elaine admired Mary's work in Robert Redford's 1979 film *Ordinary People*. "Mary is really good in that role," she said. "And listen, when you've been pegged a 'funny girl,' it can be hard to get anyone to let you do a serious, meaty role. But she did. She's got great range, and it surprised a lot of people. I think she's just terrific."

"You know she had lost her son prior to that, and Robert Redford, in an interview, said that he would often see Mary walking along the beach alone and knew that she would be great in the movie," I said.

"I didn't know that, but it makes sense."

"Were you and Mary friends?"

"Not really, but we'd see each other at this party or that party. I hear her diabetes has gotten pretty bad and she's almost blind. Bernadette and she are good friends. God, I pray for her. I hope diabetes isn't what takes her, I really don't."

After dinner, Elaine passed on the bakery counter, electing instead to stop on the way back to the Carlyle for frozen yogurt at a stand around the corner. She ordered two pints—one vanilla and one chocolate. When we got back up to her suite, she instructed me to put the yogurt into her little freezer. I asked her if there was anything else I could do for her. She said, "Nothing, darling, just let me know when you're coming back into town."

* * *

Over the next few months, I had been unable to make much contact with Elaine. A few years before I met Elaine, my mother had experienced a stroke. In the ensuing period of time, I was driving back and forth from eastern Pennsylvania to central Ohio to assist my mom and stepfather with her care. Prior to her stroke, my mom had been preparing for her retirement by collecting vintage hats. She was going to open a vintage millinery business restoring and rede-signing antique hats. Her collection had grown to over three hundred hats. With each visit, I would assist her into the electric chair that would take her upstairs to the room she had set up as her work-shop. The walls were lined, floor to ceiling, with hat boxes. She loved nothing more than to have me open the boxes, sometimes twenty to thirty at a time, so she could try on the hats and tell me what she was planning to do to bring each one back to glory. Of course, knowing that I was spending private time with Elaine, my mother and I would often mention how much Elaine would love the hats as we'd call out together, "Does anyone still wear a hat? We do!" referencing Elaine and her signature line from "The Ladies Who Lunch."

Finally, in late summer, I called Elaine and told her I was com-ing into the city and wanted to visit. When I arrived at the Carlyle a few days later and called up on the phone from the front desk, she snapped, "You know where I am." I headed up.

She met me in the hallway on the third floor wearing her walk-ing outfit and carrying a Harrods shopping bag. We headed out. This time, on a surprisingly mild August afternoon, we walked down to Thirty-Sixth Street and back along the western side of Madison Avenue. When we got to St. Patrick's Cathedral on the way back, she said she needed to stop in and light a candle. She asked if I had a dol-lar for the candle collection box. I waited while she lit the candle and sat briefly in a back pew seemingly in prayer. When we left, I asked her who she was remembering.

"My sister Georgene. She passed away in May. I've been mean-ing to light her a candle," she said.

We continued on our way up Madison Avenue to Sant Ambroeus. She ordered smoked salmon with onions and capers along with a nonalcoholic beer. I asked her about Georgene. She said Georgene was the smart one and their sister Sally, the middle sister, was the pretty one who could also dance really well. She said that she thought that her two sisters were perhaps jealous of her over the years, the success and attention her career had brought her.

"Yeah, I think my sisters were a little jealous of me, of my life-style, my fame, my success, the attention, you know. But I loved them both very much. After Mother and Daddy died, we grew closer. But it was hard with me living in New York and London and going all over the place. Georgene could be tough and was quick to judge, and I hated that. She always made me feel like I wasn't coming home enough. Sally was softer and more interested, you know what I mean?"

"Did you get along?" I asked.

"Not always, but who does? Family is one of the hardest things ever."

"Were you ever envious of your sisters?"

"Oh, boy, you bet."

"Why?"

"Well, there was a time when I was working in New York and I was pretty lonely. I didn't have any really serious boyfriends, and both my sisters were getting married and starting families. I didn't want any children, but I saw that a husband and children and a home gives you some stability, and ultimately, I think both my sisters did a better job raising their families than my mom and dad did with us."

"What was missing from your childhood?

"Nothing earth-shattering. But with my parents, especially my mother, it was 'get out from underfoot.' She didn't want to be bothered with you," she said.

"One of my favorite stories was a day when Mother told me to go out and occupy myself and I went and killed enough flies to use them to spell my name, like it was on a marquee. God, is that a story for a shrink or what? No, in our house, we were expected to do for ourselves. Mother and Daddy would do a lot of entertaining because Daddy was a big shot with the B. F. Goodrich, or as Mother liked to say, 'the GDBF Goodrich Company.' So there were cocktail and dinner parties. I loved them. I got to tend bar. I got to taste the drinks, and everyone was happy, and Mother and Daddy would be singing, with Mother at the piano. It was wonderful."

Elaine went on to tell the story of how she stole one of Georgene's boyfriends.

"His name was Jimmy Lee, and he came knocking on the door for Georgene, but Georgene wasn't home, so I answered the door. I said 'I'm sorry, Georgene is not at home, but I am, and I'm not doing anything with the rest of my life.' And he sat down on the divan with me, and we became boyfriend and girlfriend real fast. No sex, just a lot of cuddling. And I loved it. This was my first experience with any boy. At one point, Daddy called down to check on us.

"'Elaine, what's going on?' he said. 'Oh, it's okay, Daddy, we're just on our third beer.' 'Oh, okay then,' he said. Isn't that great? The message was as long as there was no horseplay or sex, drinking was just fine. That was life growing up in my house." And then after a pause, "And people wonder how it all started."

"So Jimmy and I dated. At one point, Jimmy announced he was going to Texas to get into the oil business, but he actually ended up going to New York doing some acting and writing. When I finally got myself to New York, we continued to see each other. At one point, while I was the New School with Marlon Brando, there was a heated confrontation between Marlon and Jimmy over me. I was in heaven. And I simply told Jimmy that Marlon Brando was too good a prospect to let get away and so ended the grand affair with Jimmy Lee."

"Whatever happened to him?" I asked.

"He became James Lee and went on to become a very successful screenwriter. He even won an Emmy award for that miniseries with Cicely Tyson."

"*The Autobiography of Miss Jane Pittman?*"

"No, the one about slaves coming from Africa."

"*Roots?*"

"Yes, *Roots*."

"Did you stay in touch with him?" I asked.

"Not really. Every once in a while we'd talk on the phone."

She asked me if I had made it to a production of *The Full Monty* at the Paper Mill Playhouse.

"I did indeed."

"What did you think?"

"I thought you were the funniest, and biggest and brightest thing on stage." Then taking my first stab at employing direct honesty with her, I said, "But my strongest impression afterward was that the entire production seemed beneath you."

"Yeah, I think so too," she said with casual ease and to my surprise. "But it paid well enough and wasn't the hardest night's work I've been asked to do." She paused. "And I like that you had the balls to tell me you thought it was beneath me."

When we got back to the Carlyle, she wanted to stop down in the gallery for a cappuccino nightcap. She brought up a project she's been thinking about involving the Pulitzer Prize winning *Craig's Wife* written by the American playwright George Kelly, uncle of actress and later Princess of Monaco Grace Kelly. Elaine thought she'd like to arrange a reading of the play with Cherry Jones in the lead role. Elaine was interested in playing the aunt, Ms. Austen.

"She hangs out in the background, tells it like she sees it, and stirs up trouble. Perfect for me, don't you think?" she said. "And if we could get a reading going, and do it cheap at your university, we should be able to lure a producer to consider mounting a full production. Do you know the play?"

"I don't."

"Well, read it!" she said. "There are two movie versions, one starring Rosalind Russell and another starring Joan Crawford, and they're both pretty good."

I told her I'd read it.

After escorting her up to her suite, I asked her about recent news reports that John Lahr, the *New Yorker* writer and son of comedian Bert Lahr who played the cowardly lion in *The Wizard of Oz,* who was her book writer for *At Liberty,* was suing her for royalties for subsequent cabaret performances of the show.

"Yeah, doesn't that just grab your shorts," she said. "I mean, come on. John Lahr helped me write my goddamn show and I'm grateful to him. I couldn't have done it without him. But as it was billed, I basically reworked everything he wrote. He got appropriate credit and payment. But it's my fucking life story, and if I want to perform it on tour or in small rooms, I'm going to. He can go fuck himself for all I care. End of story."

The lawsuit was eventually settled amicably.

* * *

By now, I had fallen into the pattern of calling about a month after each visit and arranging to visit about a month later. For the next visit in mid-autumn, Elaine wanted to meet me at St. Patrick's Cathedral since I was coming from the theater district. She was dressed in white capri pants, a white shirt, a light jacket, and matching hat. She was wearing sneakers. She wanted to head east to Second Street and then back up to the Carlyle to try to get her twenty to thirty blocks in for her daily walk.

"Did you read *Craig's Wife?*" she asked as we walked.

"I did, and I love the play," I said.

"It's a good play. People don't know it, but it's a great piece. And for the actress playing the lead role, it's something meaty. And I think the old aunt is fun too," she said. She mentioned again wanting to arrange a reading of the play ("no lines to memorize!") and told me to contact Cherry Jones. "She loves me, and I think she's a hell of an actress. She'd be great in that role." I told her I'd make the contact.

"You know, when I read that final scene, you know where Mrs. Craig walks through her house unknowingly dropping rose petals, I imagine rose petals falling from the sky as the stage glowed to a blazing bright white light," I said.

"Oh, god, wouldn't that be divine," she said. "That settles it, you'll direct."

I laughed.

When we got back to her suite at the Carlyle—she wanted to freshen up before dinner—she discovered that her windows had not been washed. This set Elaine off on a tear. Apparently she had been requesting that her windows get washed for over a week. "They told me they were going to clean them while I was out this afternoon on my walk," she said. "Look at them, they're fucking filthy." She called down to the front desk and demanded to know why they were still dirty.

"Don't tell me they couldn't come, I was told they'd be here this afternoon, that's why I scheduled my walk when I did. These windows are filthy. What's the use of having a corner room with a view at the Carlyle if you can't see a goddamn thing through the fucking dirt!" After asking to speak with the hotel manager on duty and being told he was unavailable, she hung up and said she'd be down to the desk shortly and to "make him available." When we got out of the elevator in the lobby, she strode straight over to the desk and began yelling about her windows. Aware that she was causing a scene in front of the other guests in the lobby, the manager tried to appease and quiet her. As he did, her ire only intensified.

"This is fucking ridiculous. I've been trying to get these windows cleaned for over a week. With what I pay to stay here, I think this is a very reasonable expectation. I really do. I am not happy about this. Not happy at all. I'm very angry!" she screamed as she walked out of the hotel. Fortunately, she was immediately recognized by a fan who feigned and fawned over her, quickly distracting her from her rage and soothing the savage beast.

At dinner, she ordered roasted chicken breast and scalloped potatoes, a favorite she confessed. She ordered a nonalcoholic beer and insisted I get a drink for myself. I ordered a nonalcoholic beer too. "Get a real one," she said. "If you want it." I stayed with my original choice.

We talked about living at the Carlyle.

"I first moved into a hotel when I was doing *Company*. I got a room in a place around the corner from the theater. It made life a lot easier. And when I moved to London and married John and worked on *Two's Company* in London, John and I lived at the Savoy, which was absolutely divine."

"Actually," she said, "when I first got to London, I stayed at the Connaught Hotel in Mayfair, which was pooh-pooh posh, let me tell you. Talk about a classy joint. It was truly divine. But it was expensive! Too expensive. So I went to the front desk to pay my bill and said I was moving out because 'I Connaught afford to stay.' So I downgraded to the Savoy, which is no downgrade, if you know what I mean. Living in a hotel—a really good hotel—is special. You feel pampered. And you should, because you've paid to be pampered. I like having fresh linens. I like having people responsible for waking me up at a certain hour. I like having a front desk to monitor my calls and guests. I like being able to order food and have it delivered. I like it all. And since I've been lucky enough to make enough money to afford it, that's how I live. So when I can't get the fucking windows cleaned, that doesn't sit well with me."

After checking her sugar levels, she decided it was safe to order a chocolate cookie and her cappuccino, both to go. She announced she was thinking of working up another cabaret act for the Café Carlyle, this time focusing on all Sondheim songs. She had just begun devising a song list with Rob, her music director.

Recalling our first meeting when I interviewed her for *The Sondheim Review*, I asked Elaine what she liked about Stephen Sondheim's songs.

"They're smart. His talent is so big, and those songs are so good. Each word of each line has a million possibilities. As an actor, you know that every time you sing it you'll be able to travel a new road. Material like that is rare, but with Steve, it's in every song."

"Why do you think he's able to tap into such potency in his writing?" I asked.

"How the hell do I know? He has talent. Talent is what it is. And it's hard to define. But you know it when you see it. And I know it—I've worked with some pretty talented writers—Noel Coward, Edward Albee—and Steve is as good as they come. I have a theory about talent," she said.

"Oh yeah, what's that?" I asked.

"I think talent is scary. I think most people are scared of people who have real talent. Most people just don't know what to do around it. They're drawn to it, but they're also scared of it. I think a lot of people feel that way about me, and I know I feel that way about other people with real, honest-to-God talent. And that's how I feel about Steve. He scares me."

"What kind of relationship do you have with Steve today?"

"None. Really. We don't stay in touch. I haven't worked for Steve in a long time, and that's the only time I can talk to him, when we're working and talking about work. I can't have a quiet sit-down with Steve, it's impossible."

"Would you like to?" I asked.

"Yes, I'd love it. I love him. But he's too guarded, and it's too frightening. But yes, I'd love to have a close relationship with him. I've always been terribly attracted to him—to him and his talent. But he and I never were able to get close. And I've often wondered why."

"Do you think he might be as wary of you as you are of him?"

Stephen Sondheim and Elaine.
Credit: Jim Spellman

"Yes. I think we're a lot alike, and we've both got a lot of bullshit we carry around, and neither one of us wants to have to deal with the other. Don't get me wrong, there have been times when he's been sweet to me, but there have been other times when he has practically ignored me, and as far as I'm concerned, that's the worst thing someone can do to me."

On the way back to the Carlyle, we passed an older woman, very petite and walking slowly with a cane. Elaine saw her coming toward us and took very specific note of her, looking her up and down and assessing the hair, the makeup, the clothing, the cane, the bag, the shoes. When we passed the woman, Elaine stopped and turned around to watch her walking, slowly, on her way.

"What's so interesting?" I said.

"Jesus, she's dripping in so much money, it's given her a limp," she said.

I chuckled and shook my head as she grabbed my arm so we could cross Madison Avenue on our way back to the Carlyle.

On her way up to her suite, the doorman handed her the *Times* and her mail. Once into her suite, there was a vase with flowers and a plate of chocolate cookies from the manager letting her know her windows had been cleaned. The bright lights of New York's night-time sky were blazing through the gleaming glass.

Elaine settled in on top of her bed with her cappuccino and asked me to open and read her mail. She received a few residual royalty checks, a notice about her insurance and retirement through Actors Equity, and a handful of fan mail. I read through it with her, and she made note of the ones to which she would respond. After an hour, I prepared to say goodbye. Before I left, she said, "Wait a minute, I want to give you Cherry's address and phone number so you can get to work on *Craig's Wife* for me."

CHAPTER 4

My next visit was a Christmas visit. After catching a bus into the city, I arrived at the Carlyle and was dazzled by the lush and elegant holiday decor. The hotel looked magical. I imagined how much Elaine must enjoy residing at a place where such resource resulted in such effortless beauty. I made my way to the front desk and called up only to have Elaine say she had changed her mind about a visit. She wasn't feeling great and would I mind if we postponed.

This was odd because Elaine typically showed great appreciation for the time I took to travel in to the city to visit with her. While she had never canceled on me in the past, I always had a sense, if we had planned a visit and she needed to cancel, that she would call to let me know before I put forth the effort to travel in. Then again, I was learning with Elaine that details can slip away quickly. So maybe she had actually forgotten I was coming.

"Honey, I've been working on this Sondheim show, and I'm just worn-out."

I was disappointed because it was just before Christmas and I had a gift for her, but I told her it was no problem and I'd call in the New Year after I had seen her new show. I wished her a Merry Christmas and left the gift at the front desk.

It was just a minute or two later, as I was walking along Madison Avenue headed back to Port Authority, that I got a call on my cell phone. Elaine said she hated to send me away and could we just have a Coke in the room and not go out for dinner.

"Fine with me," I said.

"Then come on up, darling."

When I got to her suite, she was in her white T-shirt and underpants. She made no apology and hoped I didn't mind. I told her I didn't if she didn't. We split a Diet Coke, and she checked her sugar levels. They were good.

I asked her how the Sondheim show was coming. She said it was hard work and that her memory was giving her trouble.

"I've always been very good with lyrics. Connecting one thought to another always been easy-peasy with me. But now, I finish a line and can't get the next one fast enough. It's making me fucking crazy," she said in real frustration. Then as if willing away a possible terrifying new reality, she said, "I just need to rehearse more. Harder. Till I lock it in. But Sondheim is so hard. He's so fucking hard. But once you get it, you've got something to work with, know what I mean? Some. Thing. To. Work. With."

Elaine's ability to turn around a bad thought or depressed mood by merely commanding a stricter work ethic was a skill I was noticing more and more. I got a sense that Elaine had survived in this business as long as she had by not crying in her soup—always shouldering on. It fit with her upbringing, and it certainly made sense given the difficulties associated with building a successful career as an actress.

"Do you think Sondheim will come to see the show?" I asked.

"I hope so," she said, "but you never know with him, so we'll just have to see. My sister Sally is coming in, so I'm happy about that."

"What a treat," I said.

"Yeah, it really is. I didn't get to share these types of things with Georgene and Sally much, so now that Genie is gone, I want Sally to see what I do—or at least what I'm doing now."

"I sent a letter to Cherry Jones about *Craig's Wife* and haven't heard anything back," I said.

"Well, you've got to woo her. Any good producer knows that," she chided.

"Should I try calling her directly?" I asked, wondering why Elaine wouldn't just call her herself.

"No, not yet. Send her another letter with flowers this time, and be sure to mention me. She'll respond. She better."

"Have you seen *Night Music?*" she asked, referring to the new revival of Sondheim's *A Little Night Music* starring Angela Lansbury and Catherine Zeta-Jones.

"I have," I said.

"Yeah, what did you think?"

"It was a little barren," I said, "but I thought Angela Lansbury was excellent. Have you seen it?"

"Yeah, I saw it the other night."

"What did you think?" I asked.

"It's not my favorite show of his. I thought Angie was very good, but I didn't think much of Mrs. Douglas," referring to Catherine Zeta-Jones. "She was too young and too pretty. She didn't really do anything with it. The leading man was pretty good. The rest of the performances didn't do much for me. I'm putting the death song, you know, 'Every Day a Little Death' into my act, but I'm going to speak it, not sing it."

"Really. Why?" I asked.

"Because it's such a good lyric, and I think reciting it will show it off in a new way. I tried to do this a few years back with a Dorothy Parker song, and it didn't work, but I think this time it will."

"Have you ever been offered the opportunity to play Mme. Armfeldt?" I asked. Mme. Armfeldt, an aging courtesan and lover of kings and counts, is a no-nonsense role ideally suited to many of Elaine's inherent qualities as an actress.

"No, but I could have played that role. Her song, about her love affairs, is another version of 'The Ladies Who Lunch,' don't you think?"

"I could see you in the role," I said.

"Yeah, so could I."

She announced she was feeling hungry after all and why wouldn't we just go over to Sant Ambroeus for scrambled eggs. She grabbed a pair of black stirrup pants and asked me to help her get them on. Then we worked her into a pair of calf-high leather boots. She said she was excited to wear a new sable coat and hat that she had just purchased. Once dressed and with a brown marbled pair of Marc Jacobs glasses, she looked like a million bucks, and out we went.

Elaine changed her mind on the scrambled eggs and ordered a bowl of lentil soup. I asked her what she was planning on doing for Christmas.

"Nothing, absolutely nothing. All my friends have families, and there's nothing worse than spending Christmas with other people's families. God, it's sometimes bad enough spending Christmas with your own family, don't you think? And Sally's coming in for my show in February anyway. No, I'll be right here at the Carlyle rehearsing for my show, and that suits me just fine. Maybe Rob and I will have dinner together if he doesn't go home, which he really should do."

"I have a Christmas present for you," I said.

"What is it? Open it for me."

I did. It was a box of photographs from her campus visit. Photos of her and Rob on stage together, photos of her speaking to the students, photos of students swarming her in the lobby afterward. She hated most of them because she had placed some Kleenexes in the pockets of the sweater vest she had been wearing. The Kleenexes created bulges that distorted the drape of the vest.

"It looks like I got pockets full of shit," she said.

Then I showed her one photo—my favorite of the group—featuring Elaine using the back of a student to autograph a photo of herself applying makeup. It was a great juxtaposition. She liked it, too, and, in classic Stritch fashion, told me to get notecards made of it to use as thank-you cards.

Elaine at DeSales with Kleenexes in the pockets of her sweater.
Credit: John Bell

As we walked back to the hotel, the wind had begun to pick up and, crossing Madison Avenue, her sable hat flew off her head. She went traipsing after it, whooping and hollering, stopping the oncoming taxicabs with her hands in both directions, commanding the universe to halt itself until she could retrieve her sable and get herself out of the street.

Once inside the Carlyle lobby, she wished me "Merry Christmas" and sent me on my way as she disappeared behind the elevator door on her way back up to 309.

* * *

In early spring of the new year, having caught *At Home at the Carlyle: Elaine Stritch Singin' Sondheim…One Song at a Time,* I arranged to meet with Elaine so we could talk about it.

I had enjoyed the production. My wife and I were seated off to the side this time, positioned so we could see Elaine in profile when she was facing front. From that vantage point, we could see the interaction between her and Rob as she turned her back to the audience between numbers to take a swig of water or orange juice.

After the first number, on the applause and as Rob was seguing into the second number, Elaine turned to Rob and said audibly enough for us to hear, "Are you mad at me, Rob?" He smiled and kept playing. "Better you than them," she said, referring to the audience.

We wondered what that meant and found it to be a fascinating interaction between the two, making us wonder more about their personal and professional relationship. My interpretation was that the two of them must have had some sort of disagreement that was playing out on stage. Had there been a cross word or criticism just before the show? Had there been a moment in the opening number that the two had been at cross purposes on in rehearsal and in which Elaine or Rob didn't do what the other was expecting in tonight's performance? Whatever it was, it was clear that Elaine felt Rob was not doing or giving her something she needed. Perhaps the tempo was too fast. Perhaps he didn't wait for her in a moment of rubato. Perhaps she forgot to do something and it caused a momentary misalignment, something the audience would not notice, but was obvious and important to them—or Elaine anyway. I was not going to bring this up. Most likely Elaine probably wouldn't even remember it, and if she did, I didn't imagine she'd want to talk about it. But I would have given my eye teeth to have plumbed that moment with her.

Elaine met me at the Port Authority Bus Terminal at Forty-First Street and Eighth Avenue. She had walked down from the Carlyle. We'd walk back, she said, and stop and get a bite along the way. She was carrying a Pucci shopping bag and wearing white stirrup pants and a light jacket. As usual, she had on her white walking hat and her white Marc Jacobs sunglasses. She did a quick check of her sugar level, picked up a small bottle of orange juice from a nearby convenience store, and off we went.

As usual, it was my task to carry the bag. As we walked, she revealed she had been shopping that morning and picked up a few new Pucci scarves. I asked about the scarves.

"What do you mean *what do I do with them?* I wear them. If I'm in a show and I have to do some kind of press beforehand, before I've got my hair or makeup done, I wear a fabulous scarf. Listen, the hair and makeup is the part of this business I detest. With a really great scarf and a pair of Marc Jacobs, I can go out and not have to have all the mucky muck on, you know what I mean?"

We worked our way up to Elaine's, the renowned Upper East Side bar and restaurant on the corner of Eighty-Eighth Street and Second Avenue. Elaine's was a regular hangout for the who's who of the New York arts and literary scene. Over the years, regulars such as Woody Allen, Norman Mailer, George Plimpton, Tom Wolfe, Leonard Bernstein, Jacqueline Kennedy Onassis, Kirk Douglas, Clint Eastwood, and Luciano Pavarotti gathered to enjoy Elaine Kaufman, the brassy owner, in her cigarette-smoke-hazed bar. At one point in the 1960s, Elaine Stritch, fed up with the entertainment industry, spent a short stint bartending at Elaine's Bar.

"I loved Elaine, and I really loved bartending for her. And I was a good bartender."

"How did you learn to tend bar?"

Elaine tending bar at Elaine's on the Upper East Side circa 1964.
Credit: Bettman

"What do you mean? I started making drinks at my mother and daddy's parties in Detroit at the age of fourteen. I got real good, real fast."

Elaine Kaufman, the owner, who was in her eighties, was not at the restaurant this night, but her long-time manager was, and she greeted Elaine and sat us at a quiet table in the bar. Elaine ordered a nonalcoholic beer and some soup. I ordered a nonalcoholic beer, to which Elaine said, "Go ahead and have a real drink if you want. It's fine with me." Was she sure? "Oh, come on, don't be boring. Get a drink."

I ordered a vodka martini straight up with olives, to which she said, "Jesus, you don't mess around, do you?"

Had Sally come to see her Sondheim cabaret? "Of course, what do you mean? She loved it. My sister Sally is very classy, the Café Carlyle, well, the Carlyle, period, is right up her alley. Right up Sally's alley. She loved it, and we had a great time."

When the drinks came, she asked, "Well, what did you think of the Sondheim act?"

"I reviewed the show for *The Sondheim Review*," I said. "I loved it and was struck by the spoken segues between the songs—they were really carefully constructed and well written. I remember feeling the same way about the song segues in *At Liberty* at the Café Carlyle and in the song setups when you visited campus. You're a really good writer. Do you think of yourself a writer?"

"Yes, of course. You can't have the career I've had and not develop a great appreciation for good writing. Come on. Ed Albee, Steve Sondheim, Noel Coward. You can't do much better than that. A little rubs off, you know? Wit is contagious. Yeah, you bet I'm a good writer."

"Your rendition of 'Rose's Turn' was really powerful. The energy and the force which erupts from that character has never been delivered with such razor-sharp clarity, in my humble opinion," I said.

"Not humble at all. You're right. I could have knocked that role not only out of the ballpark but out of the fucking universe if I'd had the chance to play it."

"Well, and in a room as small as the Café Carlyle, your performance was amplified even more," I told her.

"Yeah, well, coulda, woulda, shoulda. No crying about it now. That's what I like about these cabaret shows, I get to cast myself. What could be better?" she said.

* * *

As per my usual pattern, I called Elaine to schedule a visit a couple of months later. When she got on the phone, she squealed, telling me "Yes, I want you to visit. We need to have dinner. I have news." Without giving me a single hint, we set a dinner date for the following week, and she hung up.

We met at EAT diner between Eightieth and Eighty-First Streets. She asked for a booth in the back "away from everybody."

Once seated, and after she ordered her scrambled eggs and toast, I asked her about the March concert celebrating Stephen Sondheim's eightieth birthday at Avery Fisher Hall in which she, along with Bernadette Peters, Patti Lupone, Audra McDonald, Marin Mazzie, and Donna Murphy were featured in a set of Sondheim's great songs for women. Elaine sang "I'm Still Here."

"What a night! And was he ever touched. I mean he rarely shows that kind of emotion, but whooo boy, that night? What a night."

"How did you feel about your performance?"

"It was great. I've never done that song better. And that feels good, because when you know he's out there and everyone's there to celebrate him, you want to get it right. And I did. But boy, oh boy, what a day."

"Why, what happened?" I asked.

"Well, we had no fucking rehearsal. We each came in that morning to sing our song, but everything was separate. I didn't know who was performing or what they were singing—none of it. I just showed up. When I got to the theater, my red pantsuit—you know, Diane Von Furstenberg did the red clothing for each of us—was nowhere to be found. These types of things are always chaos."

"Did you know that Patti Lupone was going to sing 'The Ladies Who Lunch'"?

"Noooooooooo! I knew nothing. When Patti got up and the vamp started, I was as surprised as everyone else. I knew enough to just keep my head down, and that's what I did. When she made the crack about 'Does anyone still wear a hat' and looked at me, the audience just went wild. And my reaction was perfect…puuuuurrrrrfect. Don't you think?"

Then she revealed her big news: she had been offered the role of Mme. Armfeldt in *A Little Night Music* opposite Bernadette Peters. Angela Lansbury's contract ended in June. She was very excited about returning to a Broadway musical in a headlining role. She thought Rob Bowman, her musical director, might be able to step in as the conductor. The show was going to close in June and reopen in July with the two new leads joining the existing cast.

She was particularly taken with her negotiation. I came to learn that Elaine would negotiate many of her New York contracts herself. Everyone knew she could be reached at the Carlyle and she would often work deals herself. I assume this was her strategy to avoid paying a commission to her agent.

"I told them I'd do it for the same weekly salary that Bernadette was getting, and get this, they wasted no time telling me they were unable to offer me that amount. Isn't that great? Here I go offering to do it for as 'little as they'd pay Bernadette' and they told me they couldn't come close to offering that amount to me. Talk about a kick in the teeth. What they're offering me is nothing to sneeze at, but isn't that just great—me offering to do it for as little as they're offering Bernadette and them telling me 'fuck you.' Just great. But I'll get a car, a masseuse, a marketing allowance, and an assistant, and all that is very valuable in my eyes, you know what I mean?"

"A marketing allowance?"

"Yes, for the scarves and hats! For the interviews and all that shit."

She was particularly excited about singing Mme. Armfeldt's big number "Liaisons."

"It's a great song, don't you think? A real actor's song. And it's low, just right for my range. And hell, I'm in a wheelchair the whole time, so there's no blocking—none that I have to worry about anyway."

I asked her if she had ever worked with Bernadette Peters.

"No, I haven't. Well, we've been at certain events together or performed in concerts like this birthday thing we just did for Steve, but we've never worked together. And I think she's great. She can sing and act, and she's sexy as hell. She can play a romantic lead and a comic character role. I mean, there isn't anything she can't do. Did I say I love her? I fucking hate her."

Elaine asked if I had seen her appearance a few weeks back on *30 Rock?* I told her I had not, that I was not a fan of the show. "I'm not either," she said. "I'm not sure about Tina's humor. She's a very talented lady, but the writing does not always work. But it pays well, and I adore Alec."

Elaine and Bernadette Peters in the Broadway
rival of *A Little Night Music.*
Credit: Dario Cantatore

Did she like doing television sitcoms?

"It's okay. It pays pretty good for the amount of time you have to put into it. I loved working on *The Cosby Show.* I loved him. He was always very good to me. Now that was a show that was well written and well produced," she said.

"And I loved the role of Rudy's schoolteacher. I tried to talk them into working her into more episodes," she said, explaining that she was hoping they would make her a regular. "I only worked on the show for about two months. It could have been a lot more." After a pause, she said, "And he made a couple of innocent passes at me, which I loved. It was flattering."

* * *

At the end of the summer, Elaine and I met for a light supper at the Carlyle. It was her day off from *A Little Night Music,* and she was feeling the strain. She was tired and grumpy but, as she always did, seemed to relish the company and the attention.

Seated at a corner table in the lower gallery, she asked me if I had seen the show since its official second opening. I had. What did I think? I told her I thought Bernadette Peters was wonderful as Desiree: funny, clever, and vulnerable. I also told her how much I appreciated Bernadette's careful shaping of "Send in the Clowns."

"She's dynamite, just dynamite. So much better than the other Desiree [referring to Catherine Zeta-Jones], don't you think?" Elaine said.

I told Elaine I thought her Mme. Armfeldt was wonderfully blustery and ballsy and that Elaine was impeccable on those incredible one-liners in the script.

"It's a very good show. The writing is clever—I mean the book, not just Steve's stuff—a real classy musical story."

Knowing that Elaine was only a month or so into the run and that this role had not come easy, I asked, "How did you feel about your performance thus far in the run?"

"Oh, okay. I'm not there yet, you know. I hope you'll come back and see it in a few weeks. I'll be better. I'm still dancing around with it. Memorizing the lines has nearly killed me."

The night that I saw her performance was an early preview. Fellow actors were prompting her, and during "Liaisons," you could hear Rob Bowman calling out lines from the orchestra. Honestly, it was a little sad to see Elaine Stritch, a performer known for her ability to exact razor-sharp control, appearing a bit lost and befuddled.

She hated it when her scene partners tried to lead her to her next line. But her improvisational abilities equipped her with the ability to deflect the courtesy and make a moment of the struggle. After all, "she [Mme. Armfeldt] would struggle with age and memory too, so I just tried to make it part of the character," Elaine justified.

I had heard rumors that there had been talk of trying to coax Elaine into wearing an earpiece so she could be prompted as needed from off stage. She admitted they had tried to convince her to try it, but "the day I have to have a voice in my ear telling me what I'm doing on stage, is the day I stop because that's not acting, and I won't do it. I won't—no fucking way."

Did she feel like she had received enough rehearsal?

"Oh, no, are you kidding? I got one car ride with Trevor Nunn, and we talked character, but other than that, it was a couple of days of running scenes and a couple of runs of the show and then we were in front of a preview audience. Are you kidding? Never enough time to really do the work. You do the work in front of the audience. I'll finally get this down in about a month, until then, I'm still playing with it. And I won't apologize for *that*. That's the work and it takes time, and anyone who says they can get there faster is a fucking liar—or they're no actor."

Changing the subject, I asked her about performing at the White House in July for President Obama and the first family. The program was titled "A Broadway Celebration: In Performance at the White House," and Elaine appeared with a handful of Broadway stars. The early rumors and internet buzz was that she sang "I'm Still Here" and struggled mightily with the lyrics.

A photo of Elaine and Bernadette back stage at *A Little Night Music* that was sent to Sondheim.
Credit: Unknown/Provided by Elaine Stritch

STEPHEN SONDHEIM

December 21, 2010

Dear Bernadette and Elaine —

Your photograph moved me so much
that I'm converting. Happy Hanukkah!

Love,

[signature]

Stephen Sondheim's response.
Credit: Provided by Elaine Stritch

"It was terrifying! And I didn't sing the song as well as I know I can. I did all right, but oh my god, was I scared. And I had to take my one day off from *Night Music* to do it. But he was adorable, and it was a thrill. But thank God for Rob because I don't think I would have made it without him. That's the first time I can honestly say I don't think I could have gotten back on track by myself, and you talk about scary. And I felt so bad, so bad because I really wanted to be good that night. I was singing for the president of the fucking United States. That was a first for me, and I really wanted to show them what I can do. I was okay, but it wasn't my best, and it tears me up inside."

The impact of her failing memory was beginning to assert itself.

President Obama watching Elaine perform at the White House.
Credit: Saul Loeb

"I'm afraid of this memory thing. If I can't trust the words to be there when I get up on that stage, then I've got nothing, and I mean nothing." After a moment of silence, she said, "I think I'm just tired. With the birthday concert and then this show and the White House, it was all just too much. I'm just going to have to be more careful. I have to. It's going to have to be about me watching out for me— Elaine looking out for Elaine—that's just all there is to it."

"Is your memory improving in *Night Music* the more you run the show?"

"Oh, yes, it's fine now, and it will only improve as we keep running it. I'm not worried about it, and I'm so happy to be back in a big show. It's been a while, you know? But it feels good. It feels good to have to get to the theater and go through the preshow stuff. And the audience loves the show, and they love Bernadette and me. It's good casting. And the rest of the company has been very good to us. So in the long run, it's all worth it. But it's work."

* * *

With the start of a new school year, I wasn't able to get back to see Elaine until nearly Christmas. We met at Bemelmans Bar downstairs at the Carlyle. A very classy joint, Bemelmans was named in honor of Ludwig Bemelmans, a distinctive illustrator and artist whose work was often published in the *New Yorker, Vogue,* and *Town and Country.* The bar, like the adjacent Café Carlyle, featured murals by Bemelmans of well-known New York scenes and landmarks. The bar walls surround the well-heeled patrons with scenes of Central Park including picnicking rabbits and ice-skating elephants.

Bemelmans has always been known for its extensive drink menu and an eclectic roster of entertainment. Elaine would often stop in and, when recognized and asked, join in for a number or two.

On this night, the bar was quiet. There was no entertainment on the docket. She asked me what I wanted, and still cautious about drinking alcohol in her presence, I ordered a nonalcoholic beer. She ordered a cosmopolitan—a real cosmopolitan.

I didn't say anything and tried to hide my surprise and alarm—thinking about *A Little Night Music.* Elaine had been touting her sobriety and wearing it like a badge of honor. It was clear she was proud of the fact that she had conquered her problem. So to have her order a cocktail with me made me feel more than a little uneasy. She looked at me and said, "Do you want a real drink?" I changed my order to a gin and tonic. Her eyes softened, and she held my gaze. "I have decided that I will have half a cosmo when I want it. I don't need it, but I like knowing I'm giving myself permission to have it. I'm eighty-five, I'm not going anywhere but back to the Carlyle tonight, no show to do, and it makes me feel good to know I can have one if I want it—that I can look forward to it if I want to."

It felt as if Elaine was offering a confession, that I was perhaps the first person to know she was moving back to alcohol, her old friend. I wondered if I wasn't a safe outlet as someone who was not in her presence daily, someone who was not in her inner circle of friends, and someone in whom she sensed interest without judgment. Either way, I felt we had just stepped down a different road.

"How is *Night Music* going?" I asked.

"Great, you know they've extended until after the New Year. It's the hardest work I've ever done. The schedule is relentless, and as much as I love being back on Broadway, this is an impossible schedule to keep. It really is."

And then more news: she was going to voice the role of the ghost of the dead grandmother in the animated feature film *ParaNorman*. She had been approached and given a script, and she liked the story. The role was small, but the pay was respectable, and "I don't have to worry about hair, makeup, or costumes."

Had she done much voice-over work?

"Oh, a little here and there, but listen, with a voice like mine, I'm a cinch at this stuff. I know what to do with a script. I'm probably better in this type of work than the on-camera stuff, and we both know I'm pretty good at that."

Indeed.

And the last bit of news was the she and Rob were thinking of developing a new act featuring Elton John songs. This surprised me, but the more she talked about her affection for Elton and began lightly singing a few of his classic hits, the clearer it became that this was a fabulous idea.

In the last few years, Elaine had made unexpected career choices. In 2008 she appeared in a production of Beckett's *Endgame* at the Brooklyn Academy of Music. Her current frequent guest appearances on *30 Rock* were introducing her to a new generation of TV viewers. A cabaret act featuring Elton John songs would showcase her talent in mining the most unlikely interpretations from any song lyric. It would also attract a new breed of cabaret patron.

Classic Stritch.

"I love the idea," I said.

"Good, so do I. And so does Rob. And the Carlyle ain't cheap. I've got to keep working. And this, I think, could be good."

CHAPTER 5

It had been four months since I last visited Elaine. *A Little Night Music* closed in January, and through February and March, I was dealing with the passing of my mother. When I called Elaine to see if she was up for a visit, she said, "Where the hell you been?" When I told her of my mother's death, she didn't respond with soothing words or obligatory condolences.

Elaine knew my mom was battling leukemia. She also knew that, after trying various therapies and finding all of them intolerable, my mom had elected to discontinue all treatment. Elaine liked that. She liked that my mom had been courageous enough to make decisions and dictate the terms of her dying. Whenever Elaine spoke of aging and dying, she often mentioned courage. She liked to refer to Bette Davis's quote: "Old age ain't no place for sissies."

"How did the hospice stuff work?" Elaine asked.

"You know, I was kind of scared of it at first, but it ended up being very important and comforting."

"Do they come in twenty-four hours a day?"

"No. I had thought that too. They come in and teach the family how to provide care, and they establish a schedule for nurse visits and hygiene care. And you get access to twenty-four-hour on-call care," I told her. "My family was still responsible for providing a lot of the hour-by-hour care. And we still paid for private, in-home care to help us through the whole process."

"How much did that cost?" Elaine asked.

I told her what a typical weekly bill was running, and we both talked about how it was nearly impossible to die with grace in this world. "It just costs too damn much for most people," she said.

"What about the morphine?" Elaine asked.

"The hospice people came and trained my family on how to administer the liquid morphine. It got injected orally on an as-needed basis."

"And did that keep her comfortable?" she asked.

"It did."

"How did her eating go?" Elaine asked.

"One of my mom's most important questions—the part of the process of dying that scared her the most—was about how her body would respond when it was finally overridden by the morphine. She wanted to know if she would starve. 'Will I die of thirst?' she asked.

"The hospice team leader told my mom that for as long as she wanted food and drink she would have it and that when the body began to shut down, the body would not crave or want for food or drink. The hospice team leader tried to describe a natural shift that would occur as the body began to transition away from living, characterizing the shift as something that would be comfortable and calm."

Knowing that I was travelling on weekends for the past year to be with my mom, Elaine asked, "Were you with her when she died?"

"No, I wasn't. None of us, even her husband, were with her when she died. My aunt shared with me her theory that sometimes people, knowing how hard saying goodbye can be, wait until they are alone to actually take that last breath and let go."

"I like that," Elaine said.

I told her it had initially brought me comfort, too, but that, over the last few weeks, I was struggling with the overwhelming sense of guilt about not being there.

"Oh, come on, let yourself off the hook," she said. "You have to, your mom wouldn't want you to wallow in it." And then, after a pause, Elaine said, "I'm sorry, darling…to hear about your mom. Now when are you coming to New York?"

* * *

We set a date for the following week. We met in her suite. She wanted to go for a walk. The weather had begun to break with warmer temperatures, and we'd move our way through Central Park. As we walked, she told me she had been approached by a young filmmaker, Chiemi Karasawa, who wanted to do a documentary on her. Elaine said the young woman had been pestering her for a while, since before *A Little Night Music* closed, and Elaine had been putting her off, not sure about the project. But as we walked, she said she liked Chem, as she called her, and was thinking of doing it.

"What would it entail?" I asked.

"That's the thing. I have no idea. She says she just wants to film me doing my thing, day in day out."

"Would you like having cameras around you like that all the time?" I asked.

"Well, would *you*? Of course not."

"But…?" I goaded.

"Well, it's something I've never done, you know? Just put it all on the table, show it all and tell the truth." She reported she and Rob had a few gigs coming up taking truncated versions of *At Liberty* and *Singin' Sondheim* to small cabaret rooms around the country, including her hometown of Detroit. And even London had been calling.

"So they could follow me around, showing what I do getting ready both on and off stage. It might be good to show people how much work goes into all of this, don't you think?"

We worked our way back to her suite at the Carlyle. She wanted to catch her breath before we went out for dinner. She was going to have a cosmo and asked me if I wanted one. I told her I'd pass.

"Oh, boy, who raised *you*?" she said. "You don't turn down a drink when you're in somebody's home and they're going to have a drink themselves."

I told her I'd have one, a short one. She told me to go over to the small refrigerator where she kept her insulin supplies. There was a Tupperware pitcher about half filled with premade cosmopolitan mixed just the way she liked it. I poured two glasses. She sat and drank on the bed, and I sat on a chair I pulled up beside her. We talked further about the possible documentary and then worked our way down to EAT Diner where she ordered meatloaf, scalloped pota-toes, and another cosmopolitan.

Elaine talked about how glad she was to be able to drink a little each day and control the situation. She liked anticipating her drink and knowing she would be able to feel the way it would make her feel. She was adamant in calling herself a recovered alcoholic. "After twenty-four years of sobriety, I was curious to see if I could handle one or two drinks a day, and I can. And as far as I'm concerned, that's recovered. It's not running my life. It's just something to look for-ward to. I'm getting up in my eighties—don't you love that? 'Up in my eighties.' And I feel like a little drink each day is fine at my age. How much trouble can I get into?"

When I said good night and began my drive out of the city, I didn't have my usual feelings of excitement about being with Elaine. Tonight I felt something different. I don't know if it was sadness or what, but I felt like Elaine's sobriety had ended and that she was squarely back to drinking. Of course, I was worried about the diabe-tes. She was very careful about monitoring her sugar levels, but it was clear the return to alcohol was going to complicate her life. I tried not to judge any of this. The one thing I knew no one could get away with would be to pass judgment on Elaine Stritch. Having seen her temper, I knew judging her would be the fastest way out of her life. She'd simply not tolerate judgment or pity.

* * *

My next visit with Elaine was just prior to her opening *"At Home at the Carlyle: Elaine Stritch Singin' Sondheim… Again. Why Not?"* which was a virtual reprise of her earlier Sondheim act. She didn't want to walk, she was too tired, so we headed across the street to Sant Ambroeus.

Elaine ordered some lentil soup and bread and a nonalcoholic beer. Noting the beverage choice and ordering the same, I asked her how the show was going. She was noticeably scared about it. She told me she had been invited to perform in the Hamptons in August, and while staying at the Maidstone, one of East Hampton's most elite hotels and a place she said was "divine," she experienced a very serious hypoglycemic attack or a "hypo" as she called it. She said she lost her speech, was confused and disoriented, and was in the hospital for an extended stretch of time. I told her I was amazed to hear that because here she was looking great and getting ready to take the stage again in about a week or so.

"Well, let me tell you, this was the most terrifying thing that has ever happened to me in my entire life," she said. "I lost my speech, and when that happens, well, you know, I got nothing. That's it. It's all I've got."

Did she think this was the next step in the progression of memory loss that she encountered while singing at the White House for President Obama?

"I don't know!" she screamed. "That's just it, I don't know. That's what is so terrifying. Am I really losing my ability to remember my lines? If so, I don't know what I'll do!" After calming herself, she said, "I don't think so. That was singing at the White House for the president of the United States. Who wouldn't be nervous? And I think the Hamptons thing I can chalk up to the hypo. But I'll tell you, I'm having a terrible time with the lines in this upcoming act, and I performed it last year, so it's not a lot of new stuff. Oh boy, I'm getting scared."

After a pause, Elaine announced that she was not going to drink anymore, not even just one cosmo. It was too dangerous for her in managing her diabetes. She wasn't looking for reinforcement—she never did—but I told her I thought it was a smart decision.

"Well, good for you, but that's not what's important. I don't care what anybody thinks. This is about me. I need all my concentration just to remember my fucking lines right now. What will I do if I can't count on my memory?" she asked.

She was very concerned about being able to handle herself onstage. She was sure she could get herself out of any jam if she needed to. She knew her improvisational skills were still razor-sharp and usually just as entertaining as, if not more than, anything she could rehearse. But Elaine is a really good writer. She knows how to tell a great story and set up a song, and it was clear that her memory issues might diminish her usual moxie, the well-built packages she had rehearsed and looked forward to serving up onstage.

* * *

Over dessert of a shared piece of chocolate cake, Elaine asked me what I thought about Sondheim's recent comment on the upcoming production of *Porgy and Bess* that the American Repertory Theater, directed by Diane Paulus, was producing. Audra McDonald was going to star in the production, and there was already a lot of buzz surrounding a possible Broadway transfer. The A.R.T. was announcing judicious revisions to the piece to humanize some of the characters and was billing the production as *The Gershwins' Porgy and Bess*.

Sondheim publicly took issue with the addition of the Gershwin name to the title, noting that with a piece as groundbreaking as *Porgy and Bess*, there should be no need to reference the authors and, if the authors were going to be integrated into a new title of the show, why was DeBose Heyward, one of the authors, omitted?

"Well, it's just like Steve, to tell you the truth. He can be so goddamn sanctimonious at times. Don't get me wrong, I don't disagree with him. God knows, I love writers. I've worked with some of the best, and I want them to get their due, but come on. Steve knows full well the weight a public statement like that will carry, and I think he's causing a stink just to cause a fucking stink. And of course, he's so good at launching a public attack. He knows more about musical theater than anyone else, and he knows he'll come across smelling sweet as roses. But what a swipe at what's her name…Paulus and McDonald. This is what I'm talking about with him. You can't just sit down and talk with him. He's way over everybody's head, and he's always poking…or he's silent, and you know he disapproves. I think he does it on purpose to keep people out…at a distance. This is why he scares the shit out of me and why I don't like to be around him."

Will he come to the reprise of her act this month?

"Probably not, why would he? He came the first time around and was very nice to me, which I appreciated, but you don't push your luck with Steve Sondheim, and I don't care. I don't need him to come a second time. And I'm sure the last thing he needs is to hear Elaine Stritch sing more Sondheim songs."

* * *

Before I left that evening, she told me her sister Sally had passed away back at the end of June. Sally, she said, "was very stylish and pretty. An elegant woman. And she was very talented. Growing up she was the pretty one, and she was a marvelous dancer—a ballet dancer. But she fucked up her toes, and that shot her career as a dancer."

I told her I was sorry for her loss.

"It's just me now. The baby of the family has become the matriarch."

How did it feel?

Elaine with her sister Sally and best
friend Liz Smith at the Carlyle.
Credit: Patrick McMullan

"A little weird. I've always been the famous aunt who wasn't into the family scene as much as everyone else. Now I'm the rich old aunt—the famous, rich old aunt."

As I drove home, I was glad to hear Elaine decided drinking was not a good idea. And I was eager to see her in the Sondheim act later in the month, and to see just how serious the memory issues were and how she was handling them.

True to form, Elaine's performance in the reprise of her Sondheim act was classic Elaine. She did experience consistent memory slips but was able to charm the audience with her fight to overcome them. In fact, it is this fight against her aging that makes Elaine so fascinating. In the fight we see her greatest truth, and we admire her determination and drive. And watching Elaine Stritch improv her way out of a jam, fighting to get to the other side of the punch line, is a master class in comic timing on par with the best of all of our great comic actors and comedians.

* * *

Just before Thanksgiving, Elaine and I met for dinner at the Alex Café on Lexington between Seventy-Second and Seventy-Third Streets. Elaine ordered scrambled eggs and toast and was promising to help me eat an order of macaroni and cheese. She ordered a cappuccino.

After seeing Elaine following the Sondheim cabaret at the Carlyle, I had gone up to suite 311 to congratulate her. There were other well-wishers, so I didn't stay long. Forgetting that I had attended and stopped back after, she asked me if I had caught the show. I told her I had.

"Well, what did you think?" she asked.

I told her I thought it played just as well as the first time she presented it and that she handled the memory slips very well—using self-effacement and bickering with Rob to get her through.

"Yeah, I thought so too. I think I did okay."

She asked if I had I seen her present the show at Town Hall in October and did I know she had presented it at Music Hall in Detroit. I answered negative to both and asked how the performances went.

"Okay—not great, but good enough."

Was she able to spend time with her family while in Detroit?

"A little. I stayed at the Detroit Athletic Club and spent a little time with my nieces and nephews. And the little ones—oh my god. There's little Georgie who swears he's going to be an opera singer. An opera singer, for Christ's sake. Where does that come from?"

How did she feel about spending time with family?

"A little goes a long way, if you know what I mean. And now that Sally and Georgene are gone, I'm even more out of touch. All my nieces and nephews have their families and little ones, so it's a little loud when everybody's around. But I think they enjoy me, and I enjoy the fact that they like having me around. I'll tell you what though, I sure miss my sisters. Georgene died at ninety-two, and Sally died at ninety-one. I hope that means I've got another four or five good years ahead of me," she said. "But going home is not the same without them."

During an earlier visit, Elaine had mentioned that her mother, Mildred, had a fling with a hometown boy, Bobby Clark, who went on to become a successful comedian in the entertainment industry.

Bobby Clark was a minstrel, vaudevillian, and stage, film, and television actor who built a career as part of a comedy duo team with Paul McCullough. Clark and McCullough performed together in early variety shows including the *Ziegfeld Follies* and later went on to appear on television in the 1950s including *The Colgate Comedy Hour*.

"Mother dated Bobby before she met Daddy. She said they had a lot of fun together, but you know, Mother knew he would never amount to very much as an actor. Her father, Papa Jobe, put a quick stop to that, but Mother and Bobby remained friends. When I eventually went to New York, Bobby would check in on me, take me to see movies, and things like that. We talked a lot about comedy, timing, you know, the business. He was a very smart man."

Recalling Elaine's telling of her grand affair with Jimmy Lee, who went on to become an award-winning writer in television, I said, "I think it's rather amazing that you and your mother first dated hometown boys who then went on to have substantial careers in show business."

"What's so amazing about it?" she said. "That's just who we met and dated and how we went on with our lives."

* * *

A week after Elaine's eighty-seventh birthday, we met at the Carlyle and shared a Diet Coke. I took this as a sign that she had been serious and successful regarding her August diabetes scare and decision to not drink.

Elaine looked very sharp. She wore cream tights, a cream blouse with a cream and black man's tie, and a white sweater vest over which she wore the same brown and cream fur she wore on her visit to campus in 2008. With her black sunglasses and cream hat, she looked classy, elegant, and stylish.

"Where you been?" I asked.

"Nowhere, I've been waiting here for you. I want to go over to see one of the fashion shows over at Lincoln Center."

The New York Fashion Week was in full tilt, and she wanted to catch Nicole Miller's show. She had two tickets. Feeling desperately underdressed—not that I could ever really make myself look like I belonged at a New York fashion show—we headed out.

The show was crowded. There was a lot of buzz surrounding people I did not recognize. I assumed they were associated with the fashion industry. But I was aware of people being aware of Elaine. As was often the case, she could not enter a room without being noticed and quickly becoming the center of attention. A few designer-types came up to say hello and play the "kiss" game, a game which Elaine doesn't do cheerily.

The show did not hold Elaine's interest. She fidgeted in her Carlyle paper shopping bag that held her usual cache of supplies. She even pulled out a few prunes to eat while she was watching the show. We rushed out near the end before the final designer walk.

As we headed to dinner, she asked what I thought of the show.

"Not much," I said. "I'm not really into fashion. But I'd never been to a fashion show before, so it was interesting."

Did she see anything she liked?

"Yeah, I liked that black cashmere poncho wrap. If they've got it in cream, I may get one of each. I can get her stuff at Saks."

Abruptly, she stopped in the middle of the sidewalk, took me by both shoulders, looked me in the eye and told me she was going to leave New York.

"I am, I think I've got to. This city is just too fast for me, and if you can't keep up with it, it's no place to live."

"I'll believe it when I see it," I said, unable to imagine Elaine Stritch not living in New York. "Where are you going to go?"

"Back to Detroit," she said. "I think I'm getting ready to go back home." And just as abruptly and without any follow-up conversation, she continued walking.

At dinner, Elaine ordered a cosmopolitan. I didn't say anything. I ordered a beer. She asked for a couple of bowls of chips and pretzels from the bar. She just wanted to munch. When the savory snacks arrived along with the drinks, Elaine's warmth toward her cosmo was palpable. I took a breath and decided I was going to ask her about her previous decision not to drink.

"Well, I've just decided that what I have to do is do a better of job of controlling my diabetes rather than depriving myself of my one drink a day. That's all, just one drink."

I asked her what changes she felt she could make in monitoring her diabetes.

"Well, for one thing, I've got new monitors. These are more sensitive, and they'll wake me up if my counts go too far in either direction—up or down. And I have them monitored by someone outside who checks in with me daily. She calls me every night. And I'm just going to be more particular about what I eat, and checking my counts more regularly. I'm not convinced the drinking is causing the problem. I think the diabetes and the insulin need to be adjusted, which I've seen the doctor about, and we're making changes. So I feel good about that. My only real worry is being alone a night. So the monitor will help, and I know I've got the hotel staff standing by."

Was the fear of a hypoglycemic attack part of her thinking in wanting to leave New York?

"Maybe," she said. "If I go back home, I may need to get someone to help care for me full-time. God knows I can't afford to do that in New York. No one can. But it might come down to that, after a while...eventually."

"When did you plan to make this move?"

"Within a year. I've got my niece Midge, who's a real estate agent, on the lookout. I may make a trip this spring to see what we can find. It's a little scary and a little exciting, which tells me it's right."

She went on to say that she'd like to do one more good play on Broadway if she could before she left. She brought up *Craig's Wife* again, wondering if I had made any headway with Cherry Jones. I told her I hadn't.

"Maybe we could get Bernadette to do a reading of it with us and see if anyone would nibble at it. Bernadette would be good in that role, and she loves me. Send her a script."

"I don't have her address," I said.

"I'll give it to you when we get back to the Carlyle," she said.

Since this was the second time the play had come up in the last couple of years, it was clear she really liked it.

"Well, it's a good play," she said.

"I once heard someone describe a good play as one of those plays that every time you rehearse or perform it you can find something new in it. You'll never figure it out. Good material, whether it's a play or a song, is like carving a tunnel through a mountain. Every time you run it, you figure it out a little more, like working your way through the mountain waiting to see the light shine from the other side. With a really good play, you never get there, but each time you perform it, you're getting to know it a little bit. That's the type of play you can perform eight times a week for a really long run and never tire of it."

"Yeah, well, I've dug a few tunnels in my day," she said.

CHAPTER 6

After not being in contact for a few months, I called Elaine.

"Where you been, John?" she asked.

"Oh, busy finishing up the school year and finishing up touches on a musical. I've written a musical," I told her.

"Oh yeah, what about?

"Well, you know, it's hard to talk about what a musical is about without it sounding treacly or banal," I said.

"Oh, that good, is it?" she said in her customary sandpaper grovel.

"In a few weeks, my writing partner and I are presenting a developmental reading of it at the Pearl Studios on Eighth Avenue between Thirty-Fifth and Thirty-Sixth Streets in New York. You want to come? We'd love to have you," I said with some hesitation in my voice. *Would my writing partner want her to come? Would her presence upstage the entire event? What if she hated it and was bored?*

And yet, I invited Elaine hoping she would come because I truly felt she, more than anyone else we might invite, would provide very specific and honest feedback. Nonetheless, this invitation felt risky to me. Up until now, whatever relationship was developing between Elaine and I was personal—an acquaintanceship on its way to a friendship. And while our long walks and dinners would often involve conversation about theater or the entertainment business, none of that conversation centered around me or my work.

"Of course I'll come," she said to my surprise. And even more surprising, she actually came.

The reading featured a cast of six actors with scripts in hand while the songs were played by the composer, my writing partner Justin Fischer, from the piano. A small invited audience of about twenty people were in attendance. Elaine had walked down from the Carlyle on a warm August day wearing a white T-shirt, her very short white walking shorts, sneakers, white sunglasses, and a white hat. She was carrying two shopping bags filled with juice, insulin, monitors, cash, credit cards, her little black book, a cell phone, and a paper coffee cup recycled to carry some prunes.

I greeted her and reintroduced her to my wife and introduced her to Justin. Elaine wanted me to move her seat toward the back of the room so she could be behind the crowd. I charged my wife with keeping Elaine company while Justin and I were busy getting things ready. I had told Justin I invited Elaine and that she had said she might come but that I was very doubtful she actually would. We hadn't told the actors because we didn't want to create any false expectations.

As the actors and invited audience filtered in, they became very aware, and both excitement and nervousness escalated in equal doses. I told them she was a friend and that I had invited her but didn't alert them because I really didn't think she would be able to attend. I told them I had talked with her previously about the piece and she seemed interested and I suspected she would not participate in the talkback session following the reading but would rather give any feedback to me privately.

The reading began. Elaine was fidgety throughout, and everyone in the room was very aware of her. She was shuffling through her bag, reading her monitors, shifting in her seat, and occasionally standing to make herself more comfortable. From the onset, it would appear that she was totally uninterested in the musical, the actors, the story, and the songs. But as she was going about her business, she would laugh or hoot when a line was funny or a song really built to a great climax. I think everyone was able to acclimate to her energy while still attending to the reading.

At intermission, Elaine told me she had to leave, that her sugar levels were such that she needed to get something to eat. I asked her if she was okay or if she needed any assistance. She said she was fine and that she was going around the corner for a quick bite and would then either walk back or take a cab to the Carlyle. She went up to my writing partner and really, genuinely praised his music. This was a lovely gesture to a young composer, and it meant a lot. Just before she took off, she approached the actors, all seated up front to start the second act, and spoke with them about the story and their performances. She talked to them about how important actors were to writers in the development process and how great she felt it was that they were up there giving the material such a good showing. The actors were rapt. Elaine made her exit, and the reading continued.

About a week later, I met with Elaine at the Carlyle to talk with her about the reading. As I expected and hoped, she was brutally honest. Overall she liked the story and the score and thought both worked together very well. "It's a real original story, unlike anything I've seen in recent years. And that composer is terrific. How old is he, twelve?" she said.

The story is somewhat dark, but it has a good deal of dark humor laced throughout. Not surprisingly, she responded very positively to the humor and wanted more of it.

"You've got to find more ways to lighten it up, John. It's an interesting idea, but it needs more humor. I'd go further with that. And the title is not very good." I asked her to brainstorm with me other titles, and we came up with a few that seemed viable.

She told me the climax of the play comes too early and leaves too much time for resolution. I asked her how she knew that since she didn't stay for the second act.

"Well, I read the damn thing—you sent it to me."

I had forgotten that with the invitation, I had sent her the script. I was surprised that she took the time to read it.

"The climax comes so early that right now you've got two or three moments when the story could end but you don't end it. I think you should flesh out the characters more in act 2 and delay the climax and then choose your ending. Shouldn't be hard. The characters are all interesting, and the story is unique."

Elaine was right on every account. In fact, the talkback session focused on many of these same issues, and even before meeting with Elaine for her feedback, I had written new scenes to develop characters and relationships, which then delayed the climax. And my partner was working on a new song to capture the true ending we wanted to feature.

I loved spending this evening with Elaine in her room talking about a show—my show in this instance—and really discussing what makes for good writing. Having worked with some of the best, it was fun to hear her opinions, and I think she liked having someone with whom she could talk structure and shape, something that had come easily and instinctively for her in her career but that deserved to be questioned and understood. It was an evening that went late into the night and lasted through three short "top offs" of her cosmopolitan.

Elaine brought up Marvin Hamlisch's passing on August 6.

"Did you know him?" I asked.

"Of course, I worked with him a couple of times. What a talent—a real pianist. And he was only in his late sixties, right?"

"He was only sixty-eight," I said.

"God, you got to wonder who's calling the shots on things like that," she said.

"Did you go to the funeral?"

"No, I don't go to funerals if I can help it, especially show business funerals. A lot of kiss-kiss for its own sake, if you know what I mean."

* * *

A couple of months later, at home in Pennsylvania, my phone range at 4:45 a.m. I was up, preparing for a business trip to London.

"Hello, darling. Look, I have the name of this producer, Barry Michon, who is trying to get me to come to London to do my Sondheim show. It's in a small room called the…now wait a minute…the Pheasantry. What a dumb name. I want you to call him up while you're in London and get over to check out the room for me. Can you do that?"

"Sure, Elaine, what's his number?"

"I can't find his number, just look him up when you get there and let me know what you think about the room."

"Will do."

"Oh, good, and tell him you're there on my behalf. That should get you a free dinner or something. Have a safe trip, and I'll see you when you get back."

I was taken aback by this phone call. It had been a few weeks since I had mentioned to Elaine that I was planning to fly to London. I didn't even remember telling her which day I was leaving. So the fact that she retained the information and put it together with this offer she had received seemed rather remarkable. The other thing that made me wonder is what Elaine was doing up at four forty-five in the morning. Had she received the invitation from Mr. Michon and, then, somehow remembered I was going to London? Had she put the two together too late to call me and so set her alarm to wake up and call before I left the house? It all seemed too planned for Elaine Stritch. I still wonder about it.

I had trouble looking up Mr. Michon while I was in London. Ultimately, I didn't make contact with him, but I did leave word with an assistant that I would be attending a show at the Pheasantry on behalf of Elaine Stritch and I'd be happy to meet with him while I was there.

The Pheasantry is a little jazz club located in East London below a pizza shop. My first impression was that it was a far cry from the standard of a room like the Café Carlyle. The entertainment that evening was okay but not of the caliber that Elaine would represent. And the food left plenty to be desired.

I called Elaine from London to give her my report. Considering that she would need to travel with Rob and possibly a friend or caretaker and be housed at the Savoy, I told her that I wasn't sure the gig would be worth it to her or feel like it was up to the standard she would expect.

"Well, I couldn't do it for the money he's offering, and if he didn't bother to meet with you when you left word you were there on my behalf, I'm not going to bother with it. Thanks anyway, sweetheart, and have a good flight home."

* * *

A month later, Elaine opened the door to her residence at the Carlyle with an eye patch and a badly bruised face.

"Oh my god, what happened to you?"

"Oh, you didn't know about this? I fell on Madison Avenue and hit my head on the curb," she said.

"Oh my god. Did you damage your eye?"

"No, you twit, I'm wearing this eye patch for the fun of it. Yes, I damaged my eye, I tore my retina," she said. "There I was lying in the gutter on Madison Avenue bleeding with the cabs screaming by."

"Oh, for God's sake," I said.

"And you want to know the worst part? My dentures fell out."

And in the fullness of a major shift of emotional energy, and for the first time in the four years that I had known Elaine, she choked up and her eyes started to well with tears. I didn't know how to respond.

Commanding her composure as fast as she had lost it, she said, "It was the most terrifying thing that has ever happened to me, John. I have never felt so vulnerable, I mean really exposed. I tell you. Lying in Madison Avenue with no teeth and bleeding. Terrifying!"

I told her I was real sorry to hear about the fall and couldn't imagine how painful and scary it must have been. I gave her a hug, and she clung to me. Not long, but enough to convey a strong sense that Elaine was looking for someone, some way to get herself taken care of. I got a strong sense that she was really feeling alone and unsure.

She sat down on the bed and took off her glasses so I could get a good look at her face. The bruises were healing, and the stitches over her eye were to be removed in the next day or so.

"My eye guy thinks there won't be much of a scar, but my eyesight, well, there's no guarantee there. Right now I got nothing but blurry peripheral vision," she said. "And I was supposed to shoot a *30 Rock* episode, which we've moved to next week."

"What are you going to do about the eye?"

"I don't know. If they can cover it with makeup, maybe no one will notice. If not, Tina will have to write a fall into the script. Colleen falls and lays a great big Catholic guilt trip on Jackie," she said. "Could be kind of fun, don't you think?"

Elaine didn't want to go out. In fact, at this point in our relationship, Elaine became very skittish about leaving the Carlyle. Her eyesight had been waning, a real problem since she loved reading newspapers. While she would always upgrade the prescription in her one pair of Marc Jacobs reading glasses, the rest in her extensive collection were often outdated. She had taken to using a magnifying glass. With this fall and the loss of her peripheral vision, Elaine became very aware of her loss of depth perception. She would often feel ahead of herself if she anticipated she might be approaching a step or a change in level, and she was easily spooked if she was surprised by a loud noise.

Elaine walking in New York after her
fall and subsequent eye injury.
Credit: Arnaldo Magnani

So she had me pull some soup out of her refrigerator, and we heated it up in her microwave, and she told me to pour her a cosmopolitan. I asked her if she was taking pain medicine.

"No, just Tylenol."

We sat together and listened to the national news. Elaine was a real news hound. Whenever I was in her room, her TV either had a classic Hollywood movie or a news station blasting. The news that evening featured a story about a Russian woman named Antisa Khvichava who had died purportedly at the age of 132—the oldest living human being.

"God, can you imagine living to be 132? I'd like to see ninety-five, but I'd be fine going after that," she said.

Remembering that Elaine was supposed to kick off an impressive lineup that included Philip Seymour Hoffman, Michael Hall, Julianne Moore, and Neil LaBute at the Rubin Museum for their "Happy Talk" series, I asked if the fall happened before or after.

"Before!" she screamed. "I had to cancel. But they're going to reschedule me for December. By then I should be okay, at least if I can keep from falling on my ass."

I asked Elaine if she had been able to get her trip to Michigan in before her fall. She had. "I think I found a place," she said. It's a very nice condo in Birmingham, a very Scooby-Doo suburb of Detroit. It's surrounded by shopping and restaurants, and there's a park next door to it for my little nieces and nephews. I've put in an offer, but the owner is fighting me over the dining room chairs."

"What's so special about the dining room chairs?" I asked.

"What the fuck do I know, they're antiques, real antiques, and I guess they were very expensive. She says each chair cost her $5,000. I'm buying the condo furnished, and with an offer of 1.4 million, I want the chairs. She doesn't want to give them up."

"How long have you been waiting to hear if she'll accept your offer?" I said.

"About three weeks."

"Oh, that's ridiculous," I shot back. "You tell your agent to call her and tell her you rescind the offer and make a new offer of 1.2

million and tell her she has twenty-four hours to give you an answer. That's ridiculous."

"Should I?" she asked.

"I would," I said.

She didn't.

CHAPTER 7

It had been a month since I'd seen Elaine, and I was wondering how she was doing since her fall. I was distressed when I left her last, concerned at what seemed like her fragile state of mind. I also wanted to get the date of her rescheduled appearance at the Rubin Museum, where she was to take part in their "Happy Talk" series, figuring it would be a rare opportunity to catch her in a more "au naturel" setting, appearing onstage unscripted and unrehearsed.

Four years into my relationship with Elaine, I was still unsure of what type of relationship we had with one another. From my vantage point, it felt as though we were friends. While I wasn't part of her inner circle (I didn't see her often enough for that), I did feel that we both genuinely anticipated our visits with pleasure and liked spending time together. I enjoyed accompanying her to her favorite haunts, whether a classic New York diner or refined but low-key Upper East Side establishment. I looked forward to hearing about her upcoming gigs and found her career maneuvers fascinating. At eighty-seven, she was as hungry and opportunistic as any twenty-five-year-old. I delighted in listening to her on the phone with a producer, negotiating for a higher fee—or at the very least, a masseuse, assistant, driver, and/or wardrobe allowance.

Yes, we had a comfortable rapport, and yes, it was fun to talk to Elaine, but even after four years, I still had to steel myself for a visit. Every time I knocked on the door of room 309 in the Carlyle, I felt an uneasiness. I wondered what kind of mood I'd find her in, whether she'd need something from me that I ultimately couldn't deliver. I worried that Elaine would find me boring if I weren't funny. A quick wit and a scathing sense of humor were vital to her.

On Elaine's part, I think she enjoyed the solitary attention of a younger man. I know it may sound presumptuous to say that, but Elaine loved flirting with men. And I think she enjoyed the fact that my visits were infrequent enough so as to not interrupt her very entrenched routines but often enough to bring a degree of anticipation. At the very least, I knew she enjoyed my interest, *my* enjoyment in being with *her*.

So I called Elaine to check in and find out how her eye was healing, and to get the details of her Rubin appearance. I rang her at the Carlyle numerous times over the course of two days but got no answer. The front desk gave no indication that Elaine was out of town, offering only to forward me to her voice mail. I left two messages and didn't hear back. This alarmed me. If Elaine was ever out of town, or even if she were working and would be gone from the Carlyle, she would always leave word at the front desk about when or where callers could reach her. For the hotel to patch me through and for calls at all hours to go unanswered was very out of character.

A few days later, I got a call from a woman named Martha who was acting as Elaine's assistant. She informed me that Elaine had taken another fall at the Carlyle and ended up breaking her hip and needing a hip replacement on the right side. I was free to call Elaine at the hospital, she said, but added that she was not in the best of spirits, not because the procedure hadn't gone well—it had, and Elaine was recovering—but rather because Elaine hated being in hospitals. Also, Martha reported, the crew for Elaine's documentary had been in and out throughout the entire process as they were trying to finish up the film.

Being in a hospital meant giving up control, and Elaine was addicted to control. She did not take well to being subjected to the schedules, food, and general lack of wit and personal affection under which hospitals operate. Getting out of hospitals was always a priority whenever Elaine was unfortunate enough to be admitted.

I learned from Elaine that Martha is a professional personal assistant who worked with Angela Lansbury whenever Lansbury was in New York appearing in a Broadway show. Elaine thought Martha was one of the best assistants in the business, and so, when she needed help, she did her best to secure Martha's services.

I didn't call Elaine while she was in the hospital. I felt sure I'd find her in a bad mood, rendering me impotent on the phone, unable to provide cheer. Instead, I waited a week to get her when she was out and settled back in at the Carlyle.

When I called Elaine after her release, she actually sounded pretty good. She was relieved to be out of the hospital and back in her own environment. Martha was holding the fort, and friends were stopping by for support. She was in pain and on medication, but was getting around pretty good with a walker.

"The Rubin gig has been canceled, I assume," I said.

"Well, no, I'm going to go. It's this Wednesday, and it's sold out. I'm going." Now even though I knew that Elaine had a very high threshold for pain and discomfort and that she would tolerate a great deal in order to appear onstage in front of an enthusiastic crowd and receive a paycheck, this shocked me. I tried to imagine what it would be like to appear onstage only ten days after major surgery—a body part replacement, no less. What kind of pain would she have to navigate? How mobile was she? What would it be like to have to get in and out of a vehicle? How would she get onstage?

Of course, I didn't say any of this out loud. Elaine didn't like to think about small realities; she lived moment to moment in big, sweeping gestures.

I told her I was sorry the event was sold out, that I'd been looking forward to attending, hoping that maybe she'd been given a house seat or two that she might offer. Instead she said, "Well, come with me. God knows I can use all the help I can get. Meet me here at the Carlyle at three."

* * *

When I arrived that day and got up to her room, Elaine was there with Bella Botier, her makeup and hair designer, and she was in a rage.

Martha had just quit. "Can you believe it? Can you fucking believe it? I'm out of the hospital three days after a fucking hip replacement, I have to go onstage tonight, and she quit. Just today. Jesus fucking Christ. I've never experienced anything so unprofessional IN…MY…LIFE. Thank God you're here, because I don't know how I would be able to do this tonight. I cannot believe she did this to me. Can you?"

She fixed me with an intent look that sent liquid fear running through my veins, the kind I anticipated every time I arrived for a visit. Elaine Stritch on a tear is terrifying to anyone with polite proclivities. The launch of her unbridled vitriol could be horrifying to observe. If she were berating someone face-to-face, I always found myself wanting to reach out to the victim—the clueless waiter who had no idea of the wrath a lukewarm cup of coffee might unleash—to pacify. But I never did. For if there was one thing Elaine would not tolerate from any of her friends, it was to betray her allegiance by siding with anyone under her attack.

Before I could say anything, she started railing at Bella about getting all her supplies packed into her Carlyle shopping bag, making particular note about her pain medicine, along with her diabetes monitors, her insulin, her billfold, a bottle of orange juice, a cup of prunes, her hair and makeup supplies, etc., etc., etc. Bella worked to get the bag packed. The front desk called up to say the limousine had arrived.

"Tell them to fucking wait, I'll get down there as soon as I can. Tell them I just had hip surgery and they need to be fucking patient."

Even in this crisis, Elaine looked terrific in a black blouse with a black beaded necklace, a black hat, brown eyeglasses, and black tights. I thought the brown Marc Jacobs seemed wrong and almost suggested the black ones, but decided to steer clear of any and all land mines.

She was planning to wear a pair of black leather calf-high boots and needed help getting them on. I assisted in what was, given the tenderness of the incision at her hip, a delicate and entirely frightening maneuver. I was hyper-aware of the incision, so trying to get her foot down the shank of the boot and actually seated into the heel took effort. With each little shift and shimmy, she would cry out in pain. We were working at cross-purposes, me treading cautiously and her wanting—like ripping off a Band-Aid—to just get her foot all the way into the boot. We finally got it done, and she hobbled over to the mirror with me, turning and pivoting to check herself from many angles.

"I look pretty good, don't I?" she said.

"Spectacular, Elaine, just spectacular."

With that, I helped her with her brown sable fur, and she finished her ensemble with a pair of black leather gloves. The choice of the brown Marc Jacobs was perfectly clear. I was glad I'd kept my mouth shut.

Elaine's rant about having been left in the lurch by Martha roused again in the elevator and into the lobby. The more she cursed and shouted, the more anxious she became, alternately shouting and whimpering at her plight. Nothing Bella or I said helped.

She was in such a state that I couldn't imagine how she'd be able to go onstage in front of an audience, so before we got out of the elevator, I got in front of her, looked her squarely in the eye, and asked her if she wanted to cancel. I told her that given the circumstances, they would certainly understand.

"Nooooooo!" she screamed. "I canceled once, I'm not going to cancel again. Now let's get in the fucking car."

Getting in the fucking car was what scared me most. I suspected that once Elaine got onstage, she would be able to transition into the persona she would present to the crowd, but what I feared was what she (and Bella and I) would have to go through for the three and a half hours before. With Elaine and her walker leading the way, the Carlyle staff cleared her path and opened the doors, helping her outside to the waiting limo.

The driver and I helped Elaine into the vehicle, with her yelping and groaning with every shift of weight. Like me, the driver seemed petrified, and quickly backgrounded himself, leaving most of the work to me. Once she was inside, he put the walker into the trunk. Bella sat in the back next to Elaine with the supplies, and I sat up front next to the driver. Unbeknownst to us all, Elaine was planning a stop to see her doctor, Dr. Gideon, whose office was located at Park and Sixty-Fifth. She wanted to get a shot of vitamin B12 and have him take a look at her incision.

The driver, clearly noting the stop was not part of his contracted itinerary, but unwilling to roil Elaine, made the appropriate detour.

When we pulled up, the driver and I assisted Elaine while Bella waited in the car. I helped Elaine up the short flight of four stairs and into the office. Elaine barged into the reception area with her walker.

"Where's Dr. Gideon?" she blurted out.

"He's with a patient," said the nurse at the front desk.

"Well, get him, I don't have a lot of time," she said as another nurse intercepted and escorted her away from the patients in the waiting room and back into Dr. Gideon's private office.

After a bit of small talk about the recent hospital stay, Dr. Gideon gave her the shot, took a quick look at the incision, and told her it looked good. He asked her what pain medication she was on, and not remembering, she told him it was working fine. She said she had a supply in the car, as she was on her way to do an appearance at the Rubin. I was expecting Dr. Gideon to respond with disbelief or caution, but instead he wished her luck. Had he learned not to question Elaine? Either way, out of the office she went, back down the stairs, into the car, and on her way.

Or so I thought.

Dr. Gideon's inquiry about her medication made Elaine nervous that perhaps Bella hadn't packed it. So back in the car and overriding Bella's assurances, Elaine demanded the shopping bag and rummaged through it herself. Not finding the right pills, she went ballistic.

"Bella, it's not in here. This is the wrong fucking bottle of pills. Oh my god, what am I going to do? John, what am I going to do? I can't believe this." At that point, she started to cry.

I've always been pretty good in a crisis. My mother was a nurse specializing in psychology, so growing up, I was exposed to calm problem solving. I told the driver to pull over and turned my body squarely around to Elaine.

"If I go back to the Carlyle, will I be able to find the pills?"

"Noooo, you're not going to know where they are. Bella has to go back."

Bella, feeling terrible and fearful that she was about to be sacrificed to the gods, said she would go and get the pills and then meet us at the museum. Off she went.

I got into the back seat with Elaine. Nearly inconsolable, she went off on another tirade about Martha's betrayal. I grabbed her hand and told her everything was going to be okay and that we were going to proceed to the Rubin and get settled in. I assured here that when Bella arrived, she could get a quick bite of food and take her medication and that she would feel better. With a bit of disbelief, I was relieved to find she began to calm down a bit.

I told the driver to continue, hoping that my presence in the back with her, along with some physical contact—I was holding her hand and rubbing her arm—would be enough to quiet her fears. Things were going smoothly for a couple of blocks, but then Elaine noticed that she couldn't find one of her black leather gloves.

"Oh my god, I've lost my glove. Oh my god, not this too. I can't find my other glove!"

Dear God, no, I thought to myself as I told the driver to pull over.

"We must have left it at Dr. Gideon's office!" she lamented.

"No, I specifically picked up both of your gloves and gave them to you in the car," I said, feeling sure that I could solve this one quickly. "I saw you put them on. You must have taken them off to look for the pills. They've got to be in this car."

Once the car stopped, I looked in the shopping bag, on the floor, under the seats, on the seats, under Elaine, and her fur coat to no avail. Elaine was nearing hysteria.

"If I have lost this glove, I'm going to kill someone, and I mean *kill* someone."

I told her to calm down, that it wasn't that important, that she could always get another pair of gloves. This was the wrong thing to say. It implied to Elaine that I felt she was overreacting and inflating the problem for the sake of dramatic impact.

"Don't tell me to fucking calm down. After the day I've had. I cannot lose one of these gloves. We have to go back to Dr. Gideon's. Now!"

Partially as apology so she wouldn't turn on me, I reiterated as calmly as I could that the gloves were not at Dr. Gideon's, that I had seen her put them on.

"Well, you're wrong. They're not here. We have to go back," she demanded.

I got out of the driver's side, walked around to her side, and opened the door. Looking down between the seat and the door, I moved my hand carefully under Elaine's butt and her new right hip. I felt between the seat and the seat back. Feeling like the gods had smiled on me, I pulled out the glove.

"Oh my god. Well, how did it get there!" she wailed.

Crisis averted, we continued toward the Rubin. Still weeping and moaning, Elaine then started to flare up again over the fact that Martha quit on her. Trying to redirect, I calmly asked, "Why did she quit?"

"She said that if she was going to work for me I was going to have to show her more respect. Can you believe that? How's that for professionalism for you? The very day I have to do an appearance!"

"Did something occur between you two that upset her?"

"No. Not a goddamn thing. Show her more respect. Come on," Elaine said, as if the notion that she could be demanding, rude, or disrespectful was unimaginable.

That afternoon it was unimaginable to Elaine Stritch.

* * *

We got to the Rubin at Seventeenth Street and Seventh Avenue, and the driver double-parked. The driver and I gingerly helped Elaine out of the car and got her stabilized with her walker. She cried out in distress as cars whooshed by in the thick rush-hour traffic. Elaine had an unusual relationship with New York traffic: she feared the cars and yet had no problem walking out into traffic, waving her arms, and yelling at the drivers to slow down and give way so she could cross.

With Elaine safely on the sidewalk, I got her shopping bag and double-checked the car to make sure we had all of her supplies and belongings. I noticed that the driver double-checked my double-checking.

We went in to the Rubin, and Elaine announced her arrival to the twenty-something woman at the front desk, demanding to be taken to the green room for the night's event. The woman, who had no idea who Elaine was, asked us to wait while she made a call. After a quick phone conversation, she told us that someone would be out shortly.

After a moment or two, I was aware of a woman and a man with a video camera near us in the lobby, shooting Elaine's arrival. At first I thought it was a fan, but when Elaine became aware of them, she shouted out, "Is that you, Chem?"

It was Chiemi Karasawa and one of her cameramen. Elaine said they were going to shoot the evening in case they got anything they wanted to use for the documentary, and after Elaine got settled backstage, they were going to shoot a few clips for use as extras for the DVD or to assist in fund-raising.

Chem and her cameraman kept their distance while Elaine and I waited…and waited…and waited to be escorted to the green room. With no seating available in the lobby, Elaine had to stand with her walker, in pain, waiting to be received. I could sense her growing ire at the indignity of the moment. I also wondered, given the day so far, if she might be perfectly primed to throw a great tantrum for the benefit of the camera.

"Where's Tom?" she demanded of the poor woman at the desk, referring to the director of public programs at the Rubin, her contact for the event. "He's the fucking producer of this goddamn event. He should be here to greet me for Christ's sake."

An administrative assistant finally came forward and apologized that no one had been present to greet Elaine, stating that they weren't expecting her until six or so for the seven o'clock event.

It seems that Elaine, knowing the museum was going to send a car, had called the car company to rearrange for an early pickup so she could squeeze in her doctor's visit and the documentary interviews at the museum before her appearance. She figured she could kill all three birds with one limousine. I learned that having a car secured and paid for by a producer was a resource that Elaine was not likely to squander.

There was one problem, though. She hadn't informed Tom of her plan.

"What do you mean you weren't expecting me until six?" she snapped. "It doesn't matter, any time I arrive, you should be able to have someone greet me and help me get settled in. Tom knows I just had my hip replaced, for fuck's sake."

The assistant stood frozen, completely unprepared for Elaine's venom. I felt for her, this young bunny about to be devoured by a rattlesnake.

"Could you show us back to the green room or dressing room you have for Ms. Stritch?" I said, hoping to get Elaine off her feet and all of us out of the goddamned lobby.

The trek back to the dressing room was not a short one. When the assistant mentioned that it would involve "just a couple of flights of stairs," I nearly had a meltdown myself. With a firmer tone than I would typically use with a stranger, I said, "I'm not sure Ms. Stritch can navigate stairs. You all do know, don't you, that's she's only ten days past a hip replacement surgery?" The assistant just looked at me. Sensing that my display of frustration was helping to keep Elaine calm, I asked rather accusatorily if there was an elevator. There was. When we got to it, however, we saw that it was a tiny employees' elevator used primarily for moving collection pieces.

Not trusting its size, Elaine was absolutely terrified of it. I urged her in, telling her I thought it would be easier than the stairs, and that I'd ride up with her. She acquiesced in great, profane protest. Once we got in and closed the door, the first lurch of the industrial lift sent her into a rage. "Stop it! Stop it right now! I'm getting out. I'm not riding in this thing."

I managed to stop it, and we returned to the floor level. She got out, cursing up a storm. Her pain meds were clearly wearing off, which made me dread the stairs even more. But as calmly as possible, I steered her toward the two flights—an open stairway in the lobby. We got there and began the ascent. She held the handrail with her left hand, and I was on her other side with my hand under her fur coat, firmly gripping the waistband of her tights. We took the stairs one at a time with Elaine screaming out in pain at the top of her lungs. Other museum goers in the gift shop and café were craning their necks to see the source of the commotion.

Finally, we made our way up the last stair and back to the closet-sized dressing room ("This isn't a green room, this is just a fucking dressing room!").

"Where the hell is Bella?" she cried as I helped her get seated in front of the makeup mirror.

I called Bella. She had the pills and was in a cab on her way.

"She's just minutes away," I lied, knowing that with rush-hour traffic, it could be another half hour or more before Bella might arrive.

The administrative assistant asked if there was anything she could get for Elaine.

"Yeah, get this out of here," Elaine said, referring to the small cracker-and-cheese plate on the dressing room counter.

"What kind of hospitality crap is this? I need dinner. Get me a hot bowl of soup and a Diet Coke with lots of ice," she demanded. "And make it quick. I need food, or I'm not going to make it through this night."

The assistant, eager to accommodate, mentioned that the museum café was known for its Mulligatawny soup. Would that do?

"Well, I don't know. Get me some and we'll find out."

"Yes, Ms. Stritch," she said, scampering off.

While Elaine was waiting for the food, I helped her remove the fur coat. She went through her bag looking for her diabetes monitor. Rummaging through her packed bag typically calmed Elaine. Knowing she had her monitors, juice, prunes, and whatever else she might need, reinforced Elaine's sense of control. She checked her sugar levels, and surprisingly, they were okay. She took a few swigs of orange juice and again asked where Bella was.

Bella finally arrived with the pills, eliciting tears of relief from Elaine. And the assistant arrived with the soup and soda so Elaine could wash down the pills and get something in her stomach. Elaine wanted to be alone, so Bella and I closed the door and waited outside, in the stage's wing.

I asked Bella how she did on her errand.

"I couldn't get a cab from Dr. Gideon's back to the Carlyle, so I ran," she said. Then on the way back she had the Carlyle doorman hail her a cab, but the traffic was terrible. "And I knew Elaine would be screaming."

* * *

I'd never met Bella, although I'd heard her name before. When Elaine first came to campus, part of Elaine's negotiation with me was the surprise announcement that she needed additional money to cover the expense of having Bella come to the Carlyle early in the morning to do her hair and makeup.

I asked Bella how long she'd been working with Elaine. "Forever, or at least it feels like forever," she said. Bella had a big, round face with wide, warm eyes. It was clear that she was a kind woman who must have been flattered by Elaine's decision to use her as her personal hair and makeup artist.

Were things always this volatile?

"Oh, yes. It's always like this. Well, she's very uncomfortable right now because of her surgery, but even when she feels okay, things are always tense. She's like a scared little child. I know when she yells she's not yelling at me. She's just scared about something, and that's how it comes out. I've learned not to take it personally." I was intrigued by Bella's analogy. I had chalked up Elaine's demanding nature mostly to simple diva-dom. But this likening of Elaine to a frightened child began to increase my curiosity about the baggage she had carried through her life, baggage that had clearly informed her work.

After a few minutes, having eaten as much of the soup as she wanted, she called out, "John, where are you?"

I opened the door, and Bella and I squeezed in to the little room.

"Get this out of here," she said, referring to the soup. "It's not even hot. Do you fucking believe this place?" she said.

She wanted Bella to do her hair and makeup so Chiemi and the cameraman could come in for the interview. Bella worked quickly and efficiently while Elaine moaned quietly to herself. It was clear the medication was kicking in, but the emotional toll of the day's abandonment and the less-than-star-quality treatment waiting for her at the Rubin had bruised her soul.

Bella and I waited in the wings while Chiemi and the cameraman squeezed in.

After they got set and rolling, I heard Elaine raising her voice saying, "Tina, that is a lie!" I was afraid Elaine's rage had been sparked again by something that Chiemi had said or had reported Tina Fey had said on camera for the documentary. It sounded like Chiemi had wanted to get Elaine's response.

Elaine went on to say, "I have paid for every piece of fur I've ever had on my back, all my life. No NBC TV, no movies…I pay."

Taken aback by the strength of her retort, I was intrigued that such a combative tone might be part of the documentary.

What I came to learn is that as part of the Kickstarter promotional campaign to raise funds to finish the movie, Chiemi was planning to use a bit of interview with Tina Fey about Elaine's work on *30 Rock,* along with this retort from Elaine. Tina mentions that Elaine always wanted to wear her own clothes on *30 Rock*, often a fur coat and hat, and Tina had begun to suspect that Elaine was charging the costs of some of these furs to the show. To which Tina said, "God bless it. I hope I paid for all your hats and fur coats, because you deserve them…you sneaky bitch." After Elaine's "I pay," there was a pause, and then with a sideways turn of her head and sparkle in her eyes, she playfully says to the camera, "Sneaky bitch indeed."

After that little episode, I heard what did appear to be a real conversation between Elaine and Chiemi wherein Chiemi might have asked Elaine for suggestions of people the producers could approach about contributing money to the film. It was hard to hear Elaine's exact response, but the gist of it was that she had agreed to do the documentary but she hadn't agreed to be involved in raising money to get it funded. She suggested it would be very uncomfortable for her to approach her friends in the business to help fund a project about herself.

"My part is this, letting you film me. The rest of it is yours," she said.

After Chiemi and her cameraman exited the dressing room and went to set up in the back of the auditorium, Tom, the evening's missing-in-action producer, finally arrived.

Elaine gave him a piece of her mind, telling him, "What a lousy producer you are. I was here, and there was no one to greet me. No one to show me where to go. And I get back here, and there's this fucking sad little plate of crackers and grapes. Come on, is this amateur hour or what!"

Tom apologized profusely and asked if there was anything else she needed before the event. "It's a little late for that now, Tom," she shot back.

*　*　*

Elaine was set to appear onstage with Dr. Murali Doraiswamy, an internationally recognized expert in brain health and aging, with whom she was to engage in a freestyle conversation about the concept of happiness. Elaine would talk about it from her perspective as an actress and performer and octogenarian. Dr. Doraiswamy would speak about it from the perspective of a scientist. At approximately fifteen minutes before curtain, Dr. Doraiswamy was brought to Elaine's dressing room—the only dressing room, mind you—so they could meet one another.

"Do you think it's a good idea for us to meet and chat before we get onstage?" she said. "I thought the whole point of this was two people who have nothing in common and don't know one another talking about happiness. I don't think we should get to know one another," she said.

Dr. Doraiswamy was fine with that but did shake her hand and tell her how much he was looking forward to their conversation.

"Oh, me too, darling, me too," she said.

At that point he and Tom turned to leave, but Elaine stopped them both, asking how the introductions were going to be handled.

Tom said they'd be introduced and then come onstage at the same time and take their seats. Elaine didn't like this plan. She felt they should come from opposite sides of the stage and that they should be introduced separately, with Dr. Doraiswamy being introduced first, of course. Dr. Doraiswamy approved of that scenario, and off he and Tom went, relegated to anywhere other than Elaine's dressing room.

At approximately five minutes until curtain, the administrative assistant who had been charged to find soup knocked on the dressing room door. She was wearing a headset, serving as the stage manager. She called places and made her exit. "Oh, boy, now she's a stage manager," Elaine said as she got up and, with her walker, moved to the wing so she could see the pathway to her chair. She asked me if there were any cables on the floor in her path. I told her no; the path was level and clear. "Thank you, honey," she said.

At the "two minutes" call, something very interesting occurred. With Tom, the stage manager, and I all standing in the wing with Elaine, and Bella quickly rolling a lint brush over her black blouse and tights, Elaine got very focused and quiet. She leaned on her walker with her head down. Had she been preparing for a performance, one would imagine she was taking a few moments to quiet her nerves and review lines. But since this was a simple, unscripted conversation, the quiet focus seemed a little unusual to me.

I peered out at the audience. As Elaine had reported, the event was sold out. There was standing-room only, with people squeezed in at the back. The playwright Edward Albee and maestro James Levine were in attendance. There were possible plans for the three of them to go out for dinner afterward.

When Dr. Doraiswamy was introduced, the audience gave him a very strong, energetic round of applause. When Elaine was introduced, the house erupted. There were hoots and hollers and catcalls.

The audience was obviously filled with Elaine Stritch devotees who, like myself, figured this was going to be a rare opportunity to catch the performer in a nonscripted appearance.

When it was time for Elaine to come onstage, she appeared from the wing walking with her walker. Once she knew she was clear of the wing and all light and attention were on her, she raised a hand and, with a quick, staccato gesture, shut the audience up. While they were still on their feet, she said, "You know, tonight, I'm told, is about happiness. Well, less than ten days ago I had my right hip replaced, and I want to show you what I'm happy about tonight." With that, she moved the walker out of her way and hobbled to her seat unattended. The audience could not be contained.

In those few quiet moments before curtain, Elaine had been contemplating one of the most important things a performer must do: how to win over the audience. Elaine knew that without a script or song lyrics, her opening salvo would set the mood for the entire evening. She need not have worried about winning over *this* particular audience, but she had enough of an ego to want to make a big splash, especially at a time in her life when she might have wondered if she could muster the energy for such an appearance. A lifetime onstage had gone into those quiet moments before curtain, and the result was a demonstration, by a real pro, about how to deliver, on cue, regardless of what happens before the curtain rises.

* * *

Dr. Doraiswamy graciously greeted Elaine and helped her get settled into her chair, and the conversation began.

Elaine was charming. She flirted with her costar, calling him her leading man for the night. He deferred to her throughout. She invited him in and seemed to be interested in his scientific insights. She talked a lot about her recent fall and her eye injury in addition to the hip replacement. But she said she was happy.

She told the audience that her doctors claimed that her smooth recovery from the hip surgery was due to the strong leg muscles she had developed from frequent walks around New York City. Dr.

Doraiswamy injected that her attitude and zest for life surely contributed to her recovery and state of happiness as well.

At one point, Elaine shared with the audience that she'd recently received a copy of a letter in the mail from a fan. The letter was from Tennessee Williams to an unknown person (it was indiscernible in the copy) and included some very complimentary comments about Elaine. The fan had obviously come by the letter and wanted Elaine to have it.

In the letter, she said, "Tennessee Williams says that he thinks I would be great in his play *Sweet Bird of Youth*. He wrote that I was honest and unafraid of my talent, and he praised me for my sobriety." She went on, "The fact that this person took the time to send me this letter, and let me tell you how good it made me feel, is a real mark of goodness and, for me, happiness."

The conversation continued, and then the floor was opened for questions and answers. One of the very first questioners stood up and, speaking into the microphone, introduced herself and said she was the one who sent Elaine the letter from Tennessee Williams.

The audience gasped, and Elaine, stiff from sitting in the chair, carefully rose and hobbled over to the side of the stage. She then directed the woman up onto the stage and gave her a tearful hug. The audience again roared with approval and delight.

For the record, the letter said,

> *I've lived the better part of my life relying on a deep-seated instinct that always knew to place me in the vicinity of people who would help me, pull me through the rocky terrain that is my natural habitat.*
>
> *Every once in a while I meet someone who seems to me the perfect person to understand my particular melodramatic scenarios, someone who will listen to my fantasies and not take me too terribly seriously because they've seen deeper wells than I've ever dream of digging.*

An example that comes to mind is Elaine Stritch, an actress who did Leona (In Small Craft Warnings*) years ago in London, and would be ideal as the Princess (in* Sweet Bird of Youth*) if anyone would finally do the play as it was intended. She strikes me as intrinsically honest, and absolutely unafraid of her talent. She seems to just ride its back to whatever destination it has planned for her, and I imagine she's scared to death a lot of the times, but she's a trouper, and she laughs a lot while she's soiling her panties and thinking of an escape.*

I hear she's found an escape, for which I envy her. I can spend the rest of my life never craving another cigarette, but I absolutely cannot lick this addiction to alcohol. I wake up mornings thinking of that first drink, and I play these games with myself, as in, 'Shall I have a claret this morning? That would be unique,' or 'I haven't had a Brandy Alexander in years; today is the day to break the trend.' I seem to have no control whatsoever over this power. I have dreams of swimming in tubs and rivers and streams of alcohol. I wake up in a panic wondering if I will ever have another drink again. I once phoned up a liquor store in Key West and ordered an ungodly amount of booze, and they asked me if I was stocking a fallout shelter. I was just afraid there would be a shortage of gin and scotch.

I don't know if it's true that the creative soul is driven to drink more so than others. I somehow doubt it: it sounds like the excuse of a drunk to say, 'I am afflicted with the artists' disease,' when in fact all booze does is keep you from being anything but over-emotional and worthless. I obviously don't have the answer: talk to someone who licked it and who still bears the title of artist. I would imagine Elaine is an even better actress now than she was in that amber haze that I always associate with the best benders.

She's dear and gifted and open, and you must give her my best and ask her to offer you the advice that will keep you out of this boring swamp I've led you to.

* * *

After the event, Elaine met Ed Albee and James Levine in the lobby. There they were: Elaine leaning on her walker, Edward leaning on his cane, and James sitting in his wheelchair. The three huddled together as old friends trouping on in the face of age and infirmity. What a blazing trio of talent they represented.

Elaine begged out of dinner; she was too tired and sore. I realized that, had Elaine felt like joining them, most likely I would've been asked to come, for Elaine clearly would've needed the assistance. What a lost moment for me in that I might've been dining with Elaine, one of America's preeminent playwrights, and one of its most accomplished conductors. But alas, they said their goodbyes, and Elaine began the long trek back to the lobby to get to the waiting limo.

Once she was in the car, I was ready to say my goodbye and head to Port Authority to catch my bus home. But Elaine pleaded with me to stay and help her get settled back in at the Carlyle. I'd assumed Bella would be the one Elaine would want to assist her, but she instructed Bella to sit up front and told the driver to drop off Bella at her home before heading to the Carlyle. I felt awkward at this, as if I were replacing Bella. I wondered what Bella might have been thinking, to have this guy she'd only met that day be the one to whom Elaine was turning. Bella didn't reveal any sense of injury, however, and who knows, maybe she was relieved to put the long, trying day to bed.

On the drive to Bella's home, Elaine asked, "How did I do?" Bella and I assured her she had been tremendous, as evidenced by the audience's glee.

"Yeah, I think I did pretty good," she said.

Producer Tom had handed me an envelope to give to Elaine after the event had ended. After she opened it, she said, "Goddamn it, this is $2,000 short of what we agreed on. Now I'm going to have to call and deal with that tomorrow. Jesus Christ. Bella, darling, I'll send you a check tomorrow, okay?"

"Sure, Elaine," said Bella.

After we dropped Bella off, I asked Elaine about James Levine. I knew she'd been in a few major productions of Edward Albee's plays, so his appearance made sense to me, but I found her friendship with James interesting because, to my knowledge, she wasn't a big fan of classical music or opera.

"He came to see me in *At Liberty* fourteen times," she said. "He's one of my biggest fans, and I'm his. He saw the show twelve times in New York and then twice in Boston. He came backstage to meet me in Boston. I didn't know who he was, but he told me he wanted to take me to dinner at the Carlyle and gave me his business card. Well, when I realized who he was, I was so goddamn embarrassed. I told him, 'I really should work on getting out more.' We met for dinner at the Carlyle and have been best friends ever since. I. Love. Him. To. Death. He's been having a real hard time lately. I'm so glad he was able to come and see me tonight. I hear he might conduct again next season at the Met. God, let's say a prayer."

When we got back to the Carlyle, Elaine asked me to help her get up to her room. Once in, she checked her diabetes monitors and determined that she needed some insulin. Since her eye injury, it had become increasingly hard for her to read the settings on the injector. She asked me to double-check them before she gave herself the shot.

Feeling good about her sugar levels, she collapsed on the bed and requested that I pour her a small sip of cosmo. I asked her whether that was a good idea, given her pain medication. She answered that it had been four hours since she'd taken the pills and that she'd rather have a little drink to take the edge off than more pills. I didn't feel good about her choice, but given the day and evening she'd just experienced, I figured it wasn't my place to police her.

I poured her a very small glass of the premade concoction. After a sip or two, she said she needed help getting out of her boots; with her hip incision, she couldn't bend over enough to get them off. I assisted, again feeling very nervous about causing her any pain and discomfort. Once we got the boots off, she announced she would need my help in getting her tights off.

"Uh, okay, sure," I said, a little embarrassed at the thought of trying to help her out of her tights and undressing her down to her underwear. Elaine, of course, showed no sense of embarrassment whatsoever. She needed help, and tonight I was her helper. I suspect if I hadn't been present, she'd have called down to the front desk and asked them to send someone up. So I was going to help Elaine Stritch get undressed. After the day we'd spent together, a little indelicacy was no big deal.

So as Elaine stood up and held on to the walker, she told me to reach under the long black blouse and pull the tights down over her pelvis. I very carefully found the waistband of the tights, grasped them, and slid them downward. Once the tights had cleared her pelvis, she sat back down on the bed and told me to slowly take the tights down her legs. Averting my eyes, I did as instructed. She sighed in relief.

"All right, now I have to get out of this blouse."

I was very unsure how this was going to be navigated, but she had it all figured out. She unbuttoned the blouse and told me to fetch a white T-shirt from her dresser. "Now get my robe from the back of the bathroom door and hold it up and look away." Like a soldier in Elaine Stritch World, I was glad to receive such specific instructions. I complied, and she slipped out of the black blouse and pulled the T-shirt over her head. When finished, I helped her into the robe, found her slippers, and got her comfortably positioned back in bed with pillows under her knees.

Finally, for the first time that day, I felt like Elaine was okay—safe in her bed and able to rest. I sat beside her and told her that she'd made it through a very tough day brilliantly.

"Yeah, I think I did okay, not too bad."

At her request, I heated up some leftover scrambled eggs in the microwave and prepared a toasted Bay's English muffin with butter. While I cooked, I asked if she'd been able to shoot the *30 Rock* episode that had been postponed due to her eye injury.

"Yes," she said. "Don't you watch *30 Rock*? It aired while I was in the hospital." I confessed I didn't. "Well, you missed it, you twit," she said.

How had it gone?

"Oh, okay. They killed me off. Colleen died. I think that's all that's left for me to play, dying old women. But I don't mind."

"Hey, did you close the deal on the condo in Michigan?" I asked.

"Yes, finally!"

"Did you get the dining room chairs?" I asked.

"You bet. But she wanted it written into the contract that when I sell it, she gets first dibs on the chairs. I said, 'What the hell?' What do I care?"

Given the day she'd just endured, I hesitated but then asked when she thought she'd make the move out of New York.

"Late spring. I want to be there for the summer," she said.

It was getting late. I asked Elaine if she needed anything else. She asked me to place her medication on her bed stand along with her diabetes monitor. I gave her the remote control, and she said she was set.

"Sweetheart, thank God you came with me today. What would I have done without you?"

"If I know you, you'd have barreled through just fine. But I'm glad I was able to help. I'll call next week to check in and wish you 'Merry Christmas,'" I said.

"Oh, Merry Christmas, darling," she said.

I made my way down to the lobby. Seeing that I had a while to wait before catching the final bus home, I sat in one of the luxurious wingback chairs in front of the lobby fireplace.

This visit was almost too much to process. Being with Elaine in real distress and being forced to assist her had helped me conquer a major fear I had about her. From that point on, I was never again fearful of how I might find Elaine.

I thought about how calm Elaine became when I raised my voice in her defense about the stairs and the elevator back at the Rubin. As much as Elaine liked to be in control, this night she needed someone to take care of her, to stand up for her, to validate her victimization in the face of her growing sense of aging and vulnerability.

As for her appearance, watching her make the transition from her personal self to her stage persona was a master class in performance study.

Finally, assisting her with intimate tasks in her private room felt like a great compliment, an expression of trust. Sitting in the Carlyle lobby, exhausted and exhilarated and still not knowing where our relationship was heading, I knew, in some way or another, it was moving forward.

CHAPTER 8

After my experience with Elaine at the Rubin Museum and because of her increasing fragility, I began checking in with Elaine every couple of weeks or so by phone. In February, I drove in to the city to attend a preview of Chiemi Karasawa's first cut of her documentary titled *Elaine Stritch: Shoot Me* held in a screening room at NYU. It was a small, invited audience.

When I arrived, the room, which held about fifty seats, was nearly packed. Just before the appointed start time, Elaine walked in, with a walker and assisted by Chiemi. It was a cold and dreary day, and Elaine was decked out in fur.

When the eighty-minute screening ended, everyone stood and turned to the back row where Elaine was seated and applauded. She made a few remarks about how hard it was to watch some of what she was seeing on the screen but went on to compliment Chem about the work and thank everyone in attendance for their interest.

As the crowd broke, I passed by Elaine so she would know I was in attendance, thinking I would merely make quick contact and get on my way. But before I could say anything, she said, "Sit down. I want to know what you think as soon as everyone gets out of here."

When it was just Elaine, Chiemi, and I, I told Elaine that I thought the documentary was extremely entertaining and moving. I told Chiemi that I felt she had tapped into something very potent—messages about living, surviving, aging, and dying. I told her the movie resonated deeply not only because it provides such a direct examination of these topics but also because it does so through Elaine—someone incapable of a dishonest moment both in life and on the screen.

"Well, that's all fine and I'm glad to hear it, but I'm wearing the same fucking fur coat in almost every scene," Elaine said. "And I think we need more excerpts of me singing."

I asked Elaine what it felt like to watch something so personal projected large on a screen. She said it was hard to watch but indicated that she thought her discomfort was a sign that the movie had captured something an audience would enjoy.

After helping Elaine and Chiemi get back out to the street, I said goodbye. Elaine invited me back to the Carlyle, but I told her I had to get back to campus. She was moving pretty well, and I think a sense of excitement was beginning to build about the documentary, which both she and Chiemi were hoping would be previewed in the coming months at the Tribeca Film Festival. Elaine's spirits seemed high—always a good way to leave her.

* * *

A month later and sensing Elaine's time in New York was coming to a close, I made my way to the Carlyle to check in on her health and her plans for moving to Michigan. We met in her room and had a cosmopolitan before heading down to the gallery for soup and coffee.

Elaine was doing fairly well. Her eye was continuing to heal— at least the scar was looking better. Her eyesight wasn't improving much, and she was struggling to read the newspaper. Her TV was blasting away as usual.

Over soup, she said she was planning to leave the Carlyle at the end of May, and before she went, she was going to do one more "At Home at the Carlyle" titled *Moving Over and Out*. I asked her if she had it in her.

"I don't know!" she wailed. "But I've got a pretty big bill here to pay off, so I figure I'll give them one more week onstage and we'll call it even. The problem is, I don't think they're going to pay for an orchestra or any real rehearsal."

"So what are you going to do?" I asked.

"I don't know, I really don't know. I suppose I'll sit out there on a stool and sing some songs and tell a few stories. I think people will come out for that. I'm not going to stress out over this. I'm done. I'm going to get up there and let people know that I'm heading out and what a good time I've had. I can do that on the fly, honey, I know I can."

I assured her everyone knew she could handle a room like nobody else.

"Yeah, you're right about that," she said.

She was excited about the move. She thought the condo was going to be very nice. "Not quite as chic as the Carlyle, but pretty close." After one of her increasingly frequent, long, reflective pauses, she said, "I'm ready to leave this city. Something inside is not right being here anymore. I don't know what it is, but it's something."

I asked her how the process of packing up her room at the Carlyle was going to be handled.

"Well, I'm not taking much with me. That's the great thing about hotel living, you don't have much crap. Just my clothes and my awards and my insulin. It all gets packed up and shipped out."

"Are you going to fly to Michigan?" I asked.

"God no, are you kidding. I don't get on a plane unless it's absolutely necessary and I'm getting a lot of money. One of my nieces or nephews will pick me up, and we'll drive."

"I used to work and live in Michigan, around Ann Arbor," I said.

"Oh, good, then you've got to come to visit with me once I get settled in," she said.

I helped her upstairs with a takeaway pint of soup and some chocolate cookies, said good night, and told her I'd be there for the final bow at the Café.

"You'd better!" she said. "Oh, my movie is having its unofficial premiere at the Tribeca festival next month. Will you be able to catch it?" she called out just before I turned the corner.

"Probably not. But I've seen the early cut and I know it will be great. I'll catch the official premiere in 2014," I said.

"Okay, darling, good night."

* * *

As promised, I attended *Elaine Stritch at the Carlyle: Movin' Over and Out* the second night of the show's one-week run. Apparently the night to have attended was the opening night just the evening before when Bernadette Peters, Liza Minnelli, Tony Bennett, and Tom Hanks were in the audience. Even Elaine's stalwart pal James Levine came.

The show was mostly organized around a bowl of story prompts about Elaine's career that were circulated throughout the room by an assistant. Rob Bowman was at the piano. Elaine wore her trademark sheer black hose and white shirt. The story prompts gave Elaine a chance to do what she does best, tell stories. So the fact that the evening had not been rehearsed was not a problem—it wasn't going to be that kind of show.

Elaine sang just a handful of songs and waxed nostalgic about her time in New York and her fear about moving forward and away. On opening night, it was reported that she charmed the glitterati and apparently filled a good portion of the seventy-five-minute show with flirtatious banter with Tom Hanks.

On the second night, she seemed perhaps a little disappointed that no celebrities were in the room. Nonetheless, the audience's affection for her was palpable, and just before closing, she kissed Rob on the cheek and sang a very moving rendition of Jimmy Van Heusen and Sammy Cahn's "All My Tomorrows."

Afterward, I went up to the third floor and found Elaine and Rob in room 311, her holding pen for her Carlyle performances. "Oh my god, I thought no one was here tonight. You were here. Thank God. How was I?" she asked. "Absolutely charming," I said. "Oh my god, Rob, John says I was 'charming.' We must have stunk."

I asked how she felt about the performance. "Well, last night was over the moon. Did you hear who was here? Everybody! It was electric. Tonight I don't think it was as good, but maybe it was good enough."

I assured her she was always more than most people know how to handle. "God, ain't that the truth!" she said. "I'm leaving next week, when are you coming to Birmingham?" she said.

"I'll give you a few weeks and then I'll call and we'll set up a visit," I said.

"I have a guest room, come anytime, and I mean anytime."

CHAPTER 9

It took me a few weeks to track down Elaine's new phone number. She had left a forwarding address with the Carlyle, but either she had given them the wrong address or the person at the front desk wrote it down incorrectly. After tracking down the right address through Actor's Equity (I figured Elaine would have made certain the union had her correct contact information should royalty checks or job offers come her way) and hounding the desk staff at the Carlyle (I figured her exit was not the last they would hear of her), I finally reached Elaine by phone in her new abode.

She was in a rage.

An assistant answered the phone, and I could hear Elaine screaming in the background. Trying to calm her down and respond to whatever had triggered her tantrum, he tried to hand her off to me. I told him not to bother, that I could tell things there were crazy enough and I'd call back later. In truth, the last thing I wanted was to try to speak with Elaine when she was in such a foul mood. It would be pointless. She'd rail at me about her predicament and what was I going to do, ask her if she was up for a visit? Fat chance.

This first phone call, however, confirmed my worst fear: that the mere act of relocating would be more than Elaine could handle. Everything would be new and different, and given the fragility of her health, such a transition would be simply overwhelming—emotionally and physically. I called back later that evening and found her in a much calmer mood.

"How are you?" I asked rather hesitantly.

"Oh, I'm okay. But getting everything in place is killing me. I can't even get the fucking *New York Times* delivered. I mean honest-to-God."

"I know, Elaine. Those things all take more time and effort than you can imagine. Are there people helping you?"

"Well, yeah, for all the good they're worth," she snapped.

Afraid I'd raise her ire again, I tried to change the subject. "How's the condo, though? Is it comfortable for you?"

"Oh, it's fine. I think I'm going to like it, but right now, I mean Jesus Christ, nothing—and I mean nothing—is going right."

"Well, would you be up for a visit?" I asked, hoping the notion might cheer her spirits.

"Oh, boy, would I. When can you come?"

* * *

Elaine's condo was in a very upscale building called the Dakota tucked just off the heart of downtown Birmingham. The building overlooked Booth Park, just across the street. The building has an underground parking garage accessible by an electronic code. There is a private entrance to the condo units—there are five in the building—from the parking garage via stairs and an elevator. The front of the building features a set of concrete stairs up to the brick façade. There are three doors. The center door allows access to a central shared lobby. The door to the left is condo no. 172—Elaine's new home.

Upon entering the 2,500-square-foot condo, the smallest in the building, one is standing in a small entryway with a recessed chandelier and a small table above which hangs a mirror and two wall sconces. The table featured two high topiary trees, and each time I visited, there was always one or two of Elaine's hats, on the table, at the ready, should she need to "go out."

To the right was her formal living room, an elegant room with soft yellow walls, crowned in crisp white millwork and featuring a marble fireplace and a grand Palladian window. The living room opens to the adjoining dining room, which features those pesky dining room chairs that had been the object of great negotiation. To one side stands a grand piano upon which are displayed Elaine's Emmy and Tony awards.

"The movers unpacked all this shit and put them there, and I thought they looked divine, so I just left them."

The Dakota, Elaine's new home in Birmingham, MI.
Credit: John Bell

Beside the piano was the barstool she used in the Broadway production of *At Liberty*. It was "the one costar I liked enough to keep in touch with."

The ten-foot ceilings and cherry floors, which give the condo a deep, rich elegance, continued around the corner to a large, spacious, and elegant kitchen anchored at one end with a full, round wooden table under a black wrought-iron chandelier. Four elegant white chairs make this the central meeting place of the home.

Off the kitchen and spanning the entire back of the unit is an impressive and private six-hundred-square-foot outdoor terrace outfitted with high-end patio furniture and pedestal planters.

At the other end of the condo is a luxurious master bedroom suite that features a king-sized bed with a high mattress much like the one Elaine had at the Carlyle. And off the bedroom were a set of dual walk-in closets ("Finally enough room to have all my clothes and shoes with me!"), a master bath replete with a marble bathtub with Jacuzzi jets, steam shower, and heated floors. It is clear why Elaine would have been attracted to the place—Upper East Side all the way.

Knowing Elaine had a few friends from New York staying with her to help her get settled, I planned to stay at a nearby hotel.

* * *

When I arrived, Elaine was seated out on the terrace, enjoying the late afternoon sun. She was surrounded by Margorie McDonald, a good friend she met while doing Harold Prince's revival of *Show Boat*; Julie Keyes, another good friend; and her niece who had served as the real estate agent on the condo purchase. It was clear all three had been with Elaine for some time, and when I arrived, they all took the opportunity to scoot away knowing that someone new would hold Elaine's attention. Margie and Julie went shopping for food, and Elaine's niece excused herself to make some calls.

I asked Elaine how the past few weeks had been and how the move had gone. She reported it all went as smoothly as one could expect but, overall, she was not feeling very good about being in Michigan.

"I don't know where the fucking light switches are. I don't know where anything is. And everything has to be done. We finally got the bank account set up, and I found someone to cut my hair. But Jesus Christ, there's so much to be done. We're still trying to figure out when the trash goes out. I want to get a sleeper sofa for the study so I'll have two guest rooms when people come to visit—I think I'll need that, don't you? And I've yet to get the goddamn *New York Times* delivered. Jesus Christ, you'd think I moved to fucking Podunk Iowa or something. It's Birmingham fucking Michigan."

I tried to remind her that she had just undertaken an enormous task. "Moving is a bitch, for anyone. Let alone trying to do it at the age of eighty-seven."

"But I didn't have to do anything but drive here. All the boxes were shipped and unpacked for me," she said.

"Yes, but just getting situated and finding your routine and knowing where all the fucking light switches are is hard on anyone. You feel completely disoriented, and everything seems to take so much more effort," I said.

"I know you're right, and I know it will get easier. Right now I just have to tell myself to not give in to it. It's just going to feel bad for a while, that's that." This was one of my favorite and most admirable traits of Elaine's: her ability to recognize something was rotten and not cry about it, her ability to force herself through. I told her so.

"Well, what the hell do you think, that I'm going to go running back to the Carlyle?" she barked.

"Well, you're not the most tolerant or patient person," I wanted to but didn't dare say. Instead, I tried to change the subject by asking about the Tribeca Film Festival premiere of *Shoot Me.*

"It was divine," she said. "They loved it. It's gotten great notices, and there's even talk of it getting a possible Oscar nod in the documentary category."

After a short pause, she asked for more sunblock for her face and neck. It was a warm and humid day, and sweating up a storm, I moved my chair into the shade.

"What's wrong with you?" she snapped.

"Nothing, I just don't want to sit in the sun."

"What's wrong with the sun? I adore it," she said. "There is nothing like the sunshine in Detroit. It makes its way all the way down to you. You don't get that in New York. In New York the sun never gets all the way down to you."

After a while, we moved indoors. She wanted to show me the place. I could tell she was enjoying showing it off to me.

"And here's the guest bedroom. I'm calling it the 'Michael Feinstein' bedroom. He's promised me he's coming to visit. It's yours when you come unless Michael's here, and in that case you'll have to sleep on the sleeper sofa in the office, if I can ever find one that will fucking match the rest of the furniture. Honest to God, this is the type of shit that just kills me. This is why I've lived in fucking convents or hotels all my life."

Eventually, we settled back in to the kitchen table. Elaine's niece rejoined us and got an earful from Elaine about the front doorbell that wasn't working.

"I'm telling you, I don't pay over a million dollars for a condo in fucking Birmingham and find the doorbell doesn't work."

When told she would have to call the company that runs the maintenance on the building for the homeowners, Elaine screamed, "We've been calling the goddamn maintenance company, and nobody fucking answers the fucking phone. I mean, I tell you. This is unreal. Something's wrong here. This is why I wanted to hold $25,000 back in escrow until I got here and found that everything was working. Now if I have to pay for a bunch of stupid little things that don't work, I'm out more money. You told me I couldn't hold money back, and I know I could. And I should have. So I'm not happy. Not happy a bit."

Promising to call the maintenance company herself trying to escape, her niece made a hasty exit.

* * *

Margie and Julie returned with food just as a few of Birmingham's upper class—a couple who knew someone who knew someone else—who had called a couple days previously, stopped by to welcome Birmingham's Broadway legend. They brought a box of Cheez It crackers and a bottle of wine.

Elaine invited them in. The wine was poured. Elaine requested a cosmopolitan. Elaine made small talk and puffed her guests up for a while, and then, registering the scent in the wind, they took their cues and made a graceful exit. Once she heard the front door shut and was sure they were out of earshot, she said, "Do you believe this? A box of fucking Cheez Its. Welcome to fucking Birmingham."

Margie and Julie began to throw some dinner together. Elaine requested a second cosmopolitan.

"And I'd like it without the looks of judgment I'm getting," directing the barbed comment to Julie. "After everything I've been through the past few weeks, I don't think a drink or two at cocktail time needs to be a problem. For. Anyone."

From the early preview of *Elaine Stritch: Shoot Me*, I knew that Julie Keyes was a good friend who met Elaine in Alcoholics Anonymous. Apparently they adored one another, and I sensed that they helped keep one another in check regarding their sobriety. Julie did seem to be aware, if not concerned, of Elaine's return to alcohol.

Trying to change the subject, I asked about her return to New York for the Stella by Starlight gala at which she was honored along with George Takei and Stephen Sondheim.

"Oh, it was all right. Bernadette was there, Hal [Prince] was there, Alec [Baldwin] was there. And Steve was actually nice to me that night. But I'll tell you what, the travel in and back out, well, it's not easy. It was a little like whiplash: leaving New York, trying to get set up here, flying back to New York, then back here again. I mean… well, it was just too much. Just too much."

As the evening went on, Elaine became friendlier and her mood began to lighten as the alcohol kicked in. Sensing that she was starting to get tired, I made my exit and said good night.

"You're coming back tomorrow aren't you?" she asked.

"I'd like to if you're up to it," I replied.

"What do you mean if I'm up to it? Of course, I'm up to it. Come back and you can take us all out to dinner."

"Sounds great, I'll call before I come," I said.

"Yeah, but not before two thirty, darling."

"Oh, I know," I said.

* * *

The next day, I got to Elaine's around four. She was sitting in the kitchen with Margie and Julie. She said she didn't feel like going out for dinner but reported that there was a little Italian restaurant around the corner and we'd order in.

Having gotten up this morning for an early run, I explored Booth Park across the street from Elaine's condo complex. Beyond the public playground there is a somewhat obscure and hidden path that follows a creek along through the woods. There is an abundance of wildlife, and water fowl make daring passes through the wooded overhang onto stretches of open water. The canopy of trees keeps the pathway cool while allowing dappled pools of sunlight to break through.

I told Elaine how nice this creek-side path was and asked her if she had walked down there yet. She knew nothing about it and said she wanted to walk down. At that Margie and Julie headed out for more errands.

When we got out to the sidewalk, I pointed out the wooded area leading to the creek, but Elaine changed her mind and wanted to walk her block. 'There's a pretty church up this way,' she said. And with that, about two blocks from the Dakota, we came across Holy Name Catholic Church, a pretty little church on a beautiful, carefully kept campus. The church did not seem old. I guessed it was built in the late fifties or sixties.

"Pretty church," she said. "You think it's open?"

I went up and checked the doors—the church was unlocked. Once inside, Elaine sat in one of the back pews. She made the sign of the cross before she sat. This was the only time I saw Elaine practice a religious ritual. I don't know why—this was the second time I had been with her in a church—but I was surprised to see her make the sign of the cross.

As Elaine sat, I wandered through the quiet church, taking in the architecture and statuary. After a few moments, Elaine went up and lit five candles. I didn't ask, but I assumed she lit one candle each for her mother, her father, her two sisters, and John, her late husband. She turned to exit, and I pulled a ten-dollar bill out of my wallet for the candle box.

* * *

Back at the condo, Elaine decided she wanted to go around the corner, not for Italian food, but to try out the little bar she had noticed anchoring her new neighborhood. So with the summer sun beginning to grow long in its shadows, we headed out again. Luxe Bar and Grill was a rather swanky place outfitted in black, silver, and white. We found a spot tucked away in the back. Elaine ordered a cosmopolitan, and I ordered a gin and tonic.

Elaine reported that she was in talks with the producers of a new sitcom starring Kirstie Alley.

"They want me to play, what else, her mother!" she said.

"I can see that, you and she have similar public personas," I said.

"Public personas," she repeated with a dash of venom.

"Yeah, you know, you're both outspoken broad types. Is it an ongoing role?" I asked.

"No, just a one-week gig," she said. "And they're being really cheap about it. They aren't offering much, and I told them I can't travel alone, that they have to fly me out there with one of my assistants and all that shit."

"So you're still negotiating?" I asked.

"No, the negotiating's done. I told them what it will cost, and I'm waiting to hear from them," she said.

"Would you like to do it?" I asked.

"Sure, if they pay me what I'm worth," she said. "This is exactly the type of stuff I want to do, limited gigs for decent pay. I'd rather not have to fly, but there's no way around that living here in Michigan."

After barking at the waiter for pretzels and chips, Elaine said, "I'm not sure I've done the right thing. I don't want to go back to New York, but I'm not sure I haven't made this move a little early. I feel like I still have work in me, and I'm not sure Birmingham is going to be enough."

I told her that made sense and urged her to give it more time.

"You're right, but I've got a feeling, this may have been a mistake."

"Well, if that's the case, you can make other choices. If nothing else, the condo can be an investment. Nothing says you have to stay in Birmingham if you're not happy there," I said.

"You're right about that, it would be a good investment, wouldn't it," she said.

"Sure, real estate is always a decent investment. You'll have to hold on to the place long enough for the market to rebound, but a place like yours, in Birmingham, I would think you'd be able to make some money on it," I said.

"I hope so, darling, I really do, whether I stay here and die or go somewhere else, I'd like to be in the black," she said.

As we walked back to the condo, a few young women, college-aged, recognized her and fussed over her. She loved it. They took photos, and she signed one of their shopping bags. "We heard you moved back—welcome home," one of the girls said.

"Well, thanks, darling. I wish I could say I'm happy to be here, but the move has been terribly hard adjustment. Moving is for the birds," she said.

She was buoyed by the encounter. I could tell she was anticipating that it might be a sign of the types of encounters she hoped she'd be able to get more of in her new neighborhood.

When we got back to the Dakota, dinner was in progress. I excused myself, telling her that I wanted to get a few hours of driving in before nightfall.

"Oh, come on, you've got to stay for dinner," she said.

"I'll grab something on the way," I said.

"Okay, suit yourself, but I don't like the idea of you driving at night," she said.

"I won't. I'll drive a few hours and stop somewhere for the night."

"Okay, darling, but be careful," she insisted.

"Do you want to keep the camp stool?" I asked, hoping the notion of getting out and walking back down to the creek appealed to her.

"Oh, that would be divine." I left it in her foyer. I told her I thought I might be able to visit again in about a month.

"Anytime, darling. Just call first to make sure Michael Feinstein isn't here."

CHAPTER 10

My second trip to Birmingham to visit Elaine began at four in the morning. The drive from eastern Pennsylvania to Michigan took me along the northern route of Interstate 80, through the Pocono, Allegheny, and Appalachian mountain ridges. At sunrise, dew hung in the air as I looked out at the towering blue slopes in the distance. It was breathtaking.

Because Elaine hated flying, family members had driven from Michigan to the Carlyle to pick her up and drive her to her new home. I wondered if she'd enjoyed these views and vistas on her drive, if they'd served as a transition away from the noise of the city and toward the quieter life she would be leading.

Most of the natural splendor waned on the approach to Cleveland, Toledo, and eventually Detroit, replaced by a sense of urban, industrial decay. Driving along the Detroit beltway, I tried to imagine Elaine's childhood in this city—a childhood she often recalled with seeming fondness. I wondered what it felt like for her to have returned home after having lived such a dynamic and exciting life.

This dramatic change in Elaine's life—the move back to Michigan—fascinated me. I have always been drawn to people in the twilight of their lives, intrigued as I am by the courage and grace that one's final life stage demands. In Elaine's case, this change was as extreme as any I could imagine, especially for an eighty-eight-year-old not known for grace.

I wondered what mood Elaine might be in when I got there. I was hoping she'd be feeling more settled. This time I would be a houseguest, staying for three days. Not wanting to arrive empty-handed, I found a little flower shop around the corner and ordered a nice bunch of white lilies. I got lilies, as I knew they'd look good in her antique washbasin station. During one of my visits with her at the Carlyle, I'd complimented her on this piece. "Isn't it divine?" she said. "You should see it with long-stemmed flowers—white flowers. Forget about it."

I noticed on my previous visit to her new digs that the wash station was one of the few pieces she'd brought with her; it was set prominently in the corner of her new living room.

I pulled into the Dakota's underground parking garage at one thirty, made my way up to the inner door, and knocked. I was greeted by a caretaker, a bright-eyed young woman. Before I could introduce myself, I heard Elaine yell out from the kitchen, "Who the hell is that?"

After quickly introducing myself to the aide, I made my way to the kitchen where Elaine was reading *The New York Times*. "I see you got finally got the *Times* delivered," I said by way of greeting.

"Oh my god, look who's here—a sight for sore eyes," she said. "It only took three goddamn weeks."

I gave Elaine the flowers and a hug. "Oh, they're a knockout," she said. "And I know just where to put them."

"I thought they'd look great in the pitcher on your washbasin," I said.

"That's exactly where they're going, darling," she said, handing the lilies off to her caretaker.

After settling in to the guest room, I came back out and sat with her in the kitchen. Elaine's New York contingent had all gone back to the city, so the condo was quiet—very quiet. The caretaker was the only person with Elaine in the house. She was the first in a long line of what would become a revolving slate of personal aides.

Part of Elaine's decision to move out of New York was the realization that she needed someone with her twenty-four hours a day. Her health had just become too precarious, and she knew enough not to be alone anymore, especially at night. That kind of care would've been prohibitively expensive in Manhattan.

From what I could tell, the caretaker, who appeared to be gentle and kind, had been in the house for about a week. She and Elaine had begun the process of setting routines, but routine needs quickly turned into demands and barks. Elaine's frustration with her new surroundings and new staffing was clearly trying her patience.

This caretaker, and some of the others who were to follow, often came from ethnic backgrounds and had distinct dialects and accents, making communication challenging. Elaine often couldn't hear or comprehend some of what her caretakers were saying, resulting in quick bursts of temper.

At this point, Elaine was relying on her caretakers for everything. They cooked for her, and Elaine would tutor each new hire on just how to make her scrambled egg the way she liked it or how she wanted her hamburger cooked. They cleaned for her, and Elaine would school them on how to make the bed just the way she wanted it. They assisted her in monitoring her diabetes and injecting her insulin. They helped manage her pills and medicines. They shopped for her and assisted with correspondence. And if they lasted long enough, they eventually became a late-night confidant.

At night, Elaine's caretaker would sleep next to her in her king-sized bed. She wanted someone with her at all times—male or female. Her sleep was erratic, and the quiet times when she lay in bed, awake, were when she was most receptive to actually talking with her caretakers. She shared her insights with them and got to know them, particularly the young women she hired.

As caretakers came into Elaine's home, it was clear that most of them didn't know much about her career. But all of them had been briefed about her demanding nature. During my visits, it wasn't unusual for Elaine to chastise and berate her caretaker in front of me or any other guests who might be visiting, causing the caretaker to excuse herself in tears.

As their time with Elaine increased and they fielded calls from Bernadette Peters or Kirk Douglas, they would eventually learn the scope of her career and associations. Eventually all of them were able to see copies of the HBO production of *At Liberty* and Chiemi's *Shoot Me.* They learned quickly about the unique creature with whom their lives had intersected.

* * *

Our first point of conversation on this visit was the death of James Gandolfini in Italy just the week before at the age of fifty-one. Elaine was clearly moved by this loss, which surprised me. I knew that he was interviewed for *Shoot Me* in which he spoke about their first meeting and implied a friendly flirtation between the two, but Elaine flirted with most men. In the few years I'd spent with her, she hadn't spoken about him much. I was unaware of just how fond she was of him.

"I loved this man," she said. "And the fact that he has died is devastating. Think of all the roles he would have eventually played. He was a real actor, and I mean a *real* actor. God was he good. I can't talk about this, it's just too much—tooooooo much.

"He was with me at the Stella thing in New York last month," she said.

Elaine and James Gandolfini at the Stella by Starlight Gala.
Credit: Johnny Nunez

"Oh, I didn't realize that."

"Yes, it was his last public appearance. He told me he was about to go off to Italy for vacation. I just can't believe this. And he was so good to me that night. He came up to me and told me he thought he and I should do a production of that play for two people...you know..."

"*I Do! I Do!*" I offered.

"What? No. Not fucking *I Do! I Do!* Oh, you know the play, the one about the letters," she said.

This would become an ongoing routine between Elaine and me: her inability to remember the name of a play or a person would result in frustrated, short, angry prompts demanding that I fill in the blank. Usually, her ire would rise quickly with "Oh, come on, you know who I mean," and if you were unable to quickly fill in the blank, she would basically let you know that you were somehow intellectually deficient. But if you were able to take a good stab and miraculously arrive at the answer, she would squawk with delight and make you feel like a genius.

"Oh, A. R. Gurney's *Love Letters*."

"Yes, that's it," she said with relief.

"Oh, boy, that would have been terrific," I said.

"You're right. And James knew it, and I knew it. What I wouldn't give to have been able to do that with him. And perfect for me because there's no fucking lines to memorize." After a pause, she said, "God, I loved this man. I absolutely adored him."

James's funeral was the next day. She wasn't going, but Chiemi, her *Shoot Me* director, was going, and Elaine was looking forward to getting the report from her.

Elaine was very concerned about his thirteen-year-old son. She'd never met him and didn't know his name, but "to lose your father, at that age, can you imagine?" she said. "The next time I'm going to New York, I'm going to call him up and take him out to lunch. I want him to know that people who loved his dad care about him."

I mentioned that I was surprised to learn that James and his wife had just had a new baby and how tragic it was that this death occurred just after a new birth.

"I don't think about things like that," she said with mild rebuke. "I don't think in terms of the kid now being fatherless. The only thing about it that feels tragic to me is thinking about all the great performances that he'll never give. Everybody else says 'Oh, the poor baby,' and I don't think about it that way at all."

This seemed like a complete contradiction to her concern for James's teenage son, but I kept my opinion to myself.

Elaine went on to talk about James's weight. She expressed dismay that anyone in the entertainment industry would let themselves get so big.

"With the talent he had, if he'd have taken care of himself, the sky would have been the limit. But being so fat, well, is it any wonder he'd have a heart attack?" she said.

This was the first of a handful of conversations that Elaine and I had about obesity. I came to realize that Elaine, like so many actresses, was obsessed with her weight.

We sat for a while at the kitchen table eating pretzels. At about four thirty, while her caretaker was out checking the mail and dumping the trash, Elaine asked me to pour her a cosmopolitan. She told me there would be a prepared supply in the refrigerator. There was, but only a swallow or two was left in the little Tupperware pitcher.

"Well, make me some more. You'll have one with me, won't you?"

I told her I'd never made a cosmopolitan.

"Well, it's time you learn, don't you think?" she said.

"Okay, talk me through it," I said.

"The liquor's up there," she said, pointing to the cabinet by the laundry room door. I opened the door and found a very full supply of Grey Goose vodka, triple sec, and gin. I came to learn that Elaine had contracted with the local liquor store to deliver on demand.

"One drink is a shot of vodka, three quarters of a shot of triple sec, some cranberry juice—sugar-free—and a splash of freshly squeezed lime juice," she directed. "So multiply that times four and it should get us through the night."

I did as instructed, poured her a short one, and received a low moan of approval. I did not drink one with her, however; it was too sweet.

"What do you mean 'too sweet'?" she said mockingly. "The cranberry juice is sugar-free, for God's sake." I had a beer instead.

Elaine enjoyed her cocktail hour. She loved nothing more than just sitting at the table with something salty to munch on, a cold drink, and witty conversation. I read her the arts section of *The New York Times*, and we dished about the current gossip about upcoming shows and stars. After about an hour of this and her second cosmopolitan, Elaine got a bit tired and wanted to go back to her bedroom for a short nap. "We'll meet back here in the kitchen around seven thirty for dinner," she said. I offered to take her out for dinner, but she wasn't up for it.

"No, we'll dig something up here," she said.

When Elaine was in her bedroom, her caretakers would engage a baby monitor system that would pick up her voice if she called out for anything. She always had either news or classic movies playing loudly on her bedroom TV, so when she was back in her bedroom, the monitor would project the rather grotesque sound of Elaine's conversation with her caretaker mixed with the voices of old Hollywood forced and distorted through a cheap plastic monitor. This soundtrack was as unique and odd and fascinating as Elaine herself.

A couple of hours later, Elaine stirred and was ready to eat. I'd gone for a walk along the creek and then settled in on her patio to read *The New York Times*. She came out the kitchen, walking with her cane, her caretaker close behind. She ordered scrambled eggs and Bay's muffins for dinner.

"That all right with you, mister?" she asked.

"Sounds great. I'm a convert to these muffins now. Thomas's will never cross my lips again," I said.

"I hope not," she replied.

* * *

Over dinner Elaine talked about Steve Sondheim. She would often bring him up without prodding. She said how attracted she was to him.

"Well, not necessarily to him, but to his talent. I mean, I do think he's handsome. I don't know any other man his age half as attractive, do you? But his talent, talent like that is very attractive, don't you think?"

I did. In fact, as my relationship with Elaine evolved, I believe it was the opportunity to observe her personal and professional processes and how she funneled both into her performing that captivated me and kept me hanging around. She could be cruel, yes. She had a short fuse, yes. She was demanding, yes. But I was, as ever, intrigued by her.

"Did I ever tell you the story about Steve and P. J. Clarks on Fifth Avenue?" she asked. "Steve tells this story, and I love it. Steve says that he was at P. J. Clarks, and I walked in and ordered a Tanqueray martini straight up with two olives and a floor plan. And that, he said, was the impetus for 'The Ladies Who Lunch.' Isn't that great? Steve was somewhere in New York and told that story in front of an audience, and it brought down the house. That's how funny and famous I am: I don't even have to be present to bring down the house."

I asked Elaine about Ben Gazarra. From the little I gathered from *At Liberty* and *Shoot Me*, I sensed that he had been her real first relationship with a man. There were flirtations with Kirk Douglas, Gig Young, Jack Kennedy, and Rock Hudson, but she and Ben were more than that.

"Well, I messed that up. Biggest mistake of my life. Well, not really, I mean, I got John out of the deal, but I was pretty taken with Ben. We spent a great deal of time together. We had met at the New School."

"Did you live together?" I asked.

"Yes. Well, no. But he sure hung around a lot, if you know what I mean. I had an apartment on East Fifty-Seventh, and he was there a lot. And I loved it. I loved having someone around, you know, to go through it all with. And if I hadn't had gone to London to work on *A Farewell to Arms* and met Rock and decided to pursue Rock and thrown Ben aside, I think we might have had a go at it."

Given that Ben Gazarra was married to his first wife until 1957, the year that *A Farewell to Arms* was made, I asked Elaine if she'd been in an affair with Ben while he was married.

"Yeah, I guess, but he was separated from her. We were hoping to go to Rome to get an annulment from the pope. I even asked my uncle, the cardinal, about how to go about it. But it never came to pass. I got out there with Rock, and because he was showing some interest, Rock it was."

Was Rock really interested?

"At the time I certainly thought so. Liz Smith went out there with me, and we were both gaga for him."

"Why did Liz come with you?" I asked.

"We were best friends—had been since the early fifties," she said of the woman who went on to become the celebrated gossip columnist. "We share the same birthday, and she was not sure what she was going to do in New York, so she came as my assistant."

"Your assistant?" I asked, somewhat surprised that Elaine would've thought herself important enough to need an assistant at that point in her young career.

"Well, you know, she came along. She didn't have anything else to do, and I didn't like the idea of travelling abroad without someone with me. So it worked out good for us both." One imagines these two boisterous broads taking London by storm, but in actuality, they were both young and finding their way. They probably made a good show of it, this Hollywood starlet and her one-woman entourage. Elaine always did know how to make a favorable if not entirely realistic impression.

"And you both were vying for Rock?" I asked.

"Well, no, not really. He was flirting with me since we were in scenes together. He loved me. And after work, we'd go out and drink, and Liz would be with us, and she and I both had Scooby-Doo eyes for him. But eventually it was clear that he wasn't serious about anything. We just had a lot of fun and flirted a hell of a lot. Nothing happened." And then, after a perfectly timed pause and just the right inflection, she said, "And I think we all know why."

Elaine was ready to retreat back to her bedroom. She ordered "another of John's great cosmos for the road." "Give me a half hour to check my levels and get set in bed, and then come back. We'll talk some more."

* * *

Elaine enjoyed holding court in her bedroom. She liked being perfectly situated with the pillows and her beverage and having her guests come back and chat with her. So about thirty minutes later, I knocked on the bedroom door.

"Come on in," she said.

I sat beside her bed on a high-backed chair. I asked about her experiences working with Sondheim on *Company*.

"I didn't know what 'the ladies who lunch' meant when I got the song. I knew who rich people were, and I had a sense, growing up with some of the people in my parents' social circle, about ladies who lunch and pick their kids up from school and things like that. But I didn't really know what the song was about. Jesus Christ, I can't even talk about this, it's just too close. I haven't been away from it long enough yet."

"It's been forty years," I said.

"Yeah, but come on. This was Steve Sondheim and Hal Prince, no slouches in the musical comedy department, and let me tell you, that experience was not easy. You need time away before you can even know what you went through, you know?"

"What did you think the song was about?" I asked.

"Like I said, rich broads, Birmingham, Michigan, broads. B. F. Goodrich wives, if you know what I mean. Or as my mother would say 'GDBF Goodrich' wives.

"I mean, and this will tell how just how naive I have been throughout my whole fucking life, I didn't even know who Mahler was. I asked Steve about the lyric 'a piece of Mahler's.' I thought it was referring to a bakery in New York, some sweet treat or something.

He looked at me with those eyes that can drill right fucking through you and told me it referred to Mahler, 'a very significant classical composer.' I said 'Oh, okay,' and he looked at me and said 'I have to go to the bathroom.' That says it all. Richard Rodgers did the same thing to me. I was playing Anna in the *King and I* and asked Richard Rodgers how Anna just happened to get off the boat and know the language and culture of these people. Richard Rodgers looked at me and said 'I have to go to the bathroom.' Isn't that great? Rodgers and Sondheim clearly did their best work at the urinal.

"No, I didn't know what the fuck the song was about, not really about. So I just worked through it and brought as much of my life experience to it as I could. I've always been pretty good at that. My life experience has always been a little deeper than a lot of other people, you know?"

I did and thought this was a good summary of one of Elaine's great gifts as an actress. Whatever it was, Elaine always projected a sense that she was twenty years older in life experience than she was in real life. Some of this has to be attributed to her mother and father. By all accounts, she was raised in a household filled with Irish humor and a high, alcohol-fueled propensity for truth in all its many guises. One imagines that Elaine encountered the adult world at an early age, shaping her potent intolerance for triviality. Facing truth can be hard, but it's real. And real is what Elaine sought when she was onstage under the safety of a character. Creating a character's truth and attacking it was sport for Elaine—probably therapy too. Facing her own truth, I was coming to learn, was the hard part.

As the evening drew on, Elaine's mood seemed to dip a bit.

"I'm a little scared here," she said.

"You mean here in Birmingham? Do you still feel unsettled and disoriented?" I asked.

"Yeah, a little. I really want my health to come back. I've got to get up on my feet. I don't want to die all broken here in Birmingham. I don't want this bedroom to become my cave. When I thought about my last days, I didn't imagine being closed up in a place like this. This bedroom in Birmingham makes me sad."

I told her that if her track record was any indication, I was sure she'd recover and be getting back on her feet. Once again, she mentioned that her sisters had both lived into their early nineties, resurrecting her sense that she might still have "a few decent years left."

Again, Elaine questioned her return to Birmingham. But she was adamant that she didn't want to go back to New York. I asked if she ever thought of returning to London to live. She paused. She wasn't certain. But she seemed to enjoy that idea and whatever memories it sparked. She had a grin on her face.

"You know I met John in London, don't you?" she asked, referring to John Bay, of the family which founded and owned the Bay's English Muffin Company "We were both in *Small Craft Warnings*, and I fell completely in love with the man. We moved into the Savoy Hotel and ate at the Savoy Grill, very Scooby-Doo, if you know what I mean. It was a wonderful time in my life, personally and professionally. That's when I did *Two's Company* with Donald Sinden. It was a big hit. John was on the show a couple of times." She paused. "No, I loved London."

"How did he propose?" I asked.

"He didn't," she screamed. "I proposed to him. We were in the Savoy Gardens, and I just looked at him and said, 'John, don't you think we should get married?' And without skipping a beat, in his best Jack Benny he said, 'Why not?' and that was it. And he was so easy. He always said, 'All I want is love, love, love, a pack of cigarettes a day, and six scotches,' and I said, 'My god, you're easy. Let's get hitched.' Isn't that great?"

"When we got married, my father sent a telegram to John at the Savoy that said 'Don't forget to send muffins.' John and Daddy got along just great."

This talk of London reminded Elaine that she'd gotten another phone call from a man who was trying to get her to come to London to do cabaret at the Pheasantry. Sensing she wouldn't be able to make the trip over or endure even a short run of a show, she was clearly not interested, but I could tell the lure of London was seductive.

This led to a discussion about what type of work she might do once she got to feeling settled and strong.

I brought up her visit to my university five years earlier and how informative, entertaining, and inspiring it had been to the students. I mentioned the idea of her booking short-stint master classes, perhaps locally in the Michigan area or at universities or acting schools in New York or London if she were in the cities for other business or pleasure.

Elaine Stritch and John Bay mugging for photographers.
Credit: Frank Barratt

I could tell she was interested in the idea.

"You and Rob could make rounds, charge a decent fee, and simply do a master class on song study," I said. "You could choose a couple of songs you really feel like singing, and talk about what makes a good song good, and how you approach your interpretation of a lyric. Rob could chime in about the musical qualities. And then you could sing it and the audience will go wild. With all the musical theater training programs across the country, the notion of Elaine Stritch parlaying her performing expertise to a group of musical theater hopefuls could be a gold mine."

"How much could I charge?" she asked.

"Well, when you came to my campus, we paid you $5,000 for a couple of hours' work. If you and Rob were to do a couple of these each month, when you feel like it, you could generate $10,000 to $15,000 a month.

"Not bad for not a lot of work," she said.

"You bet. And you only have to do it when you want to, and you can sing songs you've already worked up so it wouldn't involve generating a new repertoire or learning new material," I said. "People would find it fascinating to learn about your process and to get to see how a great singer works with a great accompanist."

"I like this idea. Let's give Rob a call tomorrow and see what he thinks," she said.

All this talk had given Elaine a second wind. She wanted to get propped up in bed, and she began to channel surf. She stumbled on the movie version of *Mame*, which led to reminiscence about an audition she gave for the composer Jerry Herman. "I auditioned for the son of a bitch three times. Never got the role, but I adored him. I'd have been great in that role, don't you think?"

"Terrific," I said, meaning it and figuring she had forgotten that she played the role in 1969 in Cape Cod, the year before she starred in *Company* on Broadway.

I asked her about other roles that she'd wanted to play. "I don't do that. I really don't. I don't sit around and think about the roles I didn't play," she said.

"But surely there are roles, great female roles, you had your eye on," I prompted.

"Well, I auditioned for Gower Champion for *Hello, Dolly!* I think I'd have been pretty good with her. Champion told me to go home and keep working. He felt that I was talented but not quite ready. And Irving Berlin said the same thing about Ado Annie."

Still channel surfing, she came across a Marx Brothers movie, which got her thinking about her husband John again.

"I told you he did a better Groucho than Groucho, didn't I? Oh my god was he good. It was absolutely terrifying how good he was."

Elaine called for her caretaker to check her sugar levels. They were satisfactory. It was clear that Elaine took great pride and pleasure when her counts were stable. It seemed to reinforce for her that she was succeeding in establishing a routine and a care team to keep her safe. She would rationalize that she was comfortable drinking "just one or two a night" because she'd earned enough financial security to pay for the staffing she needed to keep her safe.

Seeing that Elaine was comfortable and settled in the bed and occupied with me, her caretaker popped in and asked, since I was with Elaine, if she could make a quick run to the grocery store. Given the caretaker's accent and Elaine's hearing loss, the communication between the two turned into a comedy of errors. Elaine wanted to know what she needed to get so late at night. "Just a few things," the caretaker replied, implying some necessities for the house.

"What necessities?" screeched Elaine.

"I need to get a few things," said her caretaker.

"I know that, why else would anyone go to the store, but what do you need?" barked Elaine, seeming suspicious.

"I need to get a personal item."

"What!" shouted Elaine.

"A personal item," said the caretaker, increasing her volume and slowing down her delivery.

"What the fuck does that mean? What kind of personal item?"

Finally throwing discretion aside, her caretaker shouted, "I need to get some tampons, Elaine." I could tell the woman was afraid that Elaine wouldn't approve of such conversation in front of a guest and was embarrassed, personally.

"Oh, for God's sake. Go. I'll be fine. But look, you have to come prepared for your shift. If he wasn't here, you wouldn't be able to just go out and leave me alone. That's just the way it is."

I felt for the aide. She clearly didn't want to reveal her specific intention in front of a man. And as a man, I confess I inwardly winced at the exposure. But as each aide would come to learn, nothing was off-limits around Elaine including private delicacies.

A little more channel surfing led to a showing of *A Long Day's Journey into Night* starring Jason Robards.

"Oh, I love this play," I said enthusiastically. "Have you done it?"

"No, never," Elaine said. "I did do the letter play with him," she said with a grin, recalling our earlier conversation and enjoying the shared shorthand.

"How did you like working with Robards?"

"He was okay, but Jesus Christ, talk about an egomaniac. He was as much a diva as anyone I've ever worked with, honest to God."

That's the pot calling the kettle black, I thought.

Elaine needed to use the bathroom. I helped her get out of bed and walked with her. When she got to her vanity, she said, "Honey, stand here and hold my hips, this hair needs help," while she fiddled with both hands to revitalize her locks. As I stood with Elaine, I flashed back to the days caring for my mother. She'd had a stroke before she developed leukemia, and I would often spend weekends, much like I was now doing with Elaine, helping out at home with her care. She, too, would stand at the basin, brushing her teeth or combing her hair. It's a strange thing for a reasonably young man to partner with an older woman as she contemplates and massages her appearance. A strange *pas de deux* providing support to a private act.

Once she was satisfied with her hair, I escorted her to the commode and exited. She didn't call for me to escort her back to the bedroom; she walked by herself and did pretty well. She had that little skip in her step with those little hand flourishes that are classic Elaine Stritch—usually a gait and punctuation she would use when she knew she was in public and being watched.

"Hey, see there, you're moving really well," I said.

"Yeah, who knows, maybe I am getting better."

She got settled back into bed and told me she really liked her physical therapist, a kind, soft-spoken Indian man named Haresh.

"He's just terrific. I adore him. He's a small, elegant man, but when he works with me and gives me my exercises, he's very clear and definite with me. If anything is going to get me back on my feet, it's Haresh. He comes tomorrow, you'll get to meet him."

* * *

The next day, knowing that Elaine wouldn't be up and about until early afternoon, I busied myself checking out some of the Birmingham scene.

I found a couple of nearby bakeries. Knowing the strength of Elaine's sweet tooth, I stopped in to get her some chocolate cookies. I also noted the nicer restaurants in the area, hoping that before too long, Elaine would feel like going out for dinner—if for no other reason than to be seen.

On my way back to the condo, I met one of Elaine's new neighbors, a dark-haired woman in her late twenties who lived in the unit directly above Elaine's. Surprised to see someone she didn't know coming up in the elevator from the gated garage, she introduced herself with the intention of finding out who I was. I said hello and told her I was a friend of Ms. Stritch's.

"Oh my god, we all just love her. I didn't know who she was at first. God, a real celebrity, right here at the Dakota." She said she was checking in with Elaine on a regular basis to see if she needed anything.

"My balcony overhangs her patio. My husband and I just lean over the railing and say hi. We can see everything she does down there. We'll keep our eye on her. She's so cute," she said. I wondered how Elaine was feeling about these neighbors who thought she was "cute."

Once inside the condo, I met the second of Elaine's new caretakers. About eighteen, she was small and timid and spoke in very broken English. My first impression was that Elaine would eat her for dinner.

I introduced myself, and she told me she'd started about a week ago and that Ms. Stritch was out on the patio sunning herself. "Oh, great, I'll join her," I said. The caretaker stammered something in broken English, which I didn't fully comprehend at first, but the gist of it seemed to be that she should check with Elaine first since Elaine was sunbathing topless.

"Oh, well, no problem. Don't interrupt her. I'll take a short break in the guest room until she's finished," I said, chuckling to myself, imagining the new neighbor and her unsuspecting husband peering down from their balcony and getting any eyeful of this feisty octogenarian sunbathing topless.

After covering herself, Elaine called out to me to join her on the patio. She requested a cosmopolitan, which she was now referring to as her "joy juice." She asked what I'd been up to, and I told her I'd strolled down to the creek and also found a great bakery.

"I brought you some chocolate cookies," I said.

"Oh, good. We'll go around the corner for dinner tonight and then come back for cappuccino and cookies," she said with a sense of glee and anticipation.

* * *

Haresh, her physical therapist, came by around four thirty. He was indeed a "small, elegant man" who had a great way with Elaine. Directing her on exercises on a portable pedal apparatus, he worked on her strength and stamina as well as muscle tone.

She enjoyed talking with him. He had a good sense of humor and seemed to marvel at her commitment to her exercises.

"You've got to get me walking—on my own—again. You know I walked everywhere in New York. When they replaced my hip, I was onstage ten days later. Everyone told me my recovery was a miracle. But the doctors told me that the muscles in my legs were so strong and developed—that's why I recovered so well. So I must get up and get walking again."

Haresh assured Elaine that she was doing great and that he was really impressed by her. A little positive reinforcement by a good-looking man went a long way with Elaine. She loved it—and him. And everyone around her was pleased that she got along so well with her therapist, because had the reverse been true, things could have gotten ugly real fast.

After her workout, Elaine invited Haresh to dinner with us. "John's paying, so come along and have a drink with us," she said. Haresh declined, citing his family waiting at home. So he said goodbye, but only after confirming the date of his next visit and Elaine's homework exercises.

Elaine wanted a small nap after Haresh left, so about an hour later, her caretaker helped her get dressed in black tights, a white shirt, and a stylish black and white derby hat. She didn't want to take her walker, so with a good grip on my arm and her cane in the other hand, we headed slowly down the Dakota front stairs and worked our way to the Italian restaurant on the corner.

A small but busy restaurant with wide windows, it was a perfect spot for people watching as the Birmingham shoppers made their way in and out of their Mercedes Benzes and up and down the stretch of shops and boutiques. When we entered the restaurant, Elaine went right up to the welcome station and announced that she was Elaine Stritch, "the Elaine around the corner who always orders out. I want that seat by the window."

I got the sense the owner had been informed that this Broadway legend had moved in to the Dakota and had been ordering food frequently. He seemed intent on giving her special treatment. Certainly everyone in the restaurant was eyeing this—as Elaine referred to herself in *At Liberty*—"existential problem in tights."

After disapproving of the hard chair that came with the table by the window, we got settled into a nice corner booth where everyone could see her and Elaine could still see the coming and goings of the jet set. Elaine ordered a cosmopolitan, giving explicit instructions to the owner. When the owner announced they only offered beer and wine, Elaine squealed, "Oh my god, what kind of joint is this? Are you kidding me?" Once she'd digested the news, she said, "Maybe we should just get the food to go and eat in."

"We're here, let's just stay and eat," I said. "Do you want a glass of wine?"

"Have you ever seen me drink a glass of wine, John?" she said, her words dripping in disdain.

"How about a beer?" I asked.

Threatening never to return, she settled for an O'Doul's nonalcoholic beer. I was afraid for the waitress when she timidly appeared, but Elaine let the moment pass and ordered eggplant parmesan and a salad.

"Now listen, honey, I want the salad chopped up fine, so tell your cook to chop it up even more than it normally is. I want it really fine, you dig?" she said. The waitress assured her she would tell the cook.

The drinks came. The food came. All was fine. The eggplant parmesan was excellent—Elaine really enjoyed it. As we ate and talked, I noted that Elaine would chew on a bit of the eggplant parmesan and then spit it out and lay the chewed-up wad on her plate. I didn't say anything but recalled the short clip in *Shoot Me* when she mentioned to Alec Baldwin that she would often chew her food and spit it out. I wondered if this was an attempt to reduce consumption and whether or not this was a regular habit with Elaine. I hadn't seen this before, so it didn't strike me as a sign of an eating disorder. I didn't ask her about it. She only ate about a third of the salad, a roll, and the eggplant, and then asked for everything to go. "We have cookies and coffee waiting," she said.

Back at the Dakota, we enjoyed our sweet treats and talked about how nice it was to look forward to food. I confessed that I often started the day by thinking about the meals I would be having and how the anticipation of food was often enough to lift my mood or carry me through my workday.

"I don't do that, but when I'm hungry, look out!" she said. "John was a real lover of food. We'd go to the Savoy Grill, and he'd order for us both—I just loved that. There are very few people I'd ever let order for me, but he knew me so well. That's what I really miss, someone knowing me *that* well.

Elaine got to talking about her final days at the Carlyle. She loved the fact that, as she exited down the elevator for the final time, all the staff in their black and white linens had been taken off their posts and lined up to say goodbye.

"I thought that was just terrific. Every one of them off post. I don't get choked up much, but that got to me," she said. "And I told them they'd all get their muffins this year for Christmas. And they will."

Ever since she'd married John Bay and entered into the Bay family muffin dynasty, Elaine kept a long list of people she liked enough to send them a box of Bay's muffins for Christmas—her version of sending Christmas cards. In her circles, Elaine was known for this, and by most accounts, the people who received them really liked them.

* * *

In the weeks since my last visit, an interview that Elaine gave to Bennett Marcus of *Vanity Fair* came out. In the interview, Elaine was quoted as saying that she was "as unhappy as anybody can be" about her move to Michigan, and in response to a question about the difference between New Yorkers and people in Birmingham, she said, "The people in New York, their humor is on a level that goes very deep, you know? Very deep, and there's not as many people in on the joke [in Birmingham] like they are in New York. You know what I'm talking about?"

A few of the local blogs and culture sites picked up on the story, and headlines started emerging locally declaring "Elaine Stritch Unhappy in 'Ham" and "Stritch Disses Michiganders." I asked if she'd gotten any fallout from the interview.

"What do you mean?" she snapped.

"Well, your comments about Birmingham were not all that flattering," I said.

"Well, what do I care?" she shouted. "And no, nobody's said a thing. I keep getting calls to attend galas and country club meetings, so I don't think it did any harm. People still want to be around the celebrity, and they always will. People like meeting famous people. I like meeting famous people. It's fun. And if anybody took offense, fuck 'em."

* * *

Later, Elaine brought up her final performance at the Carlyle and seemed somewhat unsettled by it. "I don't think it was my best," she said. She likened it to an athlete playing a final season when his body can no longer perform at the highest level.

"I don't know, I didn't sing much 'cause I was too worried about forgetting words, and I just knew I didn't have the mental stamina to fight my way through it. I see photos of me sitting there on that stool, and it just doesn't look like what I know I should be doing in front of an audience, sitting there and telling stories. I just don't know if it was worth the price they paid to see it."

I started to tell her that I thought the audience loved whatever she did because it was *her*, and then she nailed me.

"Look, John, I don't like liars. We've gotten along pretty good because I've always felt like you were straight with me."

That was all. Silence hung in the air as she just looked at me, that same gaze that drilled through me that night we first met. She was right, and she was amazingly perceptive.

"Okay," I said. "I felt like it was a diminished version of what you have always been capable of doing. Nothing fell apart, and it's always fascinating watching you improv, Elaine, but the last image New York saw of you onstage didn't feel like the Elaine we've always known and loved. And to tell you the truth, it made me a little sad. In both of your previous Café Carlyle gigs, even though you struggled with lines, you still displayed that double-barreled power you have onstage. In this one, you didn't. And I came away wishing you hadn't done it."

Elaine grabbed my hand quick and held it hard. "You're absolutely right. And I felt it. The truth is I had bills to pay at the Carlyle, and they knew a week of me saying goodbye would sell like hell. So I did it. We had no rehearsal, they wouldn't pay for it. No band. Just me and Rob. So I tried to just get out there and play it in the moment."

She paused. "Now are we straight? You don't ever lie to me," she said.

I smiled at her. "Yes, Elaine."

Another pause. "There was one moment in the show that compensated for everything else," I said.

"What?" she asked.

"The moment at the end, when you stood behind Rob and kissed him while he played the introduction to 'All My Tomorrows.'"

"Yeah, that surprised me too. And him," she said.

"Where did it come from?"

"I just thought about all we'd been through and how this was our last hurrah at the Carlyle, and well, I never really showed him how much he means to me, you know? So I kissed him, to thank him, publicly, and to let him know I loved him. He is deeply talented. Deeply talented."

"Well, it was one of the most nonperformed and nonpresented moments I think I've ever seen from you onstage. And I think everyone who saw it was deeply moved," I said.

"Well then, maybe that redeems the whole show, if it let people see how much I love Rob."

Elaine and her musical director Rob Bowman.
Credit: Barbara Davidson

I left early the next morning, dreading the long drive back to Pennsylvania but feeling good about having spent a stretch of private time with Elaine. She was reflective, willing to talk deeply about her life. She was certainly less "onstage" in this new environment. This was Elaine coping with aging, with truly ending her New York lifestyle. For as long as she would allow, I looked forward to watching her make her way through this new and yet final phase of her life.

CHAPTER 11

Since my last visit, I returned to my hometown of Springfield, Ohio, to do a little firsthand genealogy work on Elaine's ancestors. This odd coincidence between us continued to fascinate me. I was curious to know more about her mother and father and to explore any other mutuality between Elaine's life and mine.

Spending time in the local historical society, I found the gravesite location for Elaine's father's family, a small pastoral graveyard on the outskirts of town where many working-class Irish families were laid to rest. I took photos of the grave of Elaine's grandfather and the graves of her uncles and their wives. I was eager to show these to Elaine.

When I got to her condo, I found Elaine in a terrible mood. She returned from the Traverse City Film Festival to find the hot water heater broken. For the past three days, there was no hot water in the house, and it seemed that Elaine and her caretakers were battling with the condo association about getting the issue addressed. When I arrived, Elaine was insistent, demanding immediate action to get the heater fixed even though it was approximately four thirty on a Friday afternoon.

"Come in, darling. I hope you don't need a shower, because we ain't got no hot water," she barked in greeting.

"No hot water, oh my god, when did this happen?" I asked.

"We have no idea, we came back from Traverse City, and that was it. Can you believe it? I pay over a million dollars for this joint and everything is broken. And I mean everything. The dishwasher is leaking water everywhere. A cabinet door fell off the living room bookcase. We've had I don't know how many people in here messing with the air-conditioning. I mean, Jesus Christ, I'm beginning to think I've been had. I really do."

Elaine demanded that her niece who had served as her real estate agent be summoned to the house. A nephew was already en route. Before they arrived, a serviceman from a repair company recommended by the condo association knocked at the door.

"Oh, thank God. Look, I don't know what's wrong, but for what I paid for this place, I need this fixed now. I can't be here without hot water. Look at me, I'm eighty-eight years old. Please, please, please just fix it."

The serviceman made his way to the unit, tucked off the Michael Feinstein guest room, and diagnosed that Elaine needed a new hot water heater, announcing that it would cost in the range of $2,500–$3,000 installed.

Elaine went ballistic.

"You've got to fucking be kidding me!" she shouted. "How can it be shot? I just bought this place."

"Well, it looks like it's the original, and this place was built in 2002, so it's about eleven years old," said the erstwhile technician.

"Well, that's not my fucking problem," Elaine shot back, not realizing that, as a homeowner, this was her problem. Having spent the majority of her adult life living in hotels, she was accustomed to complaining and having problems fixed. On demand. The transition to homeowner was not sitting well with her.

"Since I moved into this fucking place, I have been bleeding money. I don't have this kind of money—$3,000 here, $2,000 there. I told my niece that I wanted to withhold $25,000 in escrow for the first year just in case shit like this happened. And she told me I couldn't. Well, goddamn it, I know I could and I should have. That bat I bought this place from should be paying for all of this. Do you believe this? What am I going to do?" she said, building to hysterics.

By this time one of her nephews arrived and was trying to manage the situation on Elaine's behalf. "I'm not going to pay, I'm just not," she commanded.

"Do you want me to send the repairman away then?" he asked.

"Well, yes, I'm not going to pay fucking $3,000 for hot water in a condo that cost me over a million dollars. I'm just not."

Her nephew went to tell the repairman Elaine would not be going forward with the repair. Elaine's nephew returned to inform Elaine that she would need to pay the repairman $100 for the service call.

All hell broke loose.

Erupting into searing, red-hot rage, Elaine screamed, "What the fuck are you taking about? I'm not paying him a goddamn thing. This is unbelievable."

Her nephew tried to explain the notion that service people charge a fee just for coming and diagnosing the problem. "Well then, he should have told me that when he first got here," she said. Turning to me, she said, "Do you believe this?"

"Your nephew is right, they don't come in the door without expecting at least a fee for the service call," I said.

"I've never heard of this in my life. Why didn't he tell me that when he came in. I'm not paying it!" she shouted.

The poor serviceman stood silent in the next room. He got on his cell phone and called the home office to tell them things were getting dicey. I was on the verge of paying the guy myself just to calm Elaine, but I knew that would only add fuel to the fire.

"Get him in here," she demanded. "I cannot believe you're charging me $100 for walking in here and doing nothing when you didn't even tell me, in advance, there would be a charge. Is this how you do business?" she interrogated.

He timidly repeated that there is always a service charge.

"Well, I'm not paying you $100." She grabbed her change purse, pulled out $50, and threw it on the table. "Take it and get out. Just get out."

After he left, her nephew got to work calling one of his contacts to see if they might come and look at the heater and offer a better price on a replacement. His contact agreed to come out on Friday evening. While everyone waited for his arrival, and after ordering a stiff glass of "joy juice," Elaine continued to rage on about the costs associated with owning the condo.

"I can't afford all of these bills. And they're not small. Do you have thousands of dollars you can throw around on unexpected repairs," she demanded of her nephew.

Agreeing with everything she said in an attempt to calm her, Elaine finally attacked her nephew with "Oh, stop agreeing with everything, standing there saying yes. I can't tell you how boring it is."

When the new repairman came, he agreed to a replacement for just under $2,000, and he was willing to spend the evening on the installation. Elaine agreed, and the rest of the evening was spent with the accompaniment of clanging pipes, mopped puddles, and drop cloths spread throughout the condo.

I asked Elaine if she wanted to go out for dinner. She didn't— she was in no mood for getting herself ready to be seen. Eventually her nephew left, leaving me fearful her rage might rear up again when it came time to write the check and I'd be the only one with her to cope with the outburst. Luckily about three hours later, the new hot water heater was connected and hot water was running again. That good news, along with the effect of her third glass of joy juice, seemed to soothe the savage beast. I think it also helped that the repairmen was a good-looking young man who charmed the socks off Elaine. Elaine wrote the check, and I saw the serviceman out and thanked him for his calm and quick work.

* * *

Elaine was hungry, so we had leftover lentil soup, Coca-Cola, and crackers for dinner. Around nine or so, Elaine got a call from Nicole Clark. I had been with Elaine before when this young woman called. She called regularly, if not nightly, to check in with Elaine and to check on her diabetes counts. I learned that Nicole is the daughter of actors Alexander Clark and Frances Tannehill.

"They conceived Nicole on the national tour of *Call Me Madam.* I loved them both, and Nicole has always been like family. She calls almost every night to check in on me," Elaine said.

During the phone conversation, it was clear that Nicole's mother had passed away very recently. "Well, there's nothing more you could have done, Nicole," Elaine said. "You've done everything humanly possible, and you know your mother knew how devoted you were. Every mother should be lucky to have a kid as loving as you."

Nicole was seeking advice from Elaine on how to get an obituary in the *Times.* "You let me know what they tell you. If you need me to, I'll give them a call, darling. We'll get it in, I promise. If I can do *anything* for you, I can do *that,*" she said with a sense of maternal sensitivity that I found surprising.

There was a long pause after Elaine hung up with Nicole.

"You know, I didn't go to my sister Georgene's funeral," she said rather suddenly.

"I didn't know that," I said. "Do you regret it?"

"No, well, I don't know, maybe. My nephew Frankie called and told me she died, but I was in rehearsal. I couldn't deal with it, you know, I just couldn't. And I had a good reason for not going home since I was working, you know? But ultimately, I just couldn't go. It was too big for me."

I stayed silent as she gazed intensely off into the Detroit sky just outside her kitchen window.

"One of my brothers didn't come to my mom's funeral either," I said.

"Really?" she asked.

"Yeah, I think he couldn't face it either."

"Do you hold it against him?" she asked.

"I did at first. And there are still times when I can't really believe he didn't come to his own mother's funeral. But I have realized that everyone has to grieve in their own way, and his way was on his own—alone. So I've worked hard on letting it go. Ultimately, it's between him and my mom."

"Goddamn right, it's none of your business what he chose to do."

Another pause followed.

"Did you ever tell your nephew that the reason you didn't come was because it was too hard," I said.

"Nope, never did."

Knowing that Frankie and Elaine were pretty close, I said, "I bet he's put it together. I suspect he completely understands."

"I think so too," she said.

After dinner, Elaine retired to her bedroom, requesting my presence in about an hour or so.

"Perfect. I'm going to take a hot shower," I said, unsure if it was a wise move to revisit the topic.

"Yeah, a fucking $2,000 hot shower—enjoy yourself!" she hollered as she walked pretty steadily back to her bedroom with her caretaker close behind.

* * *

About an hour later, I lightly knocked on her bedroom only to find Elaine out cold. She was sleeping soundly, so I decided to call it a night myself. About two hours later, I was awakened by what would become a common occurrence.

Since Elaine typically would sleep her mornings away, she would stir late at night—anytime between 1:00 and 4:00 a.m. It was an odd sensation to wake up in her guest room, hearing her raspy voice, amplified over the baby monitor, calling out to her caretaker to check her levels or get her a drink. Often, she could be heard walking to the kitchen for a late-night snack with her caretaker in tow, her walker tapping an aluminum rattle on the hardwood floors.

On this night, the baby monitor projected, along with a classic movie blasting in the background from the TV, Elaine having a conversation with her young caretaker beside her in the king-sized bed.

Elaine was asking the caretaker about her boyfriend, and Elaine seemed eager to dispense advice about how best to manage the opposite sex. Again it was a little odd experiencing Elaine's maternal side. After a half hour or so, the sound of conversation died down, overwhelmed by the roar of old Hollywood, which lulled all of us back to sleep.

* * *

I spent the next morning taking a run through the streets of Birmingham. I wanted to imagine Elaine in this place should her health and mobility return. Would she walk these streets with the same brio she had walked the avenues of New York? There were certainly plenty of high-end stores and trendy boutiques laced between elegant restaurants and kitschy sweet shops. There were hairstylists, dentists, jewelers, and florists. There was even a fur store and vault at which I suspected she had already registered.

This little patch of upscale Birmingham wasn't anywhere near in size to even a portion of her haunts on the Upper East Side of Manhattan, but it had a Madison Avenue feel to it—clearly a shopping district catering to Detroit's luxury set. Around a bend, I came to the Uptown Birmingham Cineplex and wondered if *Shoot Me* would be premiere here in 2014, an official welcome to Detroit's hometown girl and Broadway legend.

My run took me back to the Dakota and through Booth Park down to the creek. I recalled that quiet sun-soaked afternoon we spent here during my previous visit and hoped I might talk her into another walk this afternoon.

Elaine rose around noon or so. Her days typically began with her sitting at the kitchen table in a white T-shirt and underwear enjoying a cup of coffee and a scrambled egg with a Bay's English Muffin. She'd enjoy *The New York Times* and slowly wend her way through her mail. When I got back from the corner café where I caught up on email, she greeted me with "What have you been up to?"

"Oh, just checking out the neighborhood. Lots close by," I said.

"Yeah, not bad. A couple of interesting shops, but it ain't New York," she said.

"Elaine, our joint history in Springfield, Ohio, led me to do some genealogy work," I said, eager to share my findings.

"Oh yeah, what did you find?" she asked.

"Well, I found your family's burial plot in Calvary Cemetery in Springfield. I've got photos." She looked at the large Stritch family stone but struggled to really make out the smaller stones with each of her father's father and brothers and their wives' names. She seemed only mildly interested.

"And I found a copy of your mother's father's will."

"Oh yeah?" she asked with increased interest. "He was loaded, wasn't he? Mother came from money, or at least that's how the story always went."

"He was successful. When he died in 1928, he left most of the estate to his wife, but he did leave $5,000 to your mom and $5,000 to your uncle Howard," I said as I showed her a copy of Grandpa Louis's last will and testament.

"Hey, not bad for 1928, just before the Depression," she said. "That was a lot of money."

"And he left $500 each to 'Genie,' which we have to assume was your sister Georgene, and another $500 to Sally," I said.

"What about me, I would have been three years old in 1928," she said.

"You're not listed," I said. "I suspect he drew up the will prior to your birth and never updated it before he died."

"Go figure, just my luck," she said.

* * *

The doorbell rang. "Who's that?" she yelled to her caretaker ordering her to get the door. There was some commotion at the front door. Elaine screamed from the kitchen, "Who is it!" The caretaker came running back. "It's the delivery man," she said.

"What delivery man?" Elaine insisted.

"From the liquor store," her caretaker replied.

"Oh, well, then, my god, send him in."

The delivery man came in with a large box of liquor with multiple bottles of vodka, triple sec, and gin. He went back to his truck for a second box. Elaine chatted him up, flirting with the good-looking young man and letting him know how welcome he was. She paid him with a check and tipped him twenty dollars.

As Elaine continued with her breakfast, I asked her about the Traverse City Film Festival. "It was a smash," she said. "They loved the film, and I absolutely adored what's his name."

I was not immediately sure of who she was referring to. She lost patience and said, "Oh, come on, you know. The big guy. The fat guy."

"Oh, Michael Moore?"

"Yes, I love him. I haven't met anyone recently who I like as much as him. And he loved me."

Michael Moore, the documentary filmmaker and a Michigan native, founded the Traverse City Film Festival and enthusiastically included *Shoot Me* on the slate. He invited Elaine, and because she refused to fly, he offered to send a car to drive her the four hours each way and to put her up in a hotel.

"I had to take one of my caretakers with me, and Rob and Julie and Chiemi all met us up there," she said. "It was great. I love him, we got along just great. What is it with all of these overweight men that I meet and fall in love with," she said. "If he's not careful, he'll end up just like Gandolfini. I don't understand how people let themselves get so fat. If you're in this business, you can't afford to let it happen."

I was interested in probing her on this. "You've always been thin," I said. "Did you have to work at it?"

"No, I just tried to be careful about it," she said.

I wondered about her habit of chewing food and spitting it out.

"But I'll tell you what, I think fat people are playing Russian roulette, I really do. I mean, look what happened to James," she said. She paused and then said, "I'd rather be dead than fat."

After finishing her breakfast, we sat out on the patio in the warm sunshine. Elaine had her legs elevated on a footrest padded with a pillow and was attempting to read the *Times* as I was working on my laptop. Elaine was struggling with the paper. She held it very close and would move the paper as she attempted to read, as if she had a very narrow tunnel of good eyesight left.

I asked her if she felt that the vision in her right eye, the eye she injured in her fall on Madison Avenue, was getting any better.

"No, I've lost nearly all the vision in the eye. It's just my left eye now, and that one's never been all that great," she said.

I asked her if she'd like me to read the *Times* to her.

"Oh, you bet. That would be divine, darling."

I pulled my chair closer to her, took the paper, and worked my way through the highlights of the arts and style sections as well as the obituaries with Elaine commenting every step along the way.

* * *

During Elaine's afternoon nap, I had a chance to talk with her caretaker. Throughout the past three months, a number of caretakers had rotated through Elaine's life. By my count there were currently four caretakers on payroll providing twenty-four-hour care. There were at least two that I could account for who had, apparently, been fired. It seemed they were let go because either they couldn't stand up to Elaine's demanding expectations and occasionally abusive verbal attacks or they simply weren't sharp enough to be able to anticipate her needs and provide her with the level of keen attention she expected. Of the four who were now rotating through, they were each performing two to four twenty-four-hour, full-day shifts. Elaine didn't want to reorient to a new caretaker every single day. She preferred to settle in with one for a stretch of days.

It was clear that the four who had made it this far in the process had learned the vagaries of Elaine's personality and demanding nature. Each in their own way had begun to forge their bond with her, identifying the qualities they possessed that connected with Elaine. For one, it was a sense of humor, the ability to keep pace with Elaine's wry intellect and to spar with her. For another, it was the ability to cook food the way Elaine liked it. For another it was the ability to stay three steps ahead of Elaine and anticipate her needs. This last quality was particularly important to Elaine. She hated having to instruct her caretakers—she wanted them to perceive the lifestyle and to step up their game and provide the kind of five-star service to which she has always been accustomed.

As I talked with today's caretaker, a stylish young woman who had already developed a rather protective attitude toward Elaine, I learned that the caretakers had all agreed to dilute Elaine's vodka with water so that her "joy juice" cocktails were not full strength. So far, Elaine had not noticed the ruse, and her care team felt better in limiting Elaine's alcohol intake, not only in terms of controlling her diabetes, but also in trying to protect her ability to safely move throughout the condo.

In late afternoon, Elaine got her second wind and came out for any early cocktail. "My sexy therapist is due in a little while, and I need to get ready for him," she justified. While we waited for Haresh to arrive, we went through her mail. There was a letter from Hal Prince who was vacationing in Europe with his wife Judy.

"We're in the Alps and thank God we are! We've just returned from Venice and Rome, and all of Europe is an inferno. The streets of Venice are paved with McDonald's and KFC wrappings. But here in Megeve, it's gorgeous, pristine, and even cool," he wrote.

He went on to report that he and Judy had just sold their six-floor East Seventy-Fourth Street townhouse and "we need to make an interim move and thought we'd like to move to the Carlyle." He wondered if Elaine was still on good terms with the manager there and might assist them in negotiating "a rate for a two-bedroom apartment beginning in October through the end of the year?"

To which Elaine responded, "Yeah sure, Hal, and I'm doing just fine thank you." She chirped at her caretaker to make a note to remind Elaine to call the Carlyle tomorrow and then to call Hal.

A notecard from Stephen Sondheim began with "I hope you're happily settled in your new digs and enjoying life [a hard thing to do, but worth the effort]." She appreciated his use of the word *digs*. "That's a reference to the script for *A Little Night Music*," she said. "Desiree's digs. That's what's fun about Steve: the wordplay." Sondheim's note went on to say,

In cleaning off my desk, I came across a copy of
an extraordinary letter to you, dated December
15, 2009, by a man named Jim Grissom. It's a
reminiscence of Tennessee Williams in which he
(Mr. Williams) pays me a number of high com-
pliments. I'm almost certain that you didn't send
me the copy, but I can't remember who did. Can
you tell me who Jim Grissom is?

"I don't know what he's talking about," Elaine said. "I don't
recall any letter about Tennessee Williams, and I have no clue who
Jim Grissom is. Throw it out," she said. "No, wait, I'll call Steve
tomorrow. Take note and add that to my list for tomorrow," she said
to her caretaker.

Buried deep in Elaine's pile of mail was a script titled *Beethoven's
Treasure*. "What's this?" I asked.

"Oh, some script they want me to do. You know, it's those dog
movies. They're going to do another one," she said, referring to the
series of movies released in the 1990s featuring a St. Bernard as the
star.

"Is it a good role?" I asked.

"Are you kidding?" she said. "It's a movie about a fucking dog.
But they'll be shooting in Toronto, so that's not too bad for me, and
if they pay me enough, I might be able to afford living in this condo
for another month or two—WITH hot water.

"They're offering $65,000, which is awfully low, don't you
think," she said.

Given that the franchise fared pretty well over the years, I did
think it was fairly low. "What would you like to see?" I said.

"Well, I think $100,000 would be pretty fair, don't you?"

* * *

Elaine greeted Haresh's arrival with glee. "Oh, good, that's my
good-looking therapist." Haresh entered the kitchen, and after refill-
ing her cosmo, Elaine, Haresh, and her caretaker all retreated to the

living room where Haresh led Elaine through a thirty-minute work-out focusing on the strength and range of motion in her legs and hips. Haresh was very good at explaining each exercise and its intended outcome. Elaine liked knowing the details of what she was being asked to do. And Haresh was very good at complimenting Elaine and championing her effort. After a session with Haresh, Elaine felt renewed and very optimistic about being able to walk again.

After Haresh left, I asked Elaine if she wanted to walk down to the creek again. She didn't, stating that her workout with Haresh was all she could muster today. I was disappointed by this and each subsequent failed attempt to get Elaine out of the condo. Part of me must have thought that with a sturdy escort, she'd feel safe and strong enough to get out and navigate the streets, sidewalks, and walking paths in her new neighborhood. I also hoped that a little bit of fan recognition would buoy her spirits. I also hoped to get her back down to the creek, thinking it would be a good place for reflection, a chance for me to probe more deeply and privately. But not today.

Elaine received a few visitors, a rather wealthy couple with ties to the Birmingham Country Club and the private Cranbrook School, which was just down the road from the Dakota. They brought a bottle of wine and were thrilled to be meeting Elaine Stritch. Elaine put on the charm and immediately played the gay hostess, ordering her caretaker to pour the wine and set out bowls of pretzels and chips. Elaine peppered her new friends with questions, drawing them into conversation, and trying to get the scoop on the local country club scene.

Her guests extended an open invitation for Elaine to attend the country club's next gala event as their guest. "Everyone at the club would be so thrilled to have you with us," they assured her. Elaine liked the idea and let them know she expected them to follow up with her. Anticipating the *coup* among their social circle that arriving with Broadway legend Elaine Stritch as their guest would represent, they were absolutely giddy at the prospect. After a photo with Elaine and assurances that they would be back in touch, they made a graceful exit.

"God, talk about the ladies who lunch!" Elaine said. "But what the hell, I need the country club if I hope to meet some handsome rich man. If I'm going to live in Birmingham, the country club set is the set I need to be circulating with—even if it kills me."

For dinner Elaine requested smoked salmon with hard-boiled egg, sliced red onion, and capers. And over dessert of ice cream and a little slice of cake, our conversation turned to the Catholic church.

"Do you consider yourself a devout Catholic?" I asked.

"What do you think?" she snapped back.

"Well, I've seen you stop in a church twice now to light candles, and I know you've spent a lot of time in Catholic schools," I said.

"I was raised Catholic, and like everyone I know who is Catholic, there are parts of it that I like, you know, the candles and the ceremony and all that shit. We pick the parts that work for us, and we walk away from the stuff that doesn't. All the sex abuse shit, it makes me sick, and I'm ashamed to be associated with it. But I believe in God, and stopping in to sit and say a prayer or light a candle helps when I get just a little too full of myself, you know what I mean?"

"I don't mean to be indelicate, but you have given interviews where you've said you were a virgin well into your thirties," I said.

"Yeah, so what? That may seem odd these days, but back then, let me tell you, if you weren't married, you didn't mess around with that kind of stuff. And certainly not if my mother was your mother. You know what I mean?" she said.

"The one thing being raised Catholic did was keep me far away from sex. It's been that way all my life, and you know something, I'm glad about it. It has never been a big deal in my life, and thank God. Look at all the trouble sex causes people. Does that come from my being Catholic? I don't know. But I'm not crying about it—any of it! If you ask me, sex is highly overrated. It always has been."

CHAPTER 12

My next visit was on a September day close to noon. I knew that it would be too early to show up at Elaine's condo, so I decided to take a walk through the woods and along the creek in Booth Park. The leaves were just starting to turn, and the playful hint of cooler air whispered through the trees. I wondered how Elaine was doing and feeling, whether or not she had been out walking, perhaps here along this very path.

After killing about an hour with my feet dangling in the cool creek, I made my way to the local cupcake shop and picked up a couple of chocolate treats for Elaine and her staff and to the local floral shop for some white lilies for her wash stand.

When I arrived, Elaine was in bed sleeping, and her caretaker, a very slight young woman and new member of the team who had been alerted to my planned arrival, welcomed me into the condo.

The news was not good.

Elaine had taken a fall in her bathroom and had fractured her left pelvic bone. The fall had occurred about three weeks ago. She was doing much better after a couple of painful weeks in bed. Apparently, she was now able to move around in bed without excruciating pain, and she could transfer herself into her wheelchair to get back and forth to the kitchen.

The first two weeks, the caretaker reported, were hell. Elaine was in terrible pain, and nobody could make her comfortable. The condo was filled with screaming, moaning, and cursing. I wondered aloud if I should have come.

"Oh no, she's been looking forward to the visit and she's been doing better. She'll be glad to see you," her caretaker said almost with a sense of relief that there would be someone else in the house to distract and occupy Elaine.

After about an hour or so, Elaine began to stir in her bedroom. Actually, she began to cry out in pain as she was trying to get her caretaker to help her get to the bathroom. Hearing the commotion and concerned that perhaps the caretaker may need assistance in helping transport Elaine, I called in from outside the door, letting Elaine know I was here and asking if I could help.

"Oh my god, yes," she said. "Get in here. What are you doing out there? I fell again and broke my pelvis. Do you believe it," she said. "Broke my fucking pelvis. After falling on Madison Avenue and blinding myself and then falling in the Carlyle and breaking my fucking hip, now I fall and crack my pelvis. I mean really, do you fucking believe this? I don't know what's coming next."

"Elaine," I said. "I'm so sorry to hear this. But I hear you're getting better."

"I guess so, that's what they tell me. I can at least move around and get out of bed. But the pain, John, the pain is terrible. And there's not a goddamned thing they can do for it. 'Just lie in the fucking bed and hope the damn thing heals,' they say."

After assisting with getting Elaine in and out of the bathroom, we worked our way out to the kitchen where Elaine asked for bacon and cheese and a beer. I was surprised by this menu choice. She looked thinner, and I thought it a good sign that she was eating some high-fat food. She reported that one of her caretakers had fried up some bacon one day as a snack, and she had taken to it. "It goes great with a cocktail," she said.

I watched her eat the bacon and a few slices of cheese, and I took particular note that she wasn't spitting it back out after she chewed it. Her caretaker showed her the chocolate sweets I brought.

"Oh good, that's tonight's dessert," she said.

She seemed glad to get out of bed and to host a visitor. We settled in to some of our usual routines: reading the *Times* and going through her mail.

After that, she surprised her caretaker (and shocked me) by reporting that she felt like trying some of her bicycle pedaling exercises, so we made our way to the front living room where her little pedal therapy machine was set up. She got herself situated, moaning and screaming with each move, and then settled in with a slow steady rhythm.

Elaine was determined to work through her pain and get herself moving again. She wanted her strength, balance, and mobility back. I marveled at her ability to soldier on through the pain and keep up with her exercises.

"Haresh will be happy about this," she said.

"Happy," I said, "he'll be amazed."

"You bet," she said.

While she was exercising, I asked Elaine about an old press clipping I stumbled upon in my research motivated by her story of having played Anna in *The King and I*. I couldn't find any evidence of a Broadway or New York production of it. It made me recall Elaine's earlier comment about asking Richard Rodgers about how Anna just happened to get off the boat and know the language and culture of these people.

"Yeah, it's true. It was in the mid-1960s. In a fucking tent in New Jersey," she said.

More specifically, it was at the Music Circus in Lambertville, New Jersey, a summer stock company that did, indeed, play under a tent.

"How were you?" I asked.

"What do you mean 'how was I?'" she said. "How do you think I was?"

From her reaction, I knew my only answer could be "I bet you were great," but I really did wonder how she would translate in that role. "It's written for a soprano, isn't it?" I asked.

"No, not really. But it was a little high for me. But they took the keys down, and I was great in that role."

In fact, Gerald Krone, the general manager of the Music Circus, said in an interview, "As it turned out, she worked hard, was a wonderful Anna, and brought her solid acting strength to the role."

* * *

The afternoon was interrupted by the arrival of a childhood friend who apparently has stayed in regular contact with Elaine throughout her life. She lived close by and seemed delighted that Elaine had moved to Birmingham. This woman, very well dressed and refined, was a classic *lady who lunched*. She didn't seem like the type of person with whom Elaine would maintain ties, but old friendships can become important alliances, and if nothing else, Elaine values loyalty.

Elaine's friend had not heard about the fall and was feigning and fawning all over Elaine, telling her how great it was that she was able to be up and work on her pedaling exercises. Elaine told her about a visit earlier from the couple who invited Elaine to the country club. Elaine's friend implied that Elaine should consider being seen in such circles but cautioned—when her caretakers were out of earshot—that perhaps Elaine was not hiring the right type of people to be seen with her in public. Elaine jumped all over this.

"Oh, for fuck's sake, I don't want to hear any of the shit from you. 'Right kind of people' bullshit."

Elaine's friend seemed to take offense at this public reprimand and, after a little more small talk, made a hasty exit.

* * *

I expected Elaine to want a nap after her workout, but she was feeling energized and wanted to move back into the kitchen for dinner. Along with a cosmopolitan, she had bread and butter with ham and split pea soup. She dunked the bread in the soup, chewed it, and then spit it out. I finally decided to ask her about this practice of not swallowing her food.

"Don't you like it?" I asked.

"No, I love it, what do you mean. I just want the taste, honey, not the calories," she said.

"You don't look like you've ever had trouble with your weight, Elaine," I said.

"Well, I haven't, but you have to watch it, because it will sneak up on you, and in this business, you know what I mean?" she said.

From this point forward, I began paying more specific attention to her eating habits. It was becoming more and more clear that Elaine had become conditioned to watch her intake of food so that she could balance the caloric intake of alcohol. This was a long-embedded routine, and the more time I spent with her, the clearer it was that careful intake and lots of walking had become very important routines to help her maintain her figure.

I asked Elaine about other actresses who she admired or particular films that she liked. She mentioned that she loved Deborah Kerr in *Tea and Sympathy*. "Do you know it?" she asked.

"Sure, it's a great play. One of those midcentury plays that tiptoe around issues of sexuality," I said.

"Right. But I'm talking about the movie *Tea and Sympathy*," she said.

"Why do you like it so much?" I asked.

"I like the fact that it's about a very serious subject, a subject our society really needs to investigate more, the notion of an older woman falling in love with a young man. I think many women are attracted to this idea, but we don't talk much about it," she said.

* * *

Later that evening, over our chocolate treats, Elaine broke out in song, and once started, if she was with anyone who knew the old musical theater standards well enough, you could spend the next hour singing away. We started with the tune her father and mother would often sing to one another called "My Honey That I Loved So Well."

"It only took one martini to get them started," she said.

Then we moved on to Sondheim's "Broadway Baby" from *Follies*, and we finished with Irving Berlin's "You're Just in Love" from *Call Me Madam*. She loved these tunes. They seemed to buoy her spirit.

"You know, there's a terrific video of you singing 'You're Just in Love' on YouTube," I told her.

"What the fuck is a YouTube?"

I tried to explain it to her but decided it would be easiest to pull it up on my laptop and show her. The clip was from a 1955 broadcast of *The Colgate Comedy Hour* saluting director George Abbott who directed the Broadway production of *Call Me Madam*, which starred Ethel Merman. Elaine had been Ethel's understudy and eventually took over the role starring in the national tour.

In the clip, Elaine is performing the duet with Russell Nype, the show's original leading man. Both are dressed in black formal wear for the gala tribute. It starts rather simply, but as the piece moves on, Elaine unleashes her unmistakable ability to truly embody a song and imbue each word with clear intention and energy. By the time they both stand for the encore, Elaine is flinging her black tulle dress over her head and blowing Mr. Nype off the stage. It is Elaine at her best. And if anyone ever questioned whether she possessed a real singer's voice, this clip demonstrates a strong bright belt and keen musical instincts.

Elaine enjoyed seeing the video. She said she'd never seen it before. "But I remember that night," she said.

"You nearly blew him off the stage," I said.

"Yeah, well, that wasn't hard to do," she quipped. "You know the great thing about *Call Me Madam* for me?" she asked.

"No, what?" I said.

"Well, when I opened *Call Me Madam* in Washington, Ethel came to see it, and I was very aware of her presence. So was everyone else in the fucking theater. Can you believe she'd do that?" Elaine said in mock disbelief. "Well, the performance was fantastic, and the headline on the review the next day was 'Stritch Replaces Brass with Class.' Isn't that terrific? I loved that review."

Then after a beautifully timed pause, she said, "I still do."

* * *

When our singing had ended, I asked Elaine if she was feeling more settled here at the Dakota.

"I think so. At first, with everything being new and having so many people around me all the time, I couldn't imagine myself here, on my own. It didn't feel right, you know? But now, since I can't do a fucking thing anyway, knowing I've got a home—my place—and taking life on my own terms is feeling okay," she said. "Better anyway. Well, better until I got my fucking tax bill. Take a look at this," she said, slashing the air with the property tax bill she received.

"Do you believe that? I pay over a million dollars for this joint, everything breaks and has to be repaired, and then I get that," referring to a five-figure tax bill.

I was surprised she was surprised by it, but like so much else about this move to Michigan, I chalk it up to the fact that Elaine had no experience in real life living—mortgages and hot water heaters and the like.

I was surprised that she didn't rail on. Her caretaker freshened her cosmo, and she released the rage. Either she was beginning to accept the reality of her new position in life or she was simply too tired to fight it. I hoped it was the former and not the latter, for I suspected that when and if Elaine lost the fight, things would begin to wind down very quickly.

Later that evening, I joined Elaine in her bedroom. We watched some classic movie starring the great actress Barbara Stanwyck. Elaine liked her but had never worked with her.

"She's great, don't you think?"

"I do, and really sexy," I said.

"You're right about that."

Elaine's response got me thinking about the similarities between the two: strong, independent women with a great sense of personal style and a rather ambiguous sense of sexuality.

Elaine was a woman so steeply raised in Catholic dogma that she remained a virgin well into her thirties while actively flirting with just about every good-looking man who crossed her path, something she still does in her golden years. She's a shameless flirt. And yet here's a woman who has decried the importance of sex, who dresses in distinct masculine style, and who surrounds herself with a cadre of women. Was Elaine gay? Bisexual? None of it mattered one way or the other of course—just another interesting and illusive dimension to this fascinating woman.

* * *

The following day, I rose early and visited with friends in the area. When I got back to Elaine's, I learned that she had a scheduled photo shoot with a photographer from *The New York Times'* Detroit bureau named Fabrizio Costantini. He was coming for a shot that could be used to accompany a piece that Charles Isherwood, a theater critic and writer for the *Times*, was writing regarding Elaine's life in Michigan. Apparently, and to my surprise given the amount of pain and discomfort Elaine had been feeling, Isherwood had visited with Elaine earlier that week, spending a few days with her.

As the appointed hour drew near, Elaine's caretakers were trying to coax her into hair and makeup and a more presentable outfit. She relented by putting on black tights and her Detroit Athletic Club T-shirt and her wildest pair of black Marc Jacob eyeglasses. These choices again revealed Elaine's canny sense of media marketing. She knew a casual appearance would go over well, communicating comfort in her return to her hometown, and that the athletic club T-shirt would endear her to fellow Detroiters. She looked funky and fun.

The shoot would take place in Elaine's elegant living room, on the taupe couch in front of the large Palladium window. Once dressed, her caretaker wheeled Elaine from the bedroom to the living room where she greeted Mr. Costantini. She was taken with him—a good-looking young man—and flirted with him immediately. Once she had transferred to the couch, she demanded that they get moving on the shoot. It was clear she knew the value of getting a shot for the article, but she clearly didn't want to spend much time messing with it.

As she sat on the couch, she requested a glass of "joy juice," and she proceeded to chat with Mr. Costantini. It was clear that Elaine had learned that the best shots are shots that are a reaction to something real. The facial expression and gestures needed to be animated so the photos were capturing truthful action. In an attempt to get such shots, she tried to engage Mr. Costantini in conversation, hoping he'd shoot away as they spoke.

The problem with this particular strategy was the Mr. Costantini did not respond, offering only one-word answers to Elaine's pormpts. Quickly realizing he was not going to be the scene partner she wanted, Elaine began to do something rather fascinating.

As she sat on the couch, she began a private monologue, unspoken, during which she would animate as if in conversation. She removed her glasses; she reclined and extended her hands over her head; she lifted her head—perfectly positioned in the light, mind you—in laughter. Mr. Costantini was an experienced enough photographer to shoot these moments. And thank God he did, because it was clear Elaine was performing for him, hoping to quickly give him some interesting shots so she could be done with the whole affair.

At one point, realizing that Elaine's cosmopolitan might have been in the shots, one of her neighbors who was present motioned for the caretaker to remove the drink from the table in front of Elaine thinking that it might not be ideal for a photo of Elaine's life in Michigan to prominently feature her return to drinking.

When the caretaker attempted to take the drink away, Elaine barked, "What are you doing?"

"Nothing. I just thought we should get this out of the photograph," said the caretaker.

"Why? It's happening, isn't it?" Elaine shouted, startling everyone in the room. "Look, I'm not hiding anything. Got that. I'm here and I'm enjoying a drink, and I don't give a fuck what anyone thinks about it." The drink was returned to the table in front of her, and she held it up as if in a toast, and Mr. Costantini snapped away.

After a few more shots, Mr. Costantini suggested a shot of Elaine near the grand piano. With assistance, Elaine carefully walked to the dining room and got positioned on her *At Liberty* stool in front of the mirrored wall and next to the piano. A few more shots were taken there as Elaine again created an inner monologue to animate moments for the camera. With that, the shoot ended. Elaine was done.

Elaine moved on to the kitchen while I helped Mr. Costantini pack up his gear and get it out to his car.

"She always like that?" he asked.

"Like what," I said.

"You know, so volatile," he said.

"Often," I said. "Do you know who she is?"

"No, I just got the assignment," he said.

I often wonder what people who know nothing of Elaine think when they encounter her. Clearly she simply doesn't care, and that's part of what is so intriguing about her. I suspect some just write her off as a cranky, elderly broad. If only they knew all what lay underneath her wild psyche.

Elaine in her living room at the Dakota with that cosmopolitan.
Credit: Fabrizio Costantini

* * *

After her photo shoot, Elaine was hungry. Her caretaker prepared a big dinner with lamb shanks, roasted potatoes, and vegetables. Elaine ate very well but again spat out much of her meat after chewing it.

After dinner, with a fresh cosmo, Elaine and I and one of her neighbors went back to her bedroom and watched the DVD of the documentary of the recording of the original Broadway cast recording of *Company*.

Elaine had not seen the documentary in quite some time. As each song played, Elaine, lying in bed, would conduct the music as it coursed through her body. This is part of what makes her so captivating onstage. The music works its way into her; she gives herself over to it. As the tempo of a song would rise, she would call out little musical yelps and punctuations on the upbeat numbers, the energy bursting out of her.

And just as the documentary transitioned into her struggle to record "The Ladies Who Lunch," she said, "Here comes dummy!"

This portion of the recording session is acknowledged by most people, including Elaine, to be the highlight of the documentary.

Elaine had asked that she be scheduled to record the number last on the docket so that all the other actors wouldn't be sitting around watching. As a result, she had sung "full out" most of the day on all the group numbers, and by the time they got to "The Ladies Who Lunch," it was pretty late at night and her voice was shot.

With each take, she struggled to adjust her performance from the visual medium of the stage to the aural-only medium of the recording. And with her voice tired, she began over-singing in an attempt to muscle her way through. As the night wore on, the situation only deteriorated. It was clear Sondheim was not pleased, and Elaine, yelling at and berating herself, only made matters worse. Elaine groaned as we watched this scene in the documentary.

In contrast, however, when Dean Jones sang "Being Alive," Elaine got very still and opened her eyes wide and watched very intently.

This is the climactic moment in the musical. Bobby, the central character, realizes he would rather commit to another human being, accepting all the sacrifices such a commitment requires, than resign himself to a solitary life. The song is big and requires a big singer capable of unleashing an emotional torrent. As I watched Elaine watching Dean, I was seeing one great performer watching another great performer doing something impressive with great material, a moment of recognized artistic kinship.

"God, don't you just feel for the guy," she said. "He's bleeding up there. You know he was going through a divorce when he was doing the show, don't you? That goddamned song cut close to the bone for him. Too fucking close, if you ask me. It was painful to watch every night. But boy just look at what he did with it."

After we finished the DVD and her neighbor exited, I asked Elaine about the struggle to record "The Ladies Who Lunch." I told her I thought it was a classic case study in vocal fatigue and how little attention some performers pay it.

"Boy, oh boy, you got that right," she said. "We think we can do it all, and we're nothing but damned fools."

"The truth is that when the voice is overworked, it loses its overtone and the life energy is deadened," I said.

"You got it. And for a cast recording, that don't cut it. No way, no how," she said.

We talked about how, on one night's rest, she was able to come back the next day and do everything she wanted to do with "The Ladies Who Lunch" on the cast recording.

"I never heeded warnings back then, but boy, oh boy, after that, I paid better attention to what I could and could not do," she said. "That's why I always tell the young actors. 'Don't do eight performances a week, it'll kill you. Let the goddamn understudy do the matinees.'"

* * *

Not feeling quite right, Elaine ordered her caretaker to check her sugar levels. They were high, around 390.

Her caretaker, a kind young man in his twenties who himself had diabetes, administered insulin. In a few minutes when the counts weren't going down much, Elaine started to get scared and panicky. Her caretaker calmed her down, telling her that with the dinner she had eaten and the few drinks she had consumed, it would take a while for the insulin to kick in. The fact that he monitored his insulin daily and was very experienced in controlling his disease seemed to bring Elaine comfort. She calmed down and waited. In about a half hour, the levels were down and she was feeling better. So much better, in fact, that she wanted to go back to the kitchen for a snack.

Once settled in to her chair at the kitchen table, her caretaker poured her another small cosmopolitan on demand and set out a bowl of pretzels.

Perhaps she anticipated that I or her caretaker was judging her request for another drink given the scare over her counts, because she said, "You know, I don't mind if my counts go up because of my drinking. That I can understand. And I got these people on payroll to watch me and help me, so I don't mind it." Having seen how Elaine reacted whenever anyone judged her or lectured her about drinking, I was careful in response. "But it's still scary when it goes high," I said.

"Of course. Listen, I've had enough hypo attacks. They scare the shit out of me. But I just want to know I can control it. And I think at the age of eighty-eight I've earned the right to drink a little in the evening if I want to. I'm here in my house. I'm not going anywhere. And I proved I could get off it. And I did that to see if I had any talent without it. And guess what? I did! And I still do. So after proving I could get by without it, I don't see any problem with it now. I mean when the fuck do we give alcohol its due? I mean this, I've been thinking about this. When do we say, 'Hey, alcohol does some great things for people, it gives people courage, it helps ease pain, it makes you less lonely.' You know what I mean? I mean does anyone hear me? When does alcohol get its due? It has done a lot of good for me, I'll tell you that."

She paused.

"You don't know what to do with that, do you?" she said.

"Well, honestly, no, I don't," I said, standing up to the challenge and appreciating the invitation. "I have a bit of alcoholism in my family, and I've seen it really mess people up. So I've always been careful with it. But that said, I enjoy a cocktail, or a glass of wine, or a beer like anybody else. And I do know what you mean when you say people can find courage in it. I find that's the case with me."

"Then you know what I mean, so my point is, when do we acknowledge the goddamned good it does?" she said. "I wouldn't mind going around the country and talking about that."

Elaine was clearly in a mood to talk. As she had been doing with increased frequency, she began to think about this final phase of her life. I asked her if she believed in heaven.

"I don't know. I want to. I want to hope you get to see the people you love and things feel good…peaceful, you know?" She paused. "I hope so, I'd like to see John, and Mother and Daddy and my sisters. Yeah, I'd like that."

I asked Elaine what she thought the reaction to her passing would be.

"Oh, who the fuck cares" was her response. "John, you know me better than that by now. I don't care about that shit. Sure, it's nice when you walk down the street and someone recognizes you, but all that celebrity shit doesn't mean a fucking thing. I need the audience when I'm *on*stage, but off stage, it's just not important. I'll tell you this though, I won't be on the cover of fucking *People* magazine. You know, when famous people die and they do some glamorous portrait with their birth and death dates. That won't be me. I've never rated high enough for that, you know? I was never pretty enough for the A-list in Hollywood. That's why New York loved me. They don't care about that shit. Look at Patti Lupone. No Hollywood beauty, but she can act, and it's the talent that New York is attracted to. Same with Bernadette. Hollywood hasn't treated her well, but look at how New York treats her. No, when I pass, they might dim the lights for me on Broadway because Broadway has always loved me. But they won't name a theater after me, and *People* magazine won't come knocking."

After catching her breath and letting that topic settle, she said, "I finalized my will and signed all the papers with the funeral home."

"That's got to feel good," I said. "Knowing those details are settled."

She paused and looked me straight in the eye. "It does. It feels good knowing things are ready. When I leave the building, they'll come in here and take me away and ship me to Chicago. I'm going to be buried next to John, you know. Well, he's cremated. I don't want that. I can't stand the thought of that. I'm going to be buried, and my body will rest with John. *That* feels good. I told you what my tombstone will say, didn't I?"

"No, what?" I asked.

"The marker is one gravestone. It has Bay written across the top. John's side has the Groucho Marx quote "Hello, I must be going," and my side will say "Elaine Stritch," and then under it will be "Later." Isn't that great? I just love it. Although someone stopped by a week or so ago and told me the best goddamned story ever. At this guy's funeral, the pastor announced that the dead guy had told him, 'Just wrap me in brown paper and twine and mark me Return to Sender. Isn't that the best? I wish I'd have thought of that," she said. "'Return me to sender,' well, let's hope so, otherwise it's a fucking rotten joke to play on an awful lot of people."

Perhaps due to the intimacy of the conversation or the courage of the alcohol, I asked Elaine for something I had always been very careful about not asking of her: a photograph of the two of us together.

"Sure, darling, why not. Don't you have a photo of the two of us?" she said.

"I do not, and I'd like to have one," I said.

"Well, of course," she said.

I gave my camera to her caretaker and sidled up next to Elaine at the kitchen table. After a quick check of her hair, she began holding her hands in front of her mouth in a prayer-like fashion. I found this funny and odd and asked her what she was doing.

"Nothing, just take the damn photo," she snapped. What I realized is that, like she had with the photographer from the *Times*, she was creating the scenario for the shot, and as a testament to how well she knew how to play to a camera, the shot is terrific. It's one of my favorites. Not because I'm in it, but because she is wearing nothing but her white T-shirt. She has no makeup on and her hair, while clean and blown dry, is very casual and uncoiffed. It's a beautiful shot of Elaine, and I told her she was beautiful.

My one and only photograph of Elaine and I together.
Credit: John Bell

"Well, it's all me, as natural as they come. I've never had an ounce of work done. I don't get people who do that shit, they look so grotesque, you know?" she said.

"I couldn't agree more," I said.

"You know, you're goddamned boring—always agreeing with everything I say."

CHAPTER 13

Since I last saw Elaine, I was aware that she had continued to make the rounds to film festivals within driving distance of Birmingham. In late October, she attended the Chicago International Film Festival. Online videos of her appearance showed that while her attendant had to be in very close proximity to her throughout, she was up and able to walk and stand pretty well. And it was clear she still relished being in front of an audience. This was good to see. It looked like the pelvic fracture had healed pretty well.

I was eager to see Elaine since it had been two months since my previous visit. When I arrived, she was up and sitting at the kitchen table.

"Hey, Elaine," I said.

"Oh, hi, darling," she said.

"How have things been?" I asked.

"Well, you know. I haven't fallen on my face since you saw me last, that's something." Then after a pause, "Oh, they stole the patio furniture. Do you believe that? Do you fucking believe that?" she asked, getting angrier as she repeated it.

"Stole the patio furniture," I said in disbelief. "Who?"

"We have no fucking idea," she said. "We think they came when I was in Chicago for the film festival. Climbed right through the bushes and lifted the furniture over. Do you believe it? I mean, this place is ridiculous. Here, in Scooby-Doo Birmingham. They just walk through the hedges and rip you off. We've had to put in an alarm system and keep everything locked up tight."

"How was your trip to Chicago?" I asked.

"Oh, it was okay. It was a long drive. But they loved the film, they really did. I think this thing is going to do very well," she said.

"Every review I've read has been a rave," I said.

"I know. Pretty good," she said. "Let's hope we can make some fucking money off it."

"So your pelvis has healed?" I asked.

"It's feeling pretty good, darling," she said. "I still have to walk with the walker or the cane because I'm still a little unsteady, you know what I mean? And these guys have to stay close," she said, referring to her caretakers.

"I went to Cincinnati," she said.

"What was in Cincinnati?"

"Pam Myers directed a production of *Cabaret*."

Pam Myers was in the original production of *Company* with Elaine.

"Did you fly?" I asked.

"No, we drove. Down and back in one day."

"How was the show?"

"Oh, it was okay. But I wanted to get out of this house, you know what I mean? And if I can drive it in a day, I want to get out and do stuff. Last week, the local theater group was doing *Company*, so I went to see that," she said.

"Wow, I bet they were thrilled," I said.

"Well, of course. You bet they were," she said.

"How was the production?" I asked.

"Well, you know, it was community theater, but they did okay, but I went in there and goosed them a bit, left them feeling good about themselves."

During the cocktail hour, Elaine's nephew Frank Moran, eldest son of her sister Georgene, stopped by for a visit.

This was my first time meeting "Frankie" although I had heard his name mentioned quite a lot. In many ways, Frank is a male version of Elaine. He's long-legged and lanky and has the same sideways grin and Elaine's dancing eyes. He's also gruff and loud and loves to laugh. And drink.

Elaine ordered a cosmo for herself and beers for Frankie and me. Frank said, "I think I'll have what you're having, Lainie."

"Now this has hard liquor in it, Frankie," she warned.

Apparently Frank had had his fair share of struggles with alcohol. It seemed that Elaine, knowing he would be driving home after a while, felt obligated to offer caution. He shrugged it off. With the drinks, Elaine's caretaker stocked the table with chips, pretzels, and nuts. And as Frank chain-smoked, the drinks kept flowing. Frank and Elaine shared stories about Elaine's mother and father and Elaine's sister Georgene.

"You knew that after Mother died, my father died of a broken heart, don't you?" Elaine said to me.

"Goddamn right," Frankie said.

"When Mother died, Daddy attended the wake, and the next day, he asked if we expected anyone who hadn't been at the wake to attend the funeral. We told him we didn't expect so. So he took off his necktie, smoked a cigarette, and lay down on the bed. He didn't go to the funeral. We got word he died that afternoon while we were at the funeral. Isn't that something?" Elaine said.

"Un-fucking-believable," Frankie said. "Un-fucking-believable. But that just goes to show you how much they loved each other. Grandpa just didn't want to go on without her."

"Isn't that something?" Elaine said.

As the stories continued, Frank and Elaine would rear up in laughter and fight for control of the room. "Now shut the fuck up, Frankie," Elaine would say as she tried to correct or clarify something he was saying.

Frank told how Georgene had sent him to stay with Elaine in Hollywood during his teenage years. He told of learning to drive from Ben Gazarra and of late nights at some of Los Angeles' great night spots with Aunt Elaine.

Talk turned to Frank's mother, and they both got a bit misty-eyed. I anticipated a face-to-face acknowledgment of Elaine's having missed Georgene's funeral, but it didn't come. They both knew they loved her, and in their own way, it seemed, they acknowledged and forgave. Clearly, out of all of Elaine's nephews and nieces, the bond between these two was deep.

Elaine told a story about how when she was fourteen she wanted to go out and meet a young man named Charlie Cronin. She called him Chuck. She wanted to wear one of Georgene's dresses.

"I love my sister to death, but as kids, she could be one of the meanest people on earth."

She continued telling Frankie how she wanted to wear Georgene's hot-pink Elizabeth Arden suit for the date with Charlie. "I went up when Genie was busy doing something else and put her suit on and then snuck down out of the house. I just turned the corner near the milk coop, about to make my getaway, when there, standing in front of me, was my sister Georgene." Caught in her ruse, Elaine said she stripped out of suit right there beside the milk coop, went back upstairs got into one of her own suits, and headed off on her date.

"Genie was always studying. She was the smart one of the three of us. Genie was always trying to be the best daughter in the family, and I think, in many ways, she was."

Talk of Georgene took Frank to the topic of his younger brother George Moran, PhD. It seems that Dr. George Stritch Moran was quite an accomplished child psychologist in London.

"He moved to London in his twenties. He wanted to work at the Hampstead Clinic with Anna Freud, you know, Sigmund Freud's daughter. She kept turning him away to get more experience, and so he'd go to work at this clinic or with some organization for underprivileged children and come back to her. Finally, she let him in to study and eventually hired him," Frank said in a highly animated state.

"And then he and my father pulled together some investment scheme and made a boatload of money for the Hampstead clinic, and with that money they were able to really overhaul the buildings and grounds. And in the late 1980s, after Anna Freud died, they renamed the clinic the Anna Freud Center, and they made my little brother the director of the whole damned thing. There's a building there named in his honor."

"Does he still live in London today?" I asked, wondering if Elaine and John had spent much time visiting with him while they were living in London in the 1970s.

"No, he passed away at the age of forty-one. Forty-fucking-one," Frankie said, getting choked up. "He had Lou Gehrig's disease. My little kid brother—fucking brilliant."

As the evening and the talk wore on, it was turning into a very Irish Catholic night around Elaine's kitchen table. Both Elaine and Frank were clearly getting buzzed. Elaine was getting hungry and ordered some salad, hamburger, and sweet potato. Frank wasn't going to stay to eat—he had to get home.

Before he left, Frank and Elaine stumbled on the topic of W. C. Fields. They were both very big fans.

"You know, he didn't like to drink water," Frank said.

"I know, he wouldn't drink water because he said 'fish fuck in water,'" Elaine said in a pretty good Fields impersonation. And that started them off on a tear of great W. C. Fields's one-liners, their gales of uncontrollable laughter serving as testimony to Fields's brilliance.

"A goddamn genius," Elaine said.

"Second to none," said Frank.

Then with a kiss and a hug, Frank was on his way. "Be careful, Frankie," Elaine shouted as he walked out of the kitchen. "I will, Elaine, you know I will."

* * *

Frankie's exit was timely. Shortly thereafter, Elaine got a call from a friend reminding her he would be by to pick her up to take her to a holiday fund-raising gala and auction on behalf of the Convent of the Sacred Heart, Elaine's alma mater. Elaine and her caretaker had forgotten about the date. Elaine was due to be picked up in forty-five minutes, and there she sat, tipsy and dressed in a T-shirt and underwear.

"Oh my god, we have to go out tonight, darling," she said. "Did you bring a coat and tie?" Luckily, I had since I had driven in straight from work.

The next thirty minutes were challenging. Elaine's caretaker and a neighbor who had planned to attend with her took her back to the bedroom to get dressed. A knock-down, drag-out fight erupted regarding what Elaine wanted to wear versus what was clean and ready for her to wear. Ultimately, they settled that she would wear her standard uniform: black tights, black boots, a long white man's shirt and tie, and a pair of eyeglasses so she wouldn't have to put on makeup. Getting her dressed was a challenge due to the slight buzz she was feeling. I called in asking if anyone needed any help. The caretaker and neighbor assured me they could manage.

Once dressed, Elaine called for her brown sable coat and hat. The coat was hanging in the closet, but the matching hat was nowhere to be found.

"Oh my god, where's the hat?" she screamed. "Oh no, don't tell me they lost my sable hat. Oh my god."

"Don't worry, it's got to be here," said her caretaker. "We'll find it."

"Well, find it then. Now!"

After a frantic search that involved looking in every closet, basin, and cabinet, down in the storage compartment off the garage, and even under the beds, that hat was nowhere to be found.

"Well, call the goddamn fur vault in New York. If they forgot to send it out here, they're going to pay, and I mean pay big-time. This is unbelievable. Just fucking unbelievable," she said.

The vault was closed. Her caretakers assured her they would be called the next day and they'd figure out what happened to the hat. Elaine was not placated.

"I want them called now. What do you mean they're closed?" she screamed.

"We just tried to call, Elaine, and they're closed. There's no answer."

"Well, that's not good enough."

A second frantic search of every possible nook and cranny in the condo ensued. Once again, the hat was nowhere to be found. Still enraged about the missing hat, Elaine eventually decided to wear a simple black hat for the evening. The car was scheduled to arrive, and everyone surrounding her told her she looked terrific.

It was a very cold evening. Her caretaker suggested the car be pulled down to the underground garage so she could take the elevator down and get loaded in without being directly in the cold air. She didn't like that plan. She wanted to take the front stairs. The car was pulled up to the curb. Elaine and her walker were loaded into the car, and off the entourage went.

When we arrived at the event, in a chic two-story building, we discovered two things that made the evening challenging. First, Elaine would have to get up to the second floor. There was an elevator, but it was near the back of the building requiring a very long walk around a display of approximately twenty lit Christmas trees. The cords for the Christmas lights were taped down over the floor, making her use of the walker tricky and dangerous. And the elevator itself was small. As I learned during our night at the Rubin Museum, Elaine does not like elevators, especially small elevators that seem like service lifts. After walking all the way back to the elevator, she almost decided she would try the stairs instead, but everyone with her told her the stairs were simply too steep. The elevator it was— with a strong dose of unhappiness and resistance.

The second thing that made the evening challenging was that the event was designed as a standing cocktail event swirling around a silent auction fund-raiser. The room was crowded with people and waiters passing food and drink. There was no place for Elaine to sit. Her friend who had talked her into attending eventually secured a chair for Elaine so she could be anchored at a table. She didn't want any of the food, but she did request a cosmopolitan from the bar.

During the next twenty minutes or so, her friend brought VIPs by to meet Elaine. She was gracious and funny, but I could tell this was not the type of public recognition Elaine enjoyed. At one point, I caught her alone for a minute, and she said, "I feel like a goddamn celebrity on parade." Elaine enjoyed being recognized on the street or in a restaurant. And she loved being invited to perform. But she didn't particularly like feeling like she had been perched in place as an attraction. She finished her cosmopolitan and asked me to get her a little something from the food table.

When I returned with a little quiche, she pulled me down to her and said, "You see that guy over there?"

"Yep."

"He just asked me if you were my date."

"What did you tell him?" I asked.

"I told him you were not my date, and then he asked if you were gay. Can you believe that?"

"What did you tell him?" I said.

"I told him that as far as I knew you were not gay but that if I found out any different, he'd be the first to know."

I laughed.

"I mean do you believe that someone, anyone, would come up to someone they didn't know and ask a question like that about someone else? Tacky!"

Quoting a lyric from the musical *Chicago*, I said, "Whatever happened to class."

"You got that right," she said.

After about another ten minutes or so, Elaine was ready to leave. She was uncomfortable and was not enjoying herself. So just as quickly as she had gotten in and settled, she called for her walker and we headed back out to the car.

When we got back to the Dakota, Elaine threw her hat on the foyer table and shouted, "What a fucking disaster that was!"

I couldn't have agreed more. I actually found the experience somewhat sad. Elaine was clearly on display, and whether because she had been drinking earlier in the afternoon or whether she was just a bit disoriented by her surroundings, she seemed dazed and confused by the entire experience. The exposure was undignified.

"Yeah, it wasn't planned very well considering you were invited as a special guest. No thought had gone into your needs," I said.

"I'll say, what a waste of time," she said as I helped her off with her fur coat, hoping that the missing sable hat would not pop back into her mind.

"God, someone give me a cosmo and make it fast," Elaine called out to her caretaker who had already set out a spread of crackers and cheese, which we nibbled on as lentil soup and buttered bread were prepared. Her appetite was strong.

"I think I got around okay tonight, don't you?" she asked.

"Yes, very well. Too bad, though, that you had to do so much walking," I said, still shaking my head that better preparations hadn't been made for her visit.

"Yeah, that was the worst," she said.

"Yeah, and dodging all the Christmas tree lights—that's the part that worried me," I said.

"You and me both," she said, and then, raising her glass and in an elegant French accent, "Here's to surviving the gala of the Sacré-Cœur."

* * *

After dinner, Elaine asked me to help her prepare her mailing list for her Bay's English Muffins. Every year since she married John, she sent everyone in her little black book a box of Bay's English Muffins. No card or greeting. Everyone who received them knew they were from Elaine. So we went through a master list containing the names and addresses of people to whom she had sent muffins the previous year and justified it to the people in her little black book, making sure we updated addresses as necessary or crossed off people who had died.

The muffin list was extensive, spiked with celebrities ranging from Kirk Douglas and Barbara Cook to Elaine's doctor, lawyer, hairdresser, and of course, her nieces and nephews.

As we went through the list, Elaine struggled with some of the names. She simply couldn't remember who some of them were. So if she couldn't place them, they were scratched off the list. For those she could place, she would then decide whether or not the relationship was still "muffin-worthy."

This year she wanted to be sure that the staff at the Carlyle would receive muffins just as she promised on her final day last May.

"And we've got to send some to Alec Baldwin. Send two boxes since he and his wife just had a baby," she said.

"You know his talk show got canceled," I said.

"Already! Well, that didn't take long. How long was it on the air, about a week?" she snapped. "Well, he should have never tried to do that. His mouth gets him into trouble, and he loves messing around with all those paparazzi," she said. "I wish he'd calm down though. Maybe this new baby will do it. You know, he's a very talented actor, but most people won't give him a chance to show it—he's just too much of a hothead and a know-it-all. I love him death. I really do. But Jesus Christ, you can't trust him to bring home a quart of milk.

"Come on now, let's take a few laps," Elaine said. She liked to take a few steady-paced laps around her condo, either with the walker or without, but always with someone at her side. This time, she wanted to walk without the walker.

Using her cane, we started out. "Just stay beside me in case my legs get sneaky on me."

We made two slow laps through the hallways of the condo. "Not bad, don't you think?"

"Excellent," I said. She really was doing well, walking in nice even, wide strides in good balance.

After the third lap for which she threw the cane down and used only my arm, she said, "Okay, that's all for now, I'm going back to my boudoir, you come back and visit with me in about half an hour," as her caretaker cut in and escorted her back to the bedroom.

As Elaine was being prepared for bed, I sat out on the front steps of the Dakota. A gentle, light snow had begun to fall. The Dakota and much of downtown Birmingham was lit with holiday lights. Elaine did not have a big Christmas tree in the condo. Rather, she had two smaller artificial trees, one in her bedroom and one in the dining room.

I wondered what her Christmas would be like this year, here in Michigan, close to her family. Would she spend the day with one of her nieces or nephews and their children, or would she host a few visitors here at her place? Either way, I hoped it would be a good Christmas, one that would help her feel connected and at peace.

After about thirty minutes, I headed back to her bedroom and sat beside her.

"It's starting to snow," I said.

"Is it?"

"Yeah, do you want me to open your blinds a bit?"

"Sure, why not."

I dimmed her bedroom lights a bit so the outside lights and the snow were more visible.

"Well, that's kind of nice, isn't it?" she said.

* * *

After Elaine appeared at the Chicago Film Festival's screening of *Shoot Me*, a video excerpt from the question-and-answer session she held after the viewing appeared on YouTube. In the clip, Elaine talked very honestly about how the audience had always been her only true friend. I asked her about that.

"Well, I think it's sad, but I think it's true," she said.

"Have you not had any true friends?" I asked.

"Well, John was my best friend, there's no doubt about that. And I've had good friends. But if I tell the truth, I have to admit that I'm more comfortable in front of an audience than I am with anyone else. It's just the truth."

"What is it about that audience that feels so good?"

"I've been trying to figure that out all my life, darling."

She paused.

"The truth is, when I'm onstage, I'm in complete control. I have no doubt about anything. I know what I'm going to do. I trust my talent completely, and I know, I just always know, that I can win them over. And when I do…" She paused again. "When I do, I feel love. Real, genuine love." Another pause. "Nothing else does that for me. Nothing else ever has."

"Interesting that they're seated out in the house and you're up onstage, with the footlights between you," I said, gently.

"Close, but at a distance, is that your point? Yeah, well, that's always been the way I've wanted it. On my terms. Only as much as I can handle, know what I mean?" she said. "No, I never got the amount of love I demanded from individual people, and the truth is, the amount of love I demanded is more than anyone could deliver. But with an audience, well, that's another thing altogether."

We both sat in silence. I was feeling pretty sure that we were talking about the very essence of Elaine's power as an artist. Whatever sadness or anger she was carrying with her, performing was her way of getting it out, if even temporarily, and allowing herself to keep moving on. Performing was not just her career or passion, it was a survival necessity.

Then out of the blue, Elaine looked at me and asked why I hadn't had any children. I nearly choked. Not because it was a personal question—sitting in her bedroom watching a winter snow falling, things were beginning to feel intimate—but because Elaine rarely asked me anything about myself. Our entire relationship was based upon my interest in her.

"Well, to tell you the truth, Elaine, I think I'm just too selfish. I see all the compromises that children demand, and I've just never felt strongly enough about wanting to see what my progeny would look like to be willing to make the sacrifices. That's just not how I want to spend my life. And I'm really fortunate to have married a woman who feels the same way. That's rare, and I feel really lucky in that regard."

"That all makes perfect sense to me," she said.

"Do you regret not having children?"

"Are you kidding? I can't think of anything worse," she said without a hint of hesitation or masked regret.

* * *

The following day, after spending the morning at a local university on business, I got back to the Dakota around 2:00 p.m. Elaine was up and sitting at the kitchen table and, as usual, reading the *Times*. She seemed to be in good spirits, which was surprising given the debacle of the Sacred Heart gala the night before.

"What have you been up to?" she said.

"Oh, visiting with a couple of friends from the University of Michigan."

"Oh yeah, do you think we could try out that song study master class there?" she asked.

"Well, I didn't bring it up with them, but I know for a fact that if you and Rob wanted to go and do a master class with their students, they'd jump at the chance. No doubt about it."

"Well, it's good to hear. Let's call Rob today and see if he's up to it. Maybe we can do something in January," she said. "How much do you think we can make again?"

"Well, I bet people will pay you close to $10,000 for something like that. Hell, I paid you $5,000 and thought it was a steal," I said.

"Yeah, well, it was. But I liked you." She struggled a bit with the newspaper and asked, "What's this *Six by Sondheim* thing all about?"

"Frank Rich and James Lapine have created a documentary which looks at six of Sondheim's songs and uses interviews by Steve Sondheim to examine his writing process," I said.

"Is it any good?"

"I don't know, I haven't seen it," I said. "It's just been released on HBO, and I don't get HBO," I told her.

"Well, you usually know everything about Sondheim," she said.

It's getting good reviews. It's a documentary," I said.

"Well, it better not be too good. I don't want anything getting in the way of *Shoot Me*, if you know what I mean," she said, obviously alluding to her hope that it would get some Academy Award attention.

This sparked another conversation about Stephen Sondheim. As she had before, Elaine began ruminating on why she has not been able to strike up a deeper relationship with him.

"You know the first time I met Steve?" she said.

"No, when was that?" I asked.

"I don't know the date, but Steve and I were leaving a party given by Charles Hollerith."

Charles Hollerith was a classmate and friend of Sondheim's from their days as students at Williams College. I recognized the name from our review of her muffin list from the night before. She told me to strike him from the list because she believed he had died.

He had, in 2011. I wondered if she'd been sending muffins to him for the past two Christmases.

"Steve was waiting for me to leave. We left the party together and got into a cab, and he didn't direct the cabdriver to take me to my apartment. So I thought we were going back to his place, and I was interested, if you know what I mean. Well, we'd been eating brownies at Charlie's party, you know, brownies laced with wacky weed, so we were both feeling okay. I don't think either one of us knew they had anything in them, we just knew we were feeling loose. So the cab pulls up in front of Steve's place, and he didn't invite me in."

She said Steve simply got out of the cab, paid the cabdriver, and then said back to her, "It's not your turn yet." He then told the cabdriver to take Elaine home.

"Isn't that the meanest thing ever!" she said. "If he wasn't interested, why didn't he tell the cab to take me to my place—see me home, like a gentleman? But to take us both to his place! Well, anyone would think something was going to follow. Some sort of invitation up, you know what I mean? I've never been treated so terribly. And to say 'It's not your turn yet!' What the hell is that supposed to mean?"

"Did you have any sense that he was homosexual?" I asked.

"No, I had no idea. I never have. I mean come on, Rock Hudson! Who saw that coming? Steve Sondheim, I just thought he was as sharp and smart and cute as they come. And people hid that kind of thing back then."

"Wasn't it common knowledge among his circle of friends?" I asked.

"It wasn't to me, so there you go. Always the fucking story of my life."

"Do you think this is why you've never been invited into his inner social circle?" I asked.

"Maybe, I don't know. But I've gotten to the point where I just don't care," she said, rather unconvincingly. "You know I wrote the end of 'The Ladies Who Lunch,' don't you?"

"No, what do you mean?" I asked.

"Well, when I got it and we got to the end, it was just one 'everybody rise.' I told Steve that I thought 'rise' should be repeated a number of times and reemphasized. I told him it should be repeated seven times with each time building in intensity."

"What did he say?"

"He told me to try it, and I did, and it was terrific. It worked, and I mean *worked*," she said. "And the rest, as they say, is history. That ending brings down the house—it makes the song. And you know what? Steve never said 'thank you.'"

After a quick break to check her sugar levels, the conversation segued to Richard Rodgers. Elaine said that she visited with him the night before he died.

"It was just after I got back from London. John and I had bought our house in Nyack. I had been diagnosed with diabetes and was just starting to get off booze.

"He was a terrible alcoholic," she said. "He just didn't know or wouldn't admit it. I told him that I had finally realized I was an alcoholic and had begun attending AA meetings. I guess, I was trying to encourage him to face it before he died, to make his peace. I had enormous respect for him, he was a great composer. I'm not sure anyone—Noel Coward or Steve Sondheim—ever wrote anything as perfect as 'Something Good.' That's one terrific song." She went on saying, "Nothing comes from nothing, never ever could, so somewhere in my youth or childhood, I must have done something good. That's as good as a song gets."

Since we were in Sondheim and Rodgers territory, I asked Elaine if she had ever met Mary Rodgers Guettel, Richard Rodgers's daughter and one of Sondheim's good friends.

"Oh, of course. I always thought she was snooty and highbrow. And it was no secret she was in love with Steve. And so was I, and neither one of us got him. So no wonder we didn't like each other."

Elaine began thumbing through a Christmas catalog from Saks Fifth Avenue that had arrived in the mail. As she thumbed through the photos, she commented upon the various models, noting their stylishness and sophistication. Elaine has always had an impeccable sense of style. She dresses in expensive clothes with simple lines and in palettes that are either bold and dramatic or wonderfully soft and underestimated.

"Where did you get your sense of style?" I asked.

"Well, that's easy, from my mother. Some of her line was French, and she knew fashion. And thanks to Daddy's success a Goodrich, she could afford nice clothes. And therefore, so could me and my sisters."

In fact, her nephew Frank had mentioned that whenever Elaine got into financial trouble—overdue rent or needing clothes for this or that appearance—she would call up her mother and money would be dispatched.

"Elaine didn't want for anything in the early days before she started to make her own money. Grandma and Grandpa were always there for her, and my mom took notes of the money they sent Elaine for clothes," Frankie had said.

In the Saks catalog, she stumbled upon a very chic long white sleeveless dress designed to be worn over slacks.

"Now that's nice, don't you think," she said, showing me the photo.

"Stunning," I said.

"I've got pretty good arms. I could pull this off. And it's only $900, not bad," she said. "That's a good deal. I'd like to go shopping and get a few things. Maybe for the holidays, maybe for New York in February."

"Are you going to New York in February?" I asked.

"I think so, for the release of *Shoot Me*. Good reason to spend some money."

Elaine saw her caretaker standing out on the patio in the cold air smoking a cigarette.

"Get in here, honey, you're going to get sick. You can smoke here at the table when it's this cold. In fact, give me one. The hell with all this clean living."

This was the first time I had ever seen Elaine smoke, other than video clips from the past. Watching her smoke was interesting. She held the cigarette very far up with her fingers splayed open. I had seen this pose in photos from her past. It's a very stylish and glamorous pose that always harkened back to the glamorous movie stars from Hollywood's heyday. She seemed to really enjoy smoking the cigarette. There was no doubt that she had been a lifelong smoker. With each inhale, she relished letting the smoke trickle out and then blossoming into a waft of exhale. Elaine smoked artfully—it was a key part of her social persona and social routine.

As they smoked, her caretaker, seemingly somewhat obsessed by Rosie O'Donnell, asked her about her appearances on the comedienne's talk shows.

"Rosie was always very good to me," she said, "but I always felt like she was a bit of a phony. Working too hard to impress and not sure if you could really trust her. You know, one of those celebrities who's loving everyone just a little too much, if you know what I mean."

After working her way down half of the cigarette, she barked at her caretaker as she handed him the cigarette, "Put this thing out, it's stupid. And I'd like a little joy juice, if you please."

While the cocktail was being prepared, Elaine said she had been invited a few weeks ago to one of the local Birmingham country clubs. "Oh yeah, and tickets to the event sold out faster than anything else they have ever done there," she said, delighting in her enduring box office appeal.

"Really, what did you do?" I asked.

"Oh, I just got up and did a short little question-and-answer thing with them. And at the end, I did a little upbeat piano bar rendition of 'Silent Night'" she said.

"I bet that was terrific!" I said, wishing I could have seen it.

"It was okay," she said. "I was hoping I'd get an invitation to join the club—free of charge. But so far, none of the ladies who lunch have called me up with an offer."

I was surprised by this. I would have thought they'd have offered an immediate complimentary membership just so they could avail themselves of her fame and celebrity.

"Well, I did say 'fuck' a few times that night. It may have shocked their delicate sensibilities," she said. "I lost *Golden Girls* because I said 'fuck' in the audition. I'd have been set for life with that gig," she said as her cocktail arrived. And then, holding the drink up for a toast, she said, "And now my big mouth gets me kicked out of the Birmingham Country Club. I'll drink to that."

* * *

Over dinner of hamburgers and mashed potatoes, we talked a little bit about the psychological crime thriller *Who Killed Teddy Bear* that she made in 1965 with Juliet Prowse.

"You know, nobody liked that film. I loved it."

"It's a weird, odd film," I said.

"That's what I liked about it. I still do. And I loved Juliet Prowse. There's another actress who didn't get a chance to show what she could do. She got pegged as a singer and dancer and didn't get much else. But with *Teddy Bear,* you could see she could act."

"I like the quiet quality she brought to that role," I said.

"Exactly. And that's not easy to convey on screen. And she was really good at knowing how to step back just enough and give somebody else a scene. I liked that about her. No, I wish we'd had the chance to work together again, but it never happened. Too bad."

As we worked our way back to the bedroom, we passed the dining room table, which contained a stack of very large promotional posters for *Elaine Stritch: Shoot Me.* Elaine was very proud of this poster. It featured a photo of her in her traditional black tights and white shirt adjusting a hat as she looked into a mirror.

"This photo is sensational," I said.

"Yeah, I know," she said. "Not bad for eighty-eight."

"It's sensational, classy, and sexy as ever."

"Yeah, I think so too," she said.

"I hope I get one of these posters."

"Of course, you get one," Elaine said. She signed it "To John, with hugs and kisses. Elaine."

Back in her bedroom, Elaine talked about her mother and father coming to see her in *Who's Afraid of Virginia Woolf.* "That's the first time I can recall that they were both really impressed. I mean really impressed. They thought I was good, and they told me so."

She paused. "That meant an awful lot to me. Yep, they were over the moon, and I felt real good about it."

"I thought your mother and father were supportive. They let you go to New York at a young age and seemed to stand behind your choice to pursue acting," I said.

"Oh yeah, kind of. I mean Daddy was supportive. I'd sing for him at his cocktail parties for the tire executives. And after two or three little songs and them wanting more, I'd say 'That's all I'm going to sing,' and Daddy would say, 'That's right, unless you get paid.' So I think he knew I might be able to do something with it. But Mother was much more hesitant about it—always had been."

CHAPTER 14

As January 2014 rolled in, I was eager to visit with Elaine, hoping she was feeling strong and that she had experienced a nice holiday season. When I got to the Dakota, Elaine was asleep, and I learned from her caretaker that Elaine spent New Year's Eve in the hospital. She had not been feeling well. Her doctor came to the house and made a house call. Blood was drawn. Later that day the blood results were in, and the doctor called and said the hemoglobin count was down very low. Elaine was told to get to the emergency room as soon as possible.

Elaine's caretakers and a neighbor went with Elaine to the hospital. Tests were run. A blood transfusion was given. More tests were run the next day. Eventually a mass was found in the stomach. Elaine was diagnosed with adenocarcinoma—stomach cancer.

Elaine elected not to take chemotherapy or radiation. Her doctors told her that they believe they could get the tumor with surgery. It was scheduled for the following month. Removing the tumor would necessitate removing part of her stomach. Elaine had been told to expect a six-week recovery period. Everyone was optimistic that the surgery would be successful and she would resume her normal routines. Even if the surgery was only partially successful, her doctors reported that the stomach cancer had been developing slowly over time and shouldn't pose an immediate threat.

During the blood transfusion, Elaine needed six pints of blood. In anticipation of the surgery, Elaine was having blood drawn every two days to make sure that her iron levels and blood sugar counts were stable. Elaine hated these blood draws. They had not been going well. Elaine was wakened by the home health nurse, who, apparently like the previous nurses, had a hard time drawing the blood.

"I don't know why this is so hard for you people!" she shouted as the nurse struggled to find a vein for the draw. Calling to her caretaker, she said, "If this is what I have to go through, I'm just not going to. I'm not. That's all there is to it."

The nurse adjusted the needle, and Elaine screamed out in pain. "Oh, that hurts! Goddamn it! Get it out of me, just get it out!" Calling out to me, she said, "John, I can't do this. Why is this so hard? I need better nurses. I can't go through with this." I came in and sat next her as she drew her head to my chest.

The nurse finally hit the vein, and blood started to flow as Elaine fell into a puddle of tears and whimpers. The nurse completed the procedure and headed out.

"I don't know why these people can't do their jobs without hurting me," she snapped, making sure the nurse could hear on her way out. "I'm simply not going to do these blood tests every two days. I can't. They're hurting me," she said, crying.

Elaine's caretaker told her, "All decisions are yours, Elaine. You get to be in control. But if they can't monitor the blood levels, then they may not be able to proceed with the surgery. That's a choice you can make."

"Then, I'm not going to have the surgery, because this is just too painful. I want to call the doctor and tell him he's got to get better nurses out here or come himself. I can't keep going through this."

"We'll call tomorrow," her caretaker said.

"No!" Elaine screamed. "I want to call today—now. I need this resolved. I can't take any more." The caretaker left the room to make the call.

"Oh my god, John, what am I going to do? *What* am I going to do?"

"Well, Elaine, I think the most important thing I've heard is that you get to be in control of all of these decisions, so if you want to discontinue the blood draws, you can do that," I said.

"But then I can't have the surgery, and I need the surgery. They say the surgery can get this stuff out of my stomach. I can't just let that continue to grow."

"I think talking to the doctor is a good idea. Let him know how much trouble you've been having, and maybe there's another solution. Maybe they won't have to draw every couple of days but can just draw once a week between now and the surgery. And if so, then maybe you can just go in to the doctor's office for the draw instead of relying on the providers who come to the house," I said.

"Oh god—why is this so hard?" Elaine said.

Her caretaker returned and told Elaine the doctor was not in but that a message was left and they'd get in touch with him tomorrow.

"That's not good enough!" she wailed.

"Elaine, I'll be here tomorrow, and together we'll all make sure we get this matter fixed. The draw is over for now. We'll get this taken care of," I promised her.

To my surprise, with that Elaine began to calm down. We settled her back into the bed, and I sat and held her hand. Since this was the first I learned of the cancer diagnosis, I wanted to see if she would talk about it.

"Elaine, I'm real sorry to hear about the cancer," I said.

"What cancer?"

"Well, it sounds like from what your staff has said that you've been diagnosed with stomach cancer."

"No, it's not cancer. It's a tumor. It's been there a long time. But they think they can get it. That's why I need the surgery," she said.

I looked over at her caretaker who gave me a look as if to say *"She's not holding on to the facts lately."* I didn't push it. "Well, I'm real happy to hear they think they can get it with surgery," I said.

"Oh, me too, darling, me too. Just say your prayers," she said.

"Oh, I will, you know I will. But listen, in the last year you've come through eye surgery, a hip replacement, and a broken pelvis. If there's anyone I know who can come through this, it's you."

"I hope so, darling. I really hope so. Surgery at the age of eighty-nine, that's no small beans, you know what I mean?"

Elaine's Dexcom monitor beeped, so her levels were checked. They were fine, but the battery in the monitor was getting low, so it was replaced.

After her caretaker exited the bedroom to take care of some business in the kitchen, Elaine said she had called her lawyer in New York in order to get her will tidied up. "I needed to make a few revisions," she said. "Now everything's in order, just like I want it. If I come through the surgery and live a while, then there will be less for everyone all the way around. If I die sooner rather than later, then I know who's getting what. And I think everyone will be happy. Or at least reasonably happy. And if they aren't, that's their fucking problem, know what I mean?"

Knowing Elaine had reported that she finalized her will a few months ago, I thought it was interesting that she felt the need for revision.

"It's got to feel good to have those things settled," I said.

"Yeah, it does, darling. It feels good to know I made it and have something to give back to all the young ones, you know? On behalf of my sisters, it feels good."

"Well then, you're a lucky woman, Elaine. A lot of people don't get that," I said.

"I know—I know you're right." After a pause, she said, "You hungry, darling? Let's see if I can get myself into the kitchen. You help me."

* * *

Once in the kitchen, Elaine was in better spirit. I told her she looked good considering she had been in the hospital just a few weeks ago. She looked like she had put on a little weight, good healthy weight. Her face looked a little fuller than the last time I saw her, but perhaps that was a result of some of the medicine she was taking.

She ordered a scrambled egg, and her caretaker fried up some bacon and set out some cheddar cheese. We settled in for a nice, quiet afternoon. Given all that had been going on, I was surprised to find her in a mood to talk.

"When I was in New York, I knew it was time to leave—I didn't know why, but I felt something wasn't right. Now I know it was this cancer," she said.

I registered that she was now calmly acknowledging the cancer, and this made me wonder about her mental clarity. Was the medicine playing with her mind? Was the denial a natural part of grieving the diagnosis? Either way, I was glad she was able to acknowledge the reality of her situation.

"You know, Elaine, I often think we register, subconsciously, when something is not right within us."

"Exactly, that's what I mean. I didn't know it then, but I felt something telling me I needed to make this change. And I'm real proud I did. This move has been so hard, the hardest thing I've ever had to do, but I did it and I'm glad I did. Can you imagine if I'd been going through all of this in New York, still at the Carlyle. Whoooo boy," she said. "You know I have no vision left in my right eye, don't you?"

"You've lost all of it? You can't see anything?" I asked.

"Nothing. And there's very little left in my left eye, so reading is nearly impossible."

"Do you want me to read the *Times* to you?" I asked?

"That would be great. Maybe later tonight when I settle in back in the bedroom."

At that, she ordered a cup of coffee from her caretaker. "And don't forget to add my Bernadette sugar," she said.

"Your Bernadette sugar?" I asked.

"Oh yeah, Bernadette came to visit, did I tell you that?"

"No, that's great. For Christmas?"

"No, just a week or so ago. And she brought me a great new sweetener that's perfect for diabetics," she said.

"She stayed here at the Dakota with you?" I asked.

"Well, of course—what's wrong with you? You think I'd make Bernadette stay in a hotel? Come on, get with it."

I paused and smiled at the rebuke. "So did you and Bernadette talk about the cancer?" I asked cautiously.

"Yeah, I told her. I told her I wasn't going to go in for all the chemotherapy and radiation. Surgery, okay, but that's it. She thought I was right. She said she would do the same thing. So that was that."

"That's great that she came out to visit with you. That must have felt good," I said.

"You bet."

"So what's up with her?" I asked.

"Oh, you know, she doing pretty good. Her concerts are doing very well. She said for the first time, she feels finally set, you know financially. And I'm happy for her. That's a great feeling. You know her husband was killed in a helicopter crash. She's on her own, and I know how that feels. So to feel like you've got yourself finally set is a very big deal. I couldn't be happier for her."

"Well, I've attended her concert in the past, and it's a great show. She draws a big crowd," I said.

"I know, that's so good to hear. But look, you can't take anything for granted. She's sixty or so, and no one's writing any decent musicals anymore. There's no one out there writing for Bernadette, and there should be. It used to be that writers wrote for stars. That's what people should do for her. She's terrific. What's she going to do for the next twenty years?" she asked.

"Well, she can still play leading lady roles," I said.

"You bet she can, but who's writing any?"

"Well, if the last ten years are any indication, there's still a lot of great old musicals from the forties, fifties, sixties, and seventies that are due for revival," I said.

"Oh yeah, like what?"

"Well, I think Bernadette would be sensational as Anna in *The King and I*," I said.

Elaine roared back and clapped her hands. "My god, you're right. She'd be marvelous in that show."

"I mean, she was great as Annie Oakley in *Annie Get Your Gun,*" I said.

"That wasn't a good career move for her, and that's what I'm talking about: keeping her career moving forward."

"How did you think she did as Mama Rose in *Gypsy?*" I asked.

"Not great," she said. "She's the wrong type for Rose. And she's not a real powerhouse belter. That role needs a real belter."

"Well, you may be right about that, she did get into vocal trouble on that one," I said.

"Who doesn't? It's nearly impossible. Really, I mean come on, forget about it."

The phone rang. "Elaine Stritch's residence," her caretaker said in greeting.

"Who is it" Elaine squealed as her caretaker was giving the greeting. It was Elaine's bank. Her caretaker handed her the phone.

"Hello," she said. "Who? Oh, yeah, it's time again, is it? How much? Wait, I can't hear you, you have to speak up. Yeah, yeah, wait, how much? I can't hear you. Look, is Larry there? Yes, put him on, I'd rather deal with Larry," she said.

Apparently, Elaine had set up regular transfers from her savings or investments accounts to go into her checking account on a monthly basis to cover her expenses and to write checks to pay her staff.

"Larry. Hi, darling, how are you? Look, I don't know who these people are who are calling me. I really don't want to deal with any of them. I'd rather just deal with you, okay? Yes, that's what I'm expecting. Into the account tomorrow. Fine, darling, fine. Oh, I'm doing okay. When are you going to come by for a visit? Oh, good. Now don't forget. Okay, Larry. Good, oh good. I can't wait. I'll see you then. Don't forget."

"Who's Larry?" I asked.

"My new banker, and he's a looker. He's a bigwig at the Bank of Birmingham. He's the only one there I can understand on the phone. And I trust him. And he's not bad looking. And he must be loaded, so I've got my eye on him," she said.

Elaine got up carefully from her kitchen chair, trying to get something from the kitchen island. I rose to help her, and she waved me off. She wanted to prove to herself she could get up, balance herself, move a couple of feet unassisted, and take care of her need on her own. She made it to the island, but on her way back, one leg caught on the other as she made the turn, and she started going down. Having been very uncomfortable with her trying this maneuver on her own, I was right there, standing at the ready, and caught her as she let out a yelp. I had her full weight. She would have gone down. Her caretaker came running in from the other room.

"I'm okay," she said. "John caught me." I helped her down into the kitchen chair. "Jesus, I'm glad you were there."

"Me too," I said. Running the risk of overstepping my place, I said, "I don't think you should be trying maneuvers like that on your own, Elaine. Not yet anyway. The last thing you need now is to fall again and break a bone—with everything else you're dealing with."

"You're right, I know you're right." And then with growing frustration, she said, "It's just so fucking frustrating not being able to try a little cross to the fucking counter." After a lengthy pause, she said, "Honey, make me a cosmo. But make it a light one," she said, noting she was pulling back on the octane. "You want one?" she asked.

"Uh, maybe just a beer."

"You know where it is," she said, followed by, "I'm the only one who gets waited on in this house." We were just about to toast when the doorbell rang.

"Who the hell is that?" she yelled out to her caretaker.

"It might be Sally and Peter," her caretaker said, referring to her niece Sally who was the daughter of her sister Sally.

"Who?" she screamed.

"Sally and Peter, remember they said they might stop over?"

"No, I don't remember they were going to stop over. You didn't tell me they were going to stop over."

"No, *you* told *me* they were going to stop over," her caretaker said.

"No, I didn't. I don't know what you're talking about," Elaine said.

The doorbell rang a second time.

"Will you please answer the fucking door" Elaine barked. As the caretaker headed to the door, Elaine said, "I never know what the fuck's going on. I really don't. Do you believe this?"

It was Sally and Peter.

"Oh, hi, darling," Elaine said as Sally entered the kitchen. "And where's Peter?"

"Right here, Elaine," Peter said. "How are you?"

"Oh, I'm okay. I wish I could say better than that, but I can't, so that's just the way it is. Do you both know John?"

Having not been introduced before, I introduced myself. I had heard a lot about Sally. My sense was that Elaine was going to be relying on Sally to be the executrix of her estate.

"What do you want to drink? Peter, we've got nonalcoholic beer. Or soda, or water," she said. Peter responded that water would be fine. Sally ordered a glass of champagne, and Elaine's caretaker set out more salted munchies.

"How do you two know one another" Sally asked, somewhat curious about my presence.

I was surprised to hear Elaine say, "Oh, we've known each other forever."

"I interviewed Elaine for a magazine article about six years ago, and then I invited her to my university to do a master class for our theater students," I said.

"Oh yeah, I've heard her talk about that," Sally said.

"It was a big hit, and this guy hasn't let go since," Elaine said.

"Actually, I've been after Elaine to write a book."

"Really, that's a great idea," Sally said. "We've all told her she should write a book. She's had so many great experiences, and she's worked with everyone," Peter said.

"I agree. So I keep visiting, and with each visit, I get her to talk a little bit more about her career, how she approaches her art. All that," I said.

"Yeah, he just won't give up," Elaine said.

"Well, good for him," Sally said.

"Yeah, you're right about that," Elaine said. "I give him credit for that. And thank God he was here tonight, because I almost fell. He caught me. Can you believe that? With everything else I'm dealing with." Elaine paused and then said, "I don't know what I'm going to do."

"Well, you're not going to be up on your own, that's what you're going to do," Peter said.

Sally told the story of seeing Aunt Elaine in the original Broadway production of *Company* starring Larry Kert who had replaced Dean Jones in the role of Robert.

"It was the first time I really saw Elaine do her thing. I had heard an awful lot about her talent and the various things she had done and the people she had met in her career. But this was my first chance to really see her in action."

"Yeah, we got married shortly before that, and I hadn't met Elaine yet," said Peter.

"So when the production went on tour, we went to Toronto to see Elaine in it so she could meet Peter. We were escorted backstage," Sally said. "I introduced Peter to Elaine, and Elaine told us there was a party that evening and we were going with her."

"Oh god, I remember that. Liza was going to be there. I thought it'd be fun for you," Elaine said, referring to Liza Minnelli.

"Oh, it was. They went around the room with everyone singing portions of a song. Liza sang, and of course, she was a hit. Elaine sang and was a hit. I looked around and saw Peter heading for the door. He was trying to sneak out before it got to us," Sally said.

"Oh my god, really? That's funny." Elaine said. "That was so long ago, and yet it seems like it was just five minutes ago."

"Had you and Liza met before?" I asked Elaine.

"What do you mean? Her mother was one of my very best friends."

"Oh, that's right," I said.

"'Oh, that's right,' says the guy who's doing the book," Elaine chided.

"Well, did you ever work with her?" I asked.

"No. Not really. We were at some of the same functions, but no, I never did anything with her. To tell you the truth, I've always been bored by her," Elaine said.

"Really, why?" I asked.

"I don't know. She just bores me. Everything she does has this showbiz pizzazz draped all over it. Everything's the same. Which is a real damn shame, because her mother was not like that. Judy could act the hell out of a song. Any song. Didn't matter the style, the composer, or the story. She could just fill it, know what I mean? Just fill it. No, Liza was always too messed up. The drinking and the drugs. Always going to Amsterdam for her drugs. A lot of those stars would do that. I was never into that scene."

"You never used drugs?" I asked.

"Well, I think I had marijuana in brownies—I told you that story. But the other stuff, no way. Never interested me. Alcohol was enough. I only tried drugs once in my life, and that was just recently since I moved here to Michigan."

Sally, Peter, and I sat silent waiting...

"Yeah, Frankie brought me a joint one night a couple of months ago, and we smoked it. I didn't care for it. He thought it might give me the buzz that alcohol does without messing with my sugar levels."

"Did it?" I asked.

"I don't think so. It just made me feel very uncomfortable. Very funny...in my bones, you know? I started to hallucinate, and I didn't dig it. God, that's the last thing I'm looking for, if you know what I mean. No, drugs are not my thing, never have been."

The phone rang.

"The phone's ringing," Elaine screamed out to her caretaker. As her caretaker answered it, she yelled out, "Who *is* it?"

Her caretaker reported that a young woman named Fiona, the sister-in-law of the gentleman who decorated Elaine's condo, was outside on Elaine's doorstep with a friend and wanted to know if she could come in and say "hello."

Peter and Sally and I looked at one another, sharing the thought that this was an incredibly rude thing to do. I suspect we were also wondering if it happened frequently.

As a matter of fact, Elaine's good friend, the gossip columnist Liz Smith, had published Elaine's Michigan address in her column, encouraging Elaine's fans to send her cards and good wishes. So many people in the greater Detroit area were aware of the location of Elaine's new residence.

"Oh my god. Are they outside?" Elaine asked.

"Yes, out front," her caretaker said.

"Well, let them in, but it's going to have to be a quick hello. In and out," she said.

From the front foyer, we could hear a boisterous Fiona who apparently had been imbibing with her friend at a nearby bar before getting the idea to stop in for a visit.

"Where is she? I love this woman," Fiona shouted from the hallway leading into the kitchen as Elaine buried her head in her hand and said, "Oh god. Brace yourselves."

"There she is. Elaine, I love you. Oh, you've got company. It's a party then, isn't it?" Fiona said by way of trumpeting her arrival.

Fiona made her way over to Elaine and bent down to her from behind, throwing her arms around Elaine's neck and kissing and hugging her. "We were around the corner, and I said 'Let's go visit Elaine Stritch, she's a legend,' and here you are. Oh, god, I love you, do you know that? I absolutely love you."

Elaine eked out a "Hi, darling," and before she could say anything else, Fiona was making her way around the table introducing herself to Peter and Sally and me.

Chattering on at about a thousand miles a minute, and insisting on taking photos with Elaine, Fiona said, "Oh my god, I'm going to post this on Facebook." Crouched down next to Elaine, Fiona was hugging and kissing her, and Elaine was clearly getting uncomfortable.

"Fiona, if you hug me one more time, I'm going to fucking kill you," Elaine said. "Now, look, honey, I haven't been feeling very good and I've got company and we're about to eat, so this visit has to be short. 'Hello and goodbye' if you know what I mean."

"Oh yeah, yeah, we won't stay, I just had to see you again," Fiona said, demonstrating that she was oblivious to the hint. "Did you have a good Christmas? What did you do for New Year's Eve? God, I wish I could have spent New Year's Eve with you. I'll bet that was the party. What are you drinking, Elaine? Your joy juice? She call it her joy juice, but it's really a cosmopolitan." Fiona felt the need to instruct her companion.

It was interesting watching Elaine during this episode. It became perfectly clear how accustomed Elaine is to trying to make fans (or in this case fanatics) feel appreciated and welcomed even though, anyone who knows Elaine well can tell she is just barely tolerating the interaction. Elaine perfected this art throughout her seventy-year career.

Squealing at one of her selfie photos, Fiona shouted with glee, "Oh my god, Elaine, look at this photo. You look like a million bucks. And I don't look bad myself."

"Honey, lower your voice. You're shouting," Elaine said, beginning to show displeasure. "Look, we're just getting ready for dinner, so I'll have to ask you to excuse yourself."

"Oh, sorry. We're sorry, we didn't mean to interrupt. Okay, Elaine, we're on our way. But boy do you look good. I'll call you in a few days, and we'll set a date to party. Okay, girl? I love you."

At that, Sally and I started to show Fiona and her friend out. With each step or two out of the kitchen or down the hallway, Fiona would burst back in and shout some extended and inebriated salutation toward Elaine. We finally got the two to the foyer when Fiona saw the grand piano and Elaine's Emmy awards. She ran into the dining room, grabbing her friend by the hand, and insisted on getting selfie shots in front of the Emmy awards and in front of the marketing poster of *Shoot Me* hanging on the wall.

Finally, we were able to move the ladies on their way and shut the door. Back in the kitchen, I reported, "Fiona has left the building."

"Oh my god," Elaine said. "Now that's what a real alcohol problem looks like. That girl needs help."

"Does this happen often?" Sally asked.

"Every once in a while," Elaine said. "She's related to my decorator, so I try to be friendly. But I just don't know what to do when something like this happens. If she called and asked if she could come over, I'd have told her I wasn't up to it. But when she's on the front stoop, for God's sake, what am I supposed to do?"

Sally said, "Well, you just tell her you're not taking visitors. It's ridiculous to show up unannounced..."

"Blitzed out of your mind," Peter interrupted.

"Yes, and expect to come into someone's home. And then to carry on like that when you can see they have company," Sally finished.

"I would simply tell your decorator what happened tonight and make it clear to him that you were not pleased. This needs to be his problem to communicate to Fiona how unacceptable this is," I said.

"He's right," Sally said. "That was completely inappropriate."

Elaine's caretaker served a dinner consisting of hamburgers, garden salad, macaroni and cheese, and sweet potato. Elaine ate well. Very well. And she didn't spit out any of her food. I was glad to see that she was hungry and swallowing.

As we ate, Sally and Elaine shared a couple of stories about Elaine's mother and father.

"Mother and Daddy were something," Elaine said. "There's so much about their lives which is so romantic and so much more that's two people trying to survive one another. On their wedding night, Mother was in the bathroom getting herself ready, and Daddy could tell she was real nervous So when they got into bed, Daddy looked at her and said, 'Mildred, we don't have to do anything tonight that you don't want to do. We've got our whole lives together. We'll go nice and slow.'"

"Isn't that just the best thing ever," Sally said.

"Oh, you bet," Elaine said. "God, is that sweet, sweet, sweet.

"And when Mother was getting up in her years—God don't you just love that phrase 'up in her years'—when Mother was declining, you know, physically and mentally, Daddy made a makeshift bedroom for her in the first-floor library so she wouldn't have to go up and down the stairs. But he kept his bedroom upstairs," Elaine said. "Every night, Daddy would kiss her good night and go on up to his bedroom. Well, one night, and don't ask me how she did this, Mother worked her way up to his bedroom and got into bed with him."

"Oh god, I bet that surprised Grandpa," Sally said.

"Surprised him, it scared the shit out of him," Elaine said. "Daddy didn't know how to deal with everything Mother was going through. But to hear him tell it, this was the greatest moment, her coming up to be with him. Isn't that something? Now if that's not fucking romance, I don't know what is."

Then as if to reiterate this great love affair, Sally said to me, "Well, you know they died not twenty-four hours apart, don't you?"

"Oh my god, have I not told you that story. This is unbelievable," Elaine said. She had, but I was happy to hear it again to see if it changed.

"The day Mother died, they held a good old-fashioned Irish wake, and the next day was going to be the funeral."

"And it was a big funeral, wasn't it?" Sally asked.

"You bet it was, everyone knew Daddy and Mother," Elaine said. "So the next morning, the day of the funeral, Daddy was getting dressed, and he asked if we expected anyone at the funeral who hadn't attended the wake. We told him most likely there wouldn't be. So just then, he untied his tie, lit a cigarette, and lay back on his bed and said, 'I'm not going to the funeral then.' Well, we all went to the funeral, and somehow we got word that Daddy had collapsed or blacked out or something, and we left the funeral and went to the hospital. He died that night."

"His heart was broken," Sally said.

"Isn't that something?" Elaine said.

These stories of Elaine's mother and father seem to have coalesced into a heightened sense of romance that had risen to the level of mythology among the family members. But as with everything else about Elaine, nothing was quite that simple.

Whenever Elaine would talk of her parents, there would be a quiet underpinning of regret, that somehow she had a hard time winning her mother's approval and that her parents paid more attention to her father's career and the socializing than to their daughters. In her *At Liberty* show at the Café Carlyle, near the end, Elaine momentarily brought up her mother and father and then refused to travel down the path, deflecting with the line "But we won't go there, not tonight."

Elaine had finished a third cosmo and then switched over to beer. It was a full evening of alcohol consumption, tall tales, and laughter. Elaine seemed to need it. Nights like this were very comfortable for Elaine. I sensed this type of quiet, intimate night with friends, family, and drink brought Elaine great pleasure. As concerned as I always would be about her drinking, part of me was glad she was able to hold court. She clearly enjoyed it.

Sally and Peter eventually said their goodbyes, and Elaine wanted to retreat to the bedroom for a while. As usual, she told me to report back there to her in an hour or so, but I actually fell asleep for what must have been a couple of hours only to be awakened by the sound of Elaine and her caretaker coming from the bedroom to the kitchen. I met them in the hallway.

"Come on, John, we're going to have some soup," she said, slowly working her way back into the kitchen. Once settled, she said, "What kind of soup do we have in there?"

"Chicken and noodle," her caretaker said.

"Chicken and fucking noodle? How boring." Eyeing a hamburger leftover from dinner, she said, "Heat that hamburger up and crumble it up in the soup. Let's dress it up a bit."

So we sat and ate soup and buttered bread. Again, Elaine didn't spit anything out.

"You've been eating well. You've got your appetite," I said.

"I guess so," she said.

"A good appetite says a lot," I said.

"Oh yeah?"

"I think an appetite lets you know if a person is feeling okay, you know, really okay," I said.

She held her gaze with me for a couple of beats and said, "I'm doing okay, John, I think I'm doing okay, all things considered."

Talk turned to John Bay.

"Oh my god, well, he was the funniest man on the face of the earth. And a very good actor. He was a mimic, an excellent mimic. He used to imitate Groucho Marx. I'd come home, and he'd be dressed as Groucho and answer the door, and I swear it scared the shit out of me. He was that good."

The softening of her voice and affect made it clear that talk of John hit upon one of the real tender spots in Elaine's heart.

"He was so handsome. He looked like Jack Kennedy, and I should know because I had a date with Jack Kennedy," she said. "Actually, he was more handsome than Jack Kennedy. I was lucky to get my time with John. It went too goddamn fast, but oh my god, did we have fun."

I felt like I could advance, so I asked her how he died.

"Brain cancer, and it went fast. Very fast."

"Did John get diagnosed while you were in London?" I asked.

"No, that was just after we came back to the States. We bought a house in Nyack, an old Victorian on the Hudson. We would never have been able to afford it, but John's parents helped us out. It was bigger than we needed, but we jumped right in. Spent a goddamn fortune renovating the damn thing. It nearly sank us. And it didn't take us very long to figure out we didn't want to live in Nyack. We wanted to be in the city. And then John got sick. So…" she said, not finishing the sentence.

"So we sold the damn thing and moved back to the city. We were going to move into the city anyway. John and I would stay at the Carlyle now and then, and we both loved it, the whole Upper East Side vibe, you know? The Savoy in London and the Carlyle in New York, that's the lifestyle we wanted."

"And John was so good. He had faith and believed in God, and that was important to me. For all my shit, I've always been pretty devout myself. It may not seem like it, but it's true. And when John died, well, I had questioned it all."

No tears, just a deepening of her gaze.

"I'm sorry you didn't get more time with him."

"I am too, darling, I am too. You have no idea." And then abruptly, she said, "You know, John adored children. He was so good with them. Whenever there was a kid around, John became a child. He'd play with them, and they loved him." After a pause, she said, "If John were alive today, he'd love being here with me in Birmingham and spending time with all these grand and great-grand nieces and nephews. He'd love it."

After finishing her soup, she was ready for bed. "I just hope I can make it through the night without falling out of bed," she said.

"Have you been falling out of bed?" I asked.

"No, not while I'm sleeping. But I have been falling trying to get out of bed to get into the wheelchair or up to the bathroom with the walker." I noted her caretakers had a portable commode by the bedside.

"Do you have to work your way all the way into the bathroom?" I said.

"No, but I hate going next to the bed. If I can get up and go, that's what I'm going to do," she said. "So now, before I retire, I'm going to take one good lap around the condo, and I don't want anyone to help me," she said to the great alarm of both myself and her caretaker. As she started to rise, she waved off her caretaker.

"Now let me do this on my own," she demanded. He relented and backed away.

"Well, I don't care what you say, I'm not letting you walk these halls alone. So go ahead, but I'm right here behind you. You remember what happened earlier today, right?" I insisted.

"Oh, don't be so sanctimonious," she said. "All right, come on. Keep close."

She completed one lap and actually fared quite well. Her stride was even and balanced, and she kept her eyes straight ahead. When we got back to the bedroom, her caretaker was there to take her through the diabetes routine and to help her with her medicines.

"You know what you should do, John?" she said.

"What, Elaine?"

"You should play something on this goddamned piano. It never gets played. You should play something to serenade me to sleep. What do you say?"

"Well, I will if that's what you'd like," she said.

"Oh, good, how divine."

So as Elaine and her caretakers were busying themselves with her evening ablutions, I tickled her ivories a bit. I started out with some simple jazz improvisation just to try to help wind the evening down and because I didn't have any music with me. Finally, after things in the bedroom had settled, I played a little bit of Pachelbel's Canon in D, thinking its gentle, repetitive quality would be soothing. Sensing quiet in the bedroom, I brought the piece to a cadence hoping I'd serenaded Elaine to sleep. As I finished and stood up from the bench, I heard Elaine shout from the bedroom, "That was divine, darling! But don't stop now, I was just getting relaxed."

Not being a very skilled piano player and not having a wide repertoire of music I could play from memory, I play a few musical theatre ballads and repeated some of the jazz improv. Eventually I finished, and all was quiet in the condo. I headed to the guest room myself wondering if Michael Feinstein had ever made it out for a visit yet and imagining the music he would have played for Elaine.

* * *

The next day, Elaine rose around 1:00 p.m. and came out to the kitchen for a scrambled egg. Elaine and her caretaking team had a master calendar upon which all of Elaine's appointments, medical and social, were kept. I saw that Elaine was planning a trip to New York in mid-February.

"Are you going to New York?" I asked.

"Yes," she squealed, "for the release of *Shoot Me.* A few of these guys are going with me," she said, referring to her caretakers, "as well as one of my new neighbors. Just what I need, a goddamned entourage going with me to New York."

"When's the surgery?" I asked.

"February 24," she said. "That's a Monday, and I'll be coming back the day before on Sunday."

I thought to myself, *She's crazy. She's going to need time to recover from the trip before she goes in for the surgery*, but I didn't say a word.

"Do you have a lot of plans for your time in New York, or will you be able to take things easy?" I asked.

"Well, we'll have lots to do. I'm going to visit my dentist, my doctor, and my lawyer while I'm there, and I'm sure there will be press gigs if I want to do them. I'm supposed to do a talk at 92nd St. Y. And I know people will want to visit with me."

"Where are you staying, at the Carlyle?"

"Are you kidding? Who can afford the Carlyle?" she said. "I'm staying at the Lotus Club on Sixty-Sixth," she said. "I'm an honorary member," she said.

The Lotus Club started as a private gentlemen's club in the late 1800s catering to literary and artistic types. Over time, the club began admitting women. Past members have included Gilbert and Sullivan, Orson Wells, and Stephen Sondheim. Elaine was given one of their infamous "state dinners" in 2012 and was granted honorary lifetime membership, which means that you can reserve lodging free of charge.

"Well, I suspect that will be a good way to distract you from the surgery," I said.

"God, I hope so," she said.

"Well, and with *Shoot Me* premiering, I'm sure there will be lots of excitement."

"Yeah, probably. The *Today Show* called and wants me."

"Oh god, you'll have to get up early for that," I said.

"No, for Kathie Lee and the other gal. They come on later."

"Yeah, but not much later," I said.

"My decorator might fly in too. One more for my entourage. Oh, and he might bring his boyfriend, oh what's his name. He's so short you can't find him," she said, sending me into a gale of laughter. "You want to come?" she asked.

"Well, as much as I think *Shoot Me* is going to be very well received, I think you've got plenty of people to assist you, so I think I'll pass. And besides, school will be in session, so I'll have to teach," I said.

There was a knock at the door.

"Who's that?" Elaine asked. "You look like my neighbor," she said.

"It is your neighbor. Hi Elaine," she said.

"Oh, it's you, darling. Hi," Elaine said.

I was taken with this moment of uncertain identity. It was another quick slip of mental acuity. Not a surprise for someone of Elaine's age, but given that she was typically so sharp and witty, little moments of mental failing like this, even one that passed momentarily, illuminated her decline.

Elaine's neighbor brought by a copy of the online version of the interview column of *The New York Times Magazine.* Apparently Elaine had conducted an interview earlier in the week, and a photographer had been dispatched to the Dakota to get a photo. The photo they used is one of Elaine wearing a white man's shirt over tights. She's sitting on her *Shoot Me* stool.

"John, read it to me," she said. I did.

"Well, what do you think?" I said.

"Oh, it's okay. Kind of bland if you ask me, and the last thing I am is bland. He cut the hell out of it. I knew they would. And they kill the humor when they do. I swear to God editors are witless."

"What have you got planned for your birthday next week?" I asked.

"I turn eighty-nine this year," she said.

"Yes, I know, that's why I asked."

"Chiemi is coming in, and all my staff is coming over, and we're going to have a nice, quiet dinner party. Can you stay?"

"Unfortunately no, I have to get back to work."

"Well, too bad for you then," Elaine said. "We're going to have chocolate cake, and banana bread, and my new hairdresser, Yanni, is coming over early to do my hair. It's going to be a party. Sorry you'll miss out, mister."

Later in the afternoon, Haresh came by for a physical therapy appointment. Elaine brightens up with Haresh and tries to really give him her best. Afterward, she was feeling pretty good, and she asked me to accompany her on a walk around the block.

"If you feel up to it," I said.

"We'll take the walker, and between that and knowing you're with me, I think we should try it. It looks pretty good out there," she said, noting the bright January sunshine and somewhat milder temperatures.

Elaine lives on a rather large block, so I anticipated we'd walk up to the corner and back. To my surprise, she wanted to go all the way around. While we walked, Elaine talked about wanting to get her strength and balance back well enough to walk in New York unassisted. At one point, she had me fold up the walker and carry it on one arm while she held on to the other. She managed quite well.

"You know, you're doing pretty darn good, Elaine," I said.

"Not bad," she said. "If I can help it, I don't want to have to go to New York in a wheelchair."

Elaine stopped, and as she often would on the streets of New York, she turned her face up to the sun and soaked in the expanse of the sky.

"God, the sun feels good, especially in January," she said.

"Even in Michigan?" I asked.

"Especially in Michigan."

As we walked, we talked about her memory.

"At times it gets really bad," she said. "I think I'm coming to the end."

"The end of what?" I asked, assuming she meant her performing career.

"The end of pretend," she said. And then after a pause, "Isn't that the best word ever—*pretend*. All my life I've been living in that world, trying to get *to* something or *away* from something. I don't know. But the curtain's coming down." She paused again and then said, "You know one of my favorite parts of living a life in the musical theater?" she asked.

"No, what?"

"After the curtain call when we're walking back to the dressing room, flying high 'cause the show was good, I loved listening to the orchestra play the exit music…helping everybody, actors and audience, make their way back to reality. The end of pretend for the night. Well, now I'm in the end of pretend for my life. But I'm not sad about it. No boo-hoo. I just sense it."

"Does it scare you?" I asked.

"A little bit, you know with the surgery coming up and all, but I feel like I'm living it, it's not passing me by and I'm not fighting it. I'm making friends with it."

"That's a good way to put it," I said.

"Yep, I'm making friends with this end of pretend. God, I love that word."

When we got back to the condo, Elaine ordered a cosmo. When delivered by her caretaker, however, things turned ugly.

"What's this," she said.

"It's your cosmo, just like you like it," her caretaker said.

"It's not like I like it!" she shouted. "What's this?" she repeated, referring to the lime that was floating in the drink.

"It's a lime," her caretaker said.

"I've told you a thousand times that I don't want lime juice in my cosmopolitans anymore."

"I didn't put any of the lime juice in," her caretaker said.

"What the hell are you talking about? There's a fucking lime floating in the glass," Elaine said, growing more enraged.

"But I didn't squeeze it. It's just floating in there"

"What the fuck is inside the lime?" she said, challenging her caretaker's intelligence.

"Lime juice—but I didn't squeeze it, so the juice is not in the drink."

"But it's in the glass, and it will be eventually release into the drink, which means I'll taste it, and I don't want it. What is so hard to understand?" Elaine demanded.

Her caretaker relented. "I'll make you another one without any lime whatsoever."

"That would be nice. And can we all just agree that I won that one," Elaine said.

I wondered if this exchange and Elaine's final line was hinting that perhaps other points of disagreement had been growing more frequent in the house. If so, and given the momentary lapses in Elaine's memory, it's possible that as caretakers or friends were asserting points with Elaine, perhaps Elaine was feeling like people were second-guessing or overpowering her. Elaine demands primacy at all times.

With the lime-less cocktail in place, we settled into a reading of *The New York Times*, which contained an announcement that Meryl Streep would play the witch in the movie version of *Into the Woods*.

"I am so sick of hearing about all the roles that Meryl Streep is playing," she said. "You'd think there were no other talented actresses out there. Why is everyone so obsessed by Meryl Streep?"

I was interested in exploring this line of thought. "Well, I think most people feel that the body of work she has created over time is pretty impressive."

"So what?" Elaine said. "There are other actresses who have created impressive bodies of work."

"Well, I can't think of any who have a record of work that shows such range."

"Oh, come on. You haven't really studied good actors," she said. "Most of the people who have grown up in your lifetime aren't that good. The really good actors all have a line of great roles."

"Well, you're certainly right that modern acting is for shit. It's all about some stupid sense of false celebrity," I said.

"You got that right," Elaine said.

This got me thinking about Elaine. What were her strengths as an actress?

The most distinguishable characteristic she possesses is her personality—direct, honest, and unapologetic. Those qualities give her an undeniable force as an actress. No matter the role, the thrill of seeing Elaine perform is how her natural persona gets morphed and worked into the character. Certainly her fan base has coalesced around her persona. Some would say she's as entertaining in life as she is on stage.

Continuing on with the *Times*, I read an article about the troubles the recent Broadway production of *Spiderman* was experiencing with actors getting injured due to the rigging system used to simulate Spiderman's flight. We began talking about Julie Taymor, the director who had been released from the production.

"Who?" Elaine said.

"Julie Taymor, you know the same director of…," I started to say.

"Oh yeah, the dumb musical with the animal heads," she said. So much for her lapsing memory!

CHAPTER 15

I n mid-February, I kept my eye on news of Elaine's trip to New York for the premiere of *Shoot Me*. I was hoping she was managing okay and enjoying the attention.

She did indeed visit the *Today Show* with Kathie Lee Gifford and Hoda Kotb. She was wearing her brown sable coat and matching hat.

Elaine and the infamous brown fur hat that had gone missing.
Credit: NBC NewsWire

I was relieved to see the hat had been found and curious as to whether it had indeed been left in the New York vault, been sent to the Birmingham vault, or was somewhere in the condo. Elaine was in her wheelchair, and during the segment, she had her white sneakered feet elevated, resting on Kathie Lee's lap.

Whether intentional or not, at one point during the interview, through an opening pried open by Kathie Lee in which she asked Elaine if her tendency to speak her mind had gotten her into trouble, Elaine said "fuck," and both Kathie Lee and Hoda reacted like someone had just ran nude across the screen. In watching the clip, I had to admit that I wasn't sure that Elaine didn't drop the F-bomb on purpose. She seemed to delight slightly in Kathie Lee and Hoda's reaction, and Elaine always had an uncanny way of keeping herself in the news.

The next day, Elaine attended the screening of *Shoot Me* at the Paley Center for Media. Alec Baldwin, who was the executive producer of the documentary, introduced the film and told loving and funny anecdotes about Elaine. The clips that appeared in the following days suggested that the screening resulted in very positive responses to the film, and Elaine seemed to genuinely enjoy the acclaim and attention. If one of the goals of the trip was to distract her from the upcoming surgery, it succeeded. And there is no better medicine for Elaine Stritch than an adoring crowd.

On the Sunday evening before her Monday surgery, I called Elaine to check in.

"Oh, hi, darling," she said.

"Hi, Elaine, how did your New York trip go?"

"Well, the truth is it nearly killed me. It was too much. I'm wiped out," she said.

"Well, it looks like the film was well received," I said.

"Oh, it was, they loved it. But I think I stayed too long. I came back yesterday, and tomorrow I go in for this surgery. You know about that, don't you? I have stomach cancer."

"Oh, yes, that's why I'm calling. I want to wish you well tomorrow. I know things will go smoothly, and I'll be looking forward to visiting with you again at the Dakota after a few weeks."

"No, better medicine than that, darling, I'm telling you."

I could sense hesitation in her voice. I suspected the reality of the surgery was settling in.

"Well, I'm not going to keep you, I'm sure you're exhausted, and you need a good night's sleep. I'll be saying a couple of prayers for you tomorrow and sending good energy your way," I said.

"Oh, do, please do. A couple of really good, strong prayers, John. I feel like I may need them."

* * *

The day after the surgery, I called one of Elaine's caretakers who I knew was going to be with her through most of the process. The report was mixed.

The surgery was successful. The general report to family, caretakers, and friends was that they were able to get all the cancer. Elaine was slow in coming out of the anesthesia and had suffered severe mental degradation in the process. She was slipping in and out of reality. And perhaps most imperative, Elaine was not eating. The report was that this was fairly normal and that hopefully, as the recovery advanced, she'd begin to eat and would finally be sent home.

I called back a few days later hoping to hear that Elaine was settled in to the routine of the hospital and was eating and was making progress toward release. That was not the case.

Elaine Stritch demands control in all things. Being in a hospital and being awakened for medicine and being told when and what to eat are not conditions that sit well with her. Her caretakers report that the situation became nightmarish for everyone.

Right after the surgery, her doctors decided to medicate her to keep her calm and comfortable so the initial recovery could begin. But Elaine battled with every nurse and doctor who came near her. The pain medicine was not strong enough for her. She was hurting and mad as a hornet. She was cursing at the staff, throwing food across the room, and pulling out her IVs. She was also falling into rather deep bouts of disorientation and became very paranoid that people were out to harm her. Her caretakers reported that, at one point, one of her doctors looked her straight in the eye and told her that if she didn't start listening and obeying their care orders, they would kick her out of the hospital and give the bed to someone who wanted to be healed. To that Elaine shouted, "Fuck you."

Of course, the other unspoken factor in this process was the fact that Elaine was also going through alcohol withdrawal.

Things got so bad that the doctors finally decided that all this anger and resistance was keeping her from healing, so they induced a coma and moved Elaine into the intensive care unit to put her under and let her body heal. She was in the ICU for about two weeks.

When they finally weaned her from the Propofol and attempted again to move her into recovery, she was as irascible as before. Her voice was gone, but her anger was at full volume. She was cursing and swearing and threatening to pull out the tubes and walk out on her own. Her friends, caretakers, and family members would attempt to calm and reason with Elaine, but to no avail. Her caretakers were on shifts so that she always had one of her private team with her twenty-four hours a day.

At first she was refusing to eat. The doctors countered with a threat that if she didn't eat, they'd have to feed her intravenously. They told her until she was eating and discharging she could not be released. The doctors pushed back on her hard and refused to be bullied. Eventually, they broke her, and she started to obey and eat.

And because she's smart and has always known how to turn people into resources, Elaine began to employ humor to reconcile with the staff. She used her wit and her ability to elicit laughter to help her win affection, control circumstances, and eventually, heal. Whether she knew it or not, Elaine was relying upon laughter as a healing agent, letting it release adrenal chemicals in the brain to help her move through the experience and, eventually, to go home.

* * *

Elaine was sent home in mid-March, about three weeks or so after the surgery, and the reports upon her return were encouraging. She was thrilled to be back at the Dakota. The doctors told her to expect another six weeks of recovery before she would go back to her normal self.

She was eating, although noticeably less than before the surgery. Along with her stomach, her appetite had been reduced. She was eating small meals more frequently throughout the day. She was slowly working her way into the wheelchair so she could move into the kitchen so as not to feel completely confined to the bed. Friends and family were stopping by wishing her well.

I called about a week after her release, and her caretaker said she wanted to say hi. She sounded weak, but reasonably spirited.

"Oh, John, you just don't know what I've been through. They tell me they got all the cancer, so I'm thrilled, but you just don't know what I've been through. They nearly killed me in there," she said.

I told her that, in the short time I've known her, she has always weathered these crises miraculously and that I was very happy to hear the surgery achieved its aims and that she was home.

"When you coming to visit, darling?"

"Tell you what, I'll give you another week at home and then I'll call and we'll see if we can't find a time in the week or so after that. I want to make sure you have time just to be home and get stronger," I said.

* * *

Because of work commitments, I actually wasn't able to get to Michigan to visit with Elaine for about five weeks or so after she returned home from the hospital. While I was disappointed not to get to see her sooner, I was hopeful that I would find her stronger and fully recovered from the trauma of the surgery.

I arrived at the Dakota with my usual long-stem white lilies. Elaine was sitting up in her bed. She looked considerably thinner, especially in her arms and legs. Those endless gams began to look thin and twiglike. Much of the muscle tone was gone. It was clear she had been through a major medical procedure, one of those procedures that significantly impacts one's appearance. For the first time, Elaine looked frail and vulnerable.

As I entered, her hair was a bit disheveled, and she seemed to be searching for vision, moving her head around to make sure she was placing her subject in her increasingly limited line of vision. She seemed slightly disoriented as her caretaker announced that I had arrived.

When she finally got me into her line of sight, she said, "Oh my god, you're a sight for sore eyes. Come here, darling, it's been too long, John, just too long. You look pretty good," she said, seeming a bit more anchored. I took her hand and squeezed it tight and looked into her eyes.

"Well, you look a little thinner, but not too much worse for the wear," I said.

"Not *too* much, eh?" she said. "You sure know how to flatter a girl. What did you bring me?"

"White lilies," I said, "for your washbasin."

"Oh, good," she said. "But don't put them in the washbasin, put them in a vase and set it on the kitchen table. We'll be out there tonight—for dinner." Surprised, her caretaker stopped and gave me a look as if to say *"I'm so glad you're here, this is what she needs."*

I sat next to the bed, and she recounted the tale of the hospital visit. "The surgery was a breeze," she said. "The recovery was a fucking nightmare. You have no idea what I went through."

"Well, how are you now?" I asked.

"Well, I'm doing pretty good now. I'm feeling pretty much back to normal. All the plumbing is working."

"Are you getting up and about?"

"A little. But I'm so sore. My body is just so sore. I've been in the wheelchair a bit. Getting out into the kitchen. But I've been sleeping a lot, darling. More than usual, and you know I always sleep an awful lot anyway."

"Well, that seems right," I said. "I mean you've just come through a major operation, and the recuperation has been long. Your body is craving sleep as part of the healing."

"I guess so. But oh boy, am I glad to see you," she said.

Just then, there was a knock at the door, and bounding into the bedroom comes a brown long-haired dachshund followed by a young woman named Jody. The dachshund jumped up on the bed and was warmly greeted by Elaine.

"My god, who's this?" I asked.

"Oh, this is the newest member of the family. Julie and Chiemi got him for me. His name is Marshall Bay. That was John's middle name—Marshall," she said. "And this is Jody, she's my dog walker, and she's training the little bastard to stop peeing all over the fucking place."

"He did well today, Elaine. We're close to having him trained and under control," Jody said.

"Oh yeah, that's what you think, he crapped on the dining room rug yesterday, so I'd say we still have work to do. Isn't that right," she said, rubbing Marshall's head, "you little twit."

As I watched the interactions during this two-day visit, it was clear that Marshall's presence had brought a great deal of pleasure and calm to the house. The staff, her family and friends, and Elaine especially, all seemed to enjoy his presence.

Knowing that *Shoot Me* was scheduled to premiere in Birmingham in early April, I asked her if she had been able to attend.

"Yes, of course. It wasn't easy, but I was there," she said. "They loved it. Listen, I think it's going to do very well. There's even talk of an Oscar. Wouldn't that be something?" she said.

"You bet," I said.

"Yeah, now I just have to make it through the rest of 2014 to see if we get nominated," she said.

* * *

After a little more conversation, Elaine began to doze off. I let her sleep and had a chance to speak with her caretaker who told me that Elaine was doing very well considering how things went in the hospital. Apparently, there was very serious concern that Elaine might not make it through the recovery process. But since she's been home, she had gotten most of her spirit back and has proven to be as demanding as ever.

"That's a good sign," I said.

I also found out that Elaine fell near the end of April trying to get up out of bed on her own. She was transported to the hospital where they diagnosed another pelvic fracture. I was struck by the fact that Elaine hadn't mentioned this earlier. That's apparently why she was complaining of feeling so sore. Just like the first pelvic fracture, there was little they could do but tell her it would take four to six weeks to heal on its own.

I also found out that Elaine was scheduled to appear and sing for an induction ceremony for the Michigan Celebrity Hall of Fame on May 2. Rob Bowman and her friend Julie Keyes and her hair and makeup artist Bella Botier were flying in. Elaine's family was going to attend. Obviously, with the fractured pelvis, she wasn't feeling up to the appearance, so she sent Rob, Julie, and Bella to accept the award for her. Another singer was engaged for the gala for whom Rob offered his services as the accompanist. Together, they attended to thank Michigan for inducting Elaine into its Celebrity Hall of Fame.

The schedule for Elaine's caretakers had changed significantly. Up to the surgery, their shifts were typically two or three days around-the-clock because Elaine didn't want to have to adjust every day to another caretaker. But given the increasing demands of her care needs, now her caretakers are spending no more than twenty-four hours with her so that they can get a break and not have to try to sustain the care level for forty-eight or seventy-two hours at a time.

Additionally, there was now a camera in Elaine's bedroom monitoring her movements to alert her team if she tried to move about on her own. The camera transmitted the picture to a portable monitor so the caretaker would always have visual contact on Elaine.

I also discovered that just a few days before I arrived, Elaine was taken to the hospital with a bout of dehydration. They kept her two days and gave her IVs to get fluids into her. She was unhappy and cranky, and because of the reputation she now has with the hospital, they were eager to get her discharged and send her on her way.

* * *

After her nap, Elaine got into the wheelchair and worked her way into the kitchen. The maneuver came with lots of pain and discomfort and wailing and shouting. But she was determined. I helped where I could with the transporting and noted for myself that there didn't seem to be a consistent system in place about how to safely move her to and from the wheelchair. I wondered if each caretaker was simply winging it. And to their defense, Elaine often would dictate how she wanted the transport to go depending upon whatever position she was in at any given moment.

In the kitchen, Elaine asked for a cosmopolitan. "Just a little one, honey," she said to her caretaker. Haresh, her physical therapist, was scheduled to come for a visit, and "My joy juice helps lubricate the joints, if you know what I mean," she said.

About an hour later, Haresh arrived, and they went back to the bedroom. He was going to work with her as she lay down on the bed. Through the monitor, I could watch the session. As he always had been, Haresh was very good with her, working on range of motion and stretching exercises. She would cry out in pain, but it was her way of fighting through.

"Don't mind me," she said, "I just have to yell at the fucking pain."

As she always had, after her workout, she was energized. She came back into the kitchen and wanted to order takeout from the Italian restaurant around the corner. We ordered eggplant parmesan and "finely chopped" salad.

I was curious to see how Elaine would eat. She ate a bit of her eggplant parmesan and did not spit her food out. But she didn't eat much. She sipped her cosmopolitan over dinner but didn't drink much of it at all. There was no second round. Her caretaker told me that since the surgery, she only sips the cocktail and is consuming far less alcohol. The general feeling was that, having gone through withdrawal in the hospital, she no longer felt the urge to be perpetually buzzed.

Her caretaker also told me Elaine had been battling a urinary tract infection. She also had a recent ultrasound done on the bladder to see if she was having bladder spasms. The report was that something was found on the ultrasound and they were all waiting to find out what it might have been. Her caretaker feared it might be more cancer.

Throughout the visit, there was noticeable deterioration in Elaine's cognitive function. She would occasionally slip into momentary dementia-like confusion, inserting words that made no sense in the context of the thought she was communicating. Elaine hated feeling unsure or confused.

What was particularly interesting was that when she would fall into a moment of confusion, she didn't respond the way Elaine would typically respond, that is, by fighting to get through the memory lapse. Elaine always fought back strong when her memory betrayed her. Now when she lapsed, she just lingered in the confusion, consigned to defeat, until it passed on its own. The absence of her fight was most telling.

I read a bit from the *Times*. A notice about Kristin Chenoweth starring in a coming revival of the musical *On the Twentieth Century* elicited a "Who's that?" from Elaine. I told her she was the petite blonde who starred as the good witch in *Wicked*. "She also starred with Matthew Broderick in the recent television revival of *The Music Man*. She's got a fabulous voice. She can belt, she can sing legit opera, you name it."

"Well, I have no idea who she is," Elaine said. "And why she'd want to star in *On the Twentieth Century* is beyond me."

I read to her about James Levine's recent return to the Metropolitan Opera.

"Oh, I'm so happy to hear he's back. He's been having a tough time. They didn't know if he'd ever conduct again," she said. Elaine thanked me for taking the time to read the paper to her. "I have no vision left in my right eye and hardly any in my left," she said.

"You miss reading."

"Oh my god, you have no idea. Being able to read, opening my mail, all of it. It's a very vulnerable feeling when you don't have your sight. I've always enjoyed reading. I miss it," she said. "The arts pages, the society pages, the style pages."

I sensed that Elaine was slipping into a bout of depression. All of a sudden, she became harder to engage. She would sit and just stare ahead.

"I noticed you didn't eat much of your dinner, Elaine. Do you have your appetite?"

"I have my appetite, darling, but after I eat, I don't feel good in my stomach," she said. "You know they removed 40 percent of my stomach, don't you? I just eat small bits throughout the day."

Partly to change the subject and distract her and partly because I'd been wanting to bring it up, I showed Elaine a YouTube clip wherein she was singing "Something Very Strange" from *Sail Away* on the *Rosie O'Donnell Show*.

The song lyric refers to a woman surprised that, finally, something good was coming to her in life. Being in her seventies when she performed it on Rosie's show, the lyric carried more weight. And given that it was being sung by Elaine, who always seemed to be searching for the penultimate moment in a career of many highs and lows, her performance of the song was particularly poignant.

"I think this is a real fine performance, Elaine."

"Yeah," she said, "not too bad."

"When I watch this, I see an actress who knows how to work against the obvious meaning of the lyric. If the lyric suggests sadness or regret, she knows to keep it light until just the right moment. And then, for only an instant, she allows the character's vulnerability to break through, almost as if by denying it for most of the song, the pressure builds and it comes bursting out. And then, the actress, wisely, reins in the vulnerability with a sense of 'oh well, life is tough for us all. No crying about it."

"Well, I think that's a good observation. Crying is never very interesting to me. When I see someone cry on stage, that rarely affects me. But watching someone try not to cry, and lose control, and then pull it back in, well, that's a hell of a lot more interesting, don't you think? That's what we do in real life," Elaine said.

"That's it. It's what we do in real life, and so that actor's work rings truer. As an audience member, it feels more real," I said.

"One of my greatest gifts—if talent is a gift, and I think it is—is that I have always known exactly what an audience needs. I can't explain it, I just feel it while I'm doing it, and I know how to make sure they get what they need. And I watch other people work, and even though they may be incredibly talented, I don't really feel as if they need me or care about me as they do their thing. It leaves me unattached," Elaine said.

"Like who?"

"Oh, I don't know. Well, okay, I feel that way about Audra McDonald."

"Audra McDonald, really!" I said.

"Oh, sure, she's got a great voice, but I never feel like she needs me. Her performances leave me cold," she said.

I really enjoyed talking about acting with Elaine. It's a hard thing to talk about, to put words to, but when we did, it was always fun. And I think Elaine enjoyed it because, inevitably, it was flattering to her. She knew she was in the presence of someone who observed her work with great care.

Our visit turned, as it often did, into a songfest. She'd bring up an old standard, almost as if to test me to see if I knew it. More than I care to admit, I didn't know the song. But when I did and could volley the lyrics back at her, we'd sing away. It was a real treat, and I especially enjoyed it this night since she had been feeling a little low and singing seemed to revive her spirit.

A stack of mail was waiting. "Open my mail for me, John," she said. She received two royalty checks from the actors' union. "How much are they for?" she asked.

"One for $5.09 and one for $13.65," I said, surprised by the small amounts.

"I'll take them. Every little bit helps," she said. "Give 'em here and I'll put them in the royalty check pile."

Next, we worked our way through a stack of cards and letters from fans. Liz Smith continued to report on Elaine's health in her column, which spurred a resurgence in Elaine's fan mail. Elaine seemed to enjoy the cards and the nice wishes people were sending her. One card included a photo of Elaine at the age of eighteen, sitting in New York's Central Park reading a letter. Her bicycle is in the shot behind her. She was wearing a halter top and a pair of shorts, a very short pair of shorts.

Elaine disturbing the peace in Central Park.
Credit: *New York Daily News* Archive

The sender also included the newspaper clipping that stated that Elaine had been cited by the NYPD for appearing in the park in such revealing attire with the judge quipping that her appearance was enough to "incite a riot." To which, Elaine pled guilty, paid a $1 fine and said, "I was there all day and nothing happened."

"Oh my god, look at that. Isn't that great?" Elaine said, getting a kick out of this photo and the clipping. It took her back and seemed to remind herself of someone long forgotten. She turned quiet, lost in memory or nostalgia, staring straight ahead.

"It all goes so fast, John. That time, I hardly remember that, but I know it's me. It all goes so fast."

At that, Elaine began to wither as a cloud of sadness set in again. We sat quietly, not really saying anything. I was careful to not try to make the moment anything other than what it was. But Elaine eventually tried to snap herself out of it.

"Why don't we just change the outlook?" she said. "Right now, just change it. Let's look at life differently." With that a smile came over her face, and that energy began to twinkle again in her eyes.

"Sounds good to me, what can I do to help?" I said.

"Dye your hair," she said. "You're too young to be turning gray."

"Hey, hey, now watch it," I said. "I am anxiously waiting for my hair to turn all white like Anderson Cooper."

"You don't want to be like Anderson Cooper," she said.

"I wouldn't mind looking like Anderson Cooper, he's a good-looking guy," I said.

We playfully bantered back and forth for a few more minutes, and then her malaise settled back in.

After a moment of deep silence, I asked her, "What can I do for you, Elaine? What can I get you? Would you like a shoulder massage?"

She smiled and nodded. So I got up and began rubbing her shoulders and neck and head, which she seemed to enjoy, moaning with pleasure. She quipped, "Oh, John, marry me. I know your wife, she's a lovely woman, I'm sure she wouldn't mind sharing you."

As I rubbed her shoulders, I thought maybe what she needed was the power of touch, someone to lay hands in an attempt to make her feel better. Her shoulders were very bony, the weight loss painfully evident. As I massaged her shoulders, I thought about all the change she has endured in the past year. Just as Elaine wanted to "look at life differently" to avoid feeling down, I thought about how Elaine has always controlled her emotional landscape. Unpleasantness and obstacles were faced by barking or buying her way around them. Elaine always positioned herself so that others would deal with the disagreeable elements of life for her. Living in hotels was part of this. Whenever a problem would arise, she could just pick up a phone and have someone else take care of it.

But her return to Michigan meant that she had to face things squarely and directly. The problems of a homeowner had become hers. Health issues and establishing and paying for in-home care forced reality upon her. So much of the precious control, even if contextualized in denial, that she wielded in her life had been slowly wrestled away. Her rather sheltered and pampered lifestyle had come crashing down, and no amount of positive thinking or mere denial was sufficient in fending it off.

After the back rub, Elaine was ready to retire to her bedroom. She didn't request a follow-up meeting. I suspected sleep was going to settle in pretty deep with her this night. I said my goodbye and told her I'd be rising early in the morning but that I'd call again soon for another visit. I felt compelled not to wait—a sense of urgency had emerged.

CHAPTER 16

Even with the sense of urgency I was feeling, it was another six weeks before I was able to visit with Elaine. I had called every couple of weeks to check in, and she always urged me to visit. Her excitement pleased me because it made me feel she was still engaged and seeking interaction and stimulation. After my last visit, I had feared she might be on a path toward isolation, surrounding herself with just caretakers and family.

When I arrived, she was asleep and the condo was very quiet. Marshall Bay was still prowling the roost and seeking affection from everyone who stopped by. The old Hollywood movies, Elaine's constant soundtrack, had been replaced with easy listening music from a satellite radio station. Instrumental versions of old standards and Broadway show tunes gently provided constant, if subdued, musical accompaniment, giving the condo a rather sedate quality.

I sat and talked with Elaine's caretakers. There were now two people on every shift. I learned that since my last visit, there had been a couple of less serious falls. It had become apparent that a single caretaker was not able to attend to Elaine's cooking, errands, and housekeeping needs while also ensuring the degree of supervision needed to keep her from falling. So now, one caretaker remained stationed in her bedroom while the other attended to the various needs of the house.

The sad but not particularly surprising news is that Elaine was now under hospice care. One night a few weeks back, when one of her caretakers was in her bedroom with her and the other was in the guest room sleeping, the caretaker with Elaine woke the other caretaker reporting that he needed to leave for a brief respite to let his dog out at his home. As the other caretaker came in to Elaine's bedroom to spell the first caretaker, he did a quick check on Elaine and found that her sugar level was up to 500 and her eyes had rolled back into her head. A 911 call was immediately placed, and the EMS team arrived to provide immediate care and to transport Elaine to the hospital. One of Elaine's neighbors was awakened and rode in the ambulance.

On the way to the hospital, the EMS rider in the ambulance who was in the back with Elaine called up to the driver and reported that her heart was racing at 150 beats per minute. The sirens were turned on as the ambulance sped to the hospital. The ambulance driver alerted Elaine's neighbor that when the ambulance pulled up to the hospital, she was to stay in the cab, that medical personnel would be running to the ambulance and not to be alarmed, but that this event with Elaine was now being treated not as a blood sugar event but rather a cardiac emergency.

The medical team was able to get Elaine's cardiac and blood sugar levels stabilized, and she was released after a couple of days. On her way out of the hospital, she announced to her doctor that she would have no more of hospitals. This led to a conversation about how Elaine's wishes could be honored.

Elaine was told that since her paid staff members were not medical personnel, the only way in which her directive of not approving transport to a medical facility could be honored would be for her to enter into hospice care.

Elaine was told that hospice care was not, contrary to what many people believe, engaged only in the final stages of one's life but that it can be engaged at any point once an end-of-life condition is diagnosed.

In Elaine's case, her paid staff had to be legally protected, and the best way to ensure their protection would be to have a hospice team in place so that if medical emergencies arose, the hospice team could be called to the house to provide necessary medical attention and supervision in the home. Her doctor told her that many people live months and sometimes years under hospice care. Whether or not that was true (it certainly didn't gel with what I learned about hospice care when I went through my mother's death process), it appeased Elaine, and that was how she elected to proceed.

Over the past few weeks, Elaine's health deteriorated. She was not on pain medicine other than Tylenol. She was eating very little. The care team had begun to encourage her to drink nutrition shakes in order to keep minimal nutrients in her diet. And she had lost more weight. Her arms and legs were very skeletal, and her shoulder blades and collarbones were poking through her T-shirt. Liz Smith posted an update in her column and implored Elaine, "Eat, Elaine, eat." It was clear that cards and letters had been streaming in. They lay stacked up and unopened. Her caretaker reported that she was sleeping days on end.

Today's caretaker, one of the most earnest of the group, reported that she was concerned that even though she felt Elaine wanted to be alert and engaged, perhaps Elaine was being kept on a steady dose of anxiety medicine to keep her calm and sedated. The caretaker reported that she had not given Elaine any of the anxiety medicine today in the hope that Elaine would be alert for my visit.

Elaine was sleeping in her bedroom. I went in to sit with her. I sat near the foot of the bed and rubbed her feet gently. They were twitching involuntarily as she slept. Her breathing was steady, and her face was calm in its sleep. Every once in a while she would moan slightly. I couldn't tell if it was in response to an ache or a pain or maybe some dream she was having.

After a while and with Elaine still asleep, I decided to take a walk down to the park and the creek. This had become a peaceful and reflective place for me. I took time to absorb the news that Elaine was on hospice care and to process her significant weight loss. Having lost my mother just three years ago, this time with Elaine was resonating deeply within me. I hoped her caretaker was right that she would rouse later in the day and we'd have a chance to connect.

When I got back to the Dakota, Elaine was sitting up in her wheelchair and drinking some orange juice.

"Who's that?" she asked as I walked into the bedroom.

"It's John," her caretaker said. "Remember, he's come to visit for a couple of days."

"Oh my god, of course. John, come here, darling, let me get a good look," she said.

She smiled broadly and seemed glad to see me, very glad to have a visitor. Her caretaker left us alone.

"God, you look good, but you've lost weight," she said. "Why don't you eat a milkshake now and then?"

"Well, you should talk," I said. "You look like you're not eating as much as you should."

"I eat, I just don't eat much. But tonight, we'll have a nice dinner."

Other than her painfully obvious weight loss, Elaine actually looked pretty good. He face was full and had good color. Her hair had recently been cut, rather short, and it looked very good on her. She was well rested and eager to talk.

I took her hand and said, "It's real good to see you, Elaine. You've been on my mind a lot."

She reached out to touch me, stroking my arm and leg from her wheelchair. She seemed to want touch. She grabbed for my eyeglasses, which we dangling from my shirt collar.

"What's that?" she asked.

"Just my glasses," I said.

"What's new?" she asked.

"Oh, not much. School is out for the summer. I had to step in and direct *The Music Man* at the university because a faculty colleague got sick," I said.

"Oh god, I hate the show," she said.

"Did you ever play Marian the Librarian?" I asked.

"Are you kidding, who would want to? It's got to be one of the most boring roles ever written," she said, sounding very much like her old self.

"I couldn't agree with you more."

"Oh yeah? Well, I'm glad we agree on something," she said.

As we continued to talk, I was taken aback as Elaine occasionally slipped in and out of reality, uttering an occasional nonsense word or some odd non sequitur. Again, I wondered if this was a result of the increased medications or just sleepiness. A permanent result of the anesthesia from the cancer surgery or just aging? I was glad to see that she didn't stay in this state for long. She snapped back quickly and was as sharp and witty as ever.

"You know I'm on hospice, don't you?" she said.

"Yeah, I just heard that today," I said.

"Well, I told them no more hospitals. I'm done with all that shit. So they said the only way to pull that off was to agree to hospice, so I said, what the hell."

"Are you feeling okay?" I asked.

"Well, I've got a boatload of aches and pains. And getting in and out of bed and into the wheelchair hurts like hell. But otherwise, I'm doing okay, darling. At least I think I'm doing okay. The hospice chaplain stopped by today, and I sent him away. I hope he doesn't know something I don't," she said.

"My mom was on hospice care for quite a while, and the chaplain would stop by regularly just to check in. I don't think it implies that anything is impending," I said.

"God I hope not. And I hope he doesn't come too often, if you know what I mean," she said.

"I do, indeed I do," I said. "Well, you look pretty great. You've got good color, and I like your hair short like this."

"Yeah, I do too," she said. "Hand me the mirror. Yeah, not too bad, considering. Well, let's see if we can't get ourselves out to the kitchen."

With that, her caretakers came into the bedroom. "I want another pillow on this chair, it's too goddamn hard on my backside," she said.

In order to get her transferred onto the bed so the chair could be padded, her male caretaker, a rather beefy young guy, approached and said, "Okay, do you want to put your arms around my neck?" to which Elaine said, "Oh my god, there's that line again."

Classic Stritch.

* * *

As we worked our way to the kitchen, the caretaker who shared her concern that perhaps Elaine was being sedated more than necessary tagged along with me and indicated that Elaine's desire to get up, to go into the kitchen, and to eat a meal was further evidence that Elaine is able to be more active than perhaps she was being permitted. While I was glad to find that Elaine was indeed able to be up and mobile, I was upset at the thought that she might be automatically receiving medication intended to be used on an as-needed basis.

We settled in around the kitchen table. She asked for "some joy juice—a short one." Her caretaker announced that the dinner menu would be roasted chicken and gravy, a sweet potato, and some broccoli. "Sounds divine," she said anticipating the meal. Her caretaker smiled broadly.

"Here, read me the *Times,* John," she said.

"There's a new high-powered revival of Edward Albee's *A Delicate Balance* headed for Broadway this fall," I announced.

"You're kidding? Who's in it?" she asked.

"Glenn Close and John Lithgow," I said.

"Who's playing Claire?"

"Uh, looks like Lindsay Duncan," I said.

"Who's that?"

"I don't know," I confessed. "So what do you think?"

"Well, I think Glenn will be pretty good. I don't think Lithgow is right, he's a funny guy but he'll go for the gags, and that will kill that show," she said.

"I'm sorry I never had a chance to see you in the play."

"Oh, I am too, John. That was the best work I ever did."

After working our way through the newspaper, I made my way through another hefty stack of fan mail. One card came with a bulge in it. I opened it up to find a polished black rock.

"What the hell is that?" Elaine asked.

"It's a rock, Elaine."

"A rock?"

"Yep, a rock. Do you want me to read the letter?"

"Well, I think you better," she said.

"Dear Elaine Stritch, I have admired your work for many years. I saw you in *Sail Away*…"

"Oh my god, he goes way back," she interrupted.

"And have been a fan ever since. I've attended the New York theater for many years and always brought a polished rock to give to the stars of the productions. I've given them to Lauren Bacall, Katherine Hepburn, Jerry Orbach, Ethel Merman, and Angela Lansbury. I tried to get one to you after *Show Boat* in the early nineties but didn't see you at the stage door. I've been reading about your recent health issues and wanted to finally send you this rock. Thanks for the many great memories over the years."

"Well, it's nice of him to want to send it to me. It obviously means more to him that it does to me. What am I supposed to do with a rock," she said. "Where does he live?"

"In Pt. Ewen, New York," I said.

"You mean Pt. Huron," she said, correctively.

"No, it's Pt. Ewen," I said.

"There is no Pt. Ewen, it's Pt. Huron," she said, thinking we were referring to a city in Michigan.

"No, it's Ewen," I said. "E-W-E-N. In New York."

"Never heard of it," she said. "But they've got pretty rocks. Here, darling," she said, handing the rock to her caretaker, "throw this away."

I was glad at Elaine's attempt to correct me. Jousting with me over words was her feisty nature coming through. Elaine was always a careful listener. If you said something wrong, like a firm grammar instructor, she would call you on it and chide you for it.

Dinner was brought to the table. Elaine was hungry and ate well. She praised her caretaker on the cooking, and together we sat, enjoying the food and laughing and talking about her caretaker's young son and how he was doing in school. Elaine enjoyed the updates and seemed to enjoy playing surrogate grandma.

After dinner Elaine requested another back rub. I rubbed her shoulders gently, not finding much muscle. Unsatisfied with the depth of the touch, she barked, "Oh, come on, get in there."

I rubbed a little more forcefully, and she groaned in both pleasure and pain.

"Don't mind the groans," she said. "I have to release the pain, darling. It feels good, keep on."

As I continued the massage, Elaine talked about how, coming out of the stomach surgery, she needed to get her voice back, to sing, as a way to release the pain and feeling whole again. "Without your voice, you're shut down," she said, whimpering and groaning. "That's the worst feeling of all. So I sing and I yell, and that's just the way it is."

"I hear you," I said, rubbing a little harder.

"Oh, goddamn it, that's too hard," she said.

"Sorry," I said. "You want to sing?"

"Sure, start something," she said.

Standing there rubbing her shoulders, I started "The Little Things You Do Together" from *Company*. It seemed somewhat apropos.

It's the little things you do together,
Do together,
Do together,
That make perfect relationships.

It's sharing little winks together,

"No, that's not the next lyric," she snapped.

"Well, what is?" I asked.

"I don't know," she said.

"Well, I'm going on. Come on along," I said. She joined in with me.

It's sharing little winks together,
Drinks together,
Kinks together,

That make marriage a joy.

And then with relish, she leaned into

Uh-huh…
Kiss-kiss…
M-hm…

She loved these little impromptu singing sessions. I started a good old standby, "You're Not Sick You're Just in Love."
I don't need analyzing…
"That not the way it starts," she reprimanded. "It's '*you* don't need.'"
I restarted, and she joined right in.

You don't need analyzing
It is not so surprising
That you feel very strange but nice
Your heart goes pitter-patter
I know just what's the matter
Because I've been there once or twice

Put your head on my shoulder
You need someone who's older
A rubdown with a velvet glove
There is nothing you can take
To relieve that pleasant ache
You're not sick, you're just in love

We finished with a bit of flourish and a little harmony. And we laughed. Her caretaker watched as she was cleaning up the dinner dishes, and I could tell that there had been very little of this type of activity in the house for the past few weeks and she was glad to see Elaine up and talking and eating and singing.
"Do you like your voice, Elaine?" I asked.
"No, not really. I never have."

"But you love singing," I goaded.

"Oh yes, I love it. It's like flying," she said, echoing something she told my students when she first visited campus those years ago.

"You don't have to have a great, classically trained voice to tell a great story. My voice was never very pretty in the pure sense of the word. But I always had the ability to be truthful, and that, in my opinion, is what makes a great singer. Not everyone can be Renee Fleming," she said, referring to the opera singer. "And who would want to?"

Eventually, all sung out, Elaine retreated to the bedroom to rest, requesting my presence in an hour or so. As she got back to the bedroom and her attendant helped transfer her to the bed, there were lots of screaming and shouting. But eventually, things quieted down and the monitor projected the sound of some great old Turner Classic movie.

Elaine took a long, two-hour snooze. When she woke up and got her sugar levels checked and a refill on her cosmopolitan, she called for me to join her.

She had stumbled upon the movie version of Lillian Hellman's *The Children's Hour* starring Audrey Hepburn, Shirley MacLaine, and James Garner.

"You ever see this one?" she asked.

"No, but I've done the play."

"Oh really. Directed it?"

"No, I played Dr. Cardin."

"I could see you in the role."

"I wish you had," I said. "Is the movie any good?"

"Not bad. Shirley MacLaine is pretty good. And Jim Garner is playing your role," she said. "Now there's a good-looking man."

"Did you ever work with him?" I asked.

"No, but I would have liked to," she said. "I had my eye on him early on, but he eventually got married, and I think they've stayed married all this time. But I liked his looks and his sense of humor. He and I would have gotten along just fine." She paused. "But then I wouldn't have met John, so everything happens for a reason. Noel Coward always used to say that. 'Stritchie, everything is due its course,' he'd say. He told me *Goldilocks* was a flop so I could do *Sail Away*. Noel taught me to never worry about what might have been. Just keep focused on what might come next."

"Tell me about *Goldilocks*," I said, eager to cover the territory of her early career. Elaine's first leading role on Broadway was in 1958 in Walter and Jean Kerr and Leroy Anderson's *Goldilocks*.

"What's to tell? It was a flop, a total disaster," she said. "And that's when I met Noel. He came and saw the show and knew it was no good, but he thought I was talented, and he wrote *Sail Away* for me."

"Did you know while you were working on *Goldilocks* that it wasn't a good show?" I asked.

"On some level, you get a sense. But in this business, you don't really know until it opens and the critics chime in. And you never know about critics, sometimes they love the worst crap and hate really good work. And *Goldilocks* was interesting because the other critics seemed to enjoy slamming Walter Kerr."

Walter Kerr was a major theater critic in New York, eventually rising to the position of chief drama critic of *The New York Times*.

"But no, the show wasn't any good, and I really disliked working with Agnes de Mille," she said.

"Really? Why is that?" I asked.

"She didn't like me. I wasn't a trained dancer, and I questioned her on some of the movements she was giving me. We never got along, and I'm happy to report I never worked with her again.

"Noel saw it and decided then and there he wanted me for *Sail Away*. No, I was glad to get out of *Goldilocks* and move on to *Sail Away* with Noel Coward, if you know what I mean," she said. "And in *Sail Away*, I started as the comic lead, but when the romantic lead wasn't cutting it, he combined the parts, canned her, and gave it all to me. I loved it."

Noel had caught a September 1958 performance of *Goldilocks*. His diary entry stated:

> It was frankly one of the most idiotic, formless, amateur productions I have ever seen. The music

is entirely dull, the lyrics overburdened with effort and the book non-existent. The production is grandiose and fabulously expensive. It has already cost $500,000; Aggie deMille's ballets are not really good enough, and the cast, with the exception of Elaine Stritch, is lamentable.

Clearly Elaine made a deep impression. When Coward began work on *Sail Away*, he wrote the part of Mimi Paragon, the hapless cruise director, for her. And by all accounts, Stritch was a shining light.

"*Sail Away* was a big deal for you. Your first real Broadway splash," I said.

"Yeah, I think so. After *Goldilocks, Sail Away* was my real coming out. And I got both parts because an opera singer couldn't act, so there's another one in the win column for an actor who can sing."

But early in the rehearsal period, before the parts were combined, Coward wrote in his diary that Stritch was

> wildly enthusiastic and very funny. She will, I am sure, be wonderful as Mimi, but I foresee leetle clouds in the azure sky. She is an ardent Catholic, and has been "in analysis" for five years! Oh dear, a girl with problems. However, I think I shall be able to manage her. If I can, all will be fine and dandy, if not ze scenes zay will be terribile. I must engage an expert understudy.

The original romantic leading lady in *Sail Away* was to be played by opera singer Jean Fenn. When she began rehearsals, Coward wrote,

> I have taken a really immense liking to her. She is direct, simple, completely *un*tiresome and has taken the trouble to learn the part accurately… Her voice is perfectly glorious.…Elaine Stritch is

now my only problem.... Something tells me she may be going to be tiresome. She certainly has a reputation for it. I don't think bitchy and vile like some, but complicated and difficult.

While the show was in Boston for its out-of-town tryouts, it became clear that Fenn was miscast. In his diary, Noel Cowart wrote, "Fenn is beautiful, suburban, frigid and sings competently." He went on to write,

> What is awful for the poor bitch is that Stritch and the show are so strong that it really only matters to *her* [Fenn] if she comes across or not. She is cursed with refinement and does everything 'beautifully.' Oh dear, how I long for her to pick her nose or fart and before I am through with her, she'll do both.

Well, even Noel Coward couldn't work his magic. Fenn was fired, and the roles were combined and given to Stritch.

The show opened strong in New York. Two weeks after the New York premiere, in a letter to Elaine from Jamaica, Coward wrote,

> Darling Stritchie,
>   I hope you are well, that your cold is better; that you are singing divinely; that you are putting on weight; that you are not belting too much;... that you are delivering my brilliant material to the public in the manner in which it *should* be delivered; that you are not making too many God-damned suggestions; that your breath is relatively free from the sinful taint of alcohol.

"Tell me about Noel Coward," I said.

"He was divine. I adored him," she said. "The thing about Noel was that he got me. He didn't love everything about me, but he got me, and that meant a lot to me. He was one of the first really big players in this business that got me. And I felt okay with him. Safe."

It seems Coward did get Elaine. When *Sail Away* premiered in London, he took her with him. The show premiered at the Savoy Theater, and it was during this stint that Elaine first got a taste of the Savoy Hotel. Noel Coward put his leading lady up in grand style.

During the London rehearsal period he wrote,

> Poor darling Stritch, with all her talents, is almost completely confused about everything. She is an ardent Catholic and never stops saying fuck and Jesus Christ. She is also kind, touching and loyal and, fortunately, devoted to me. She is also, like most Americans, dreadfully noisy.

"He got me, and I loved him," Elaine said.

"And doing *Sail Away* in London was your first stay at the Savoy, right."

"Right, and I loved it. When I went over for *Company* and John and I got married and I stayed for *Two's Company*, John and I stayed at the Savoy."

"Did you like living in London?" I asked.

"I loved it. That was the best decade of my life. *Two's Company* was a big hit, and John and I loved being there. The city was classy, and we both were very well known. And the shopping, in Mayfair, oh boy, it puts Manhattan to shame. The English are so much more refined. John loved it. He'd go and spend nights in the pubs—all around London. And everyone he met became his best friend. And when he'd start his impersonations, forget about it. He had everyone in the place eating out of his hand. They loved his Groucho. He did Groucho better than Groucho."

"Did you and John ever meet Groucho?"

"John did. Groucho was in London for a BBC interview, and he went to the studio to meet him. John idolized everything about Groucho. Thought he was the best. You know, Groucho died just three days after Elvis died. In the London newspapers, they covered Elvis, but they didn't go crazy like they did in the States. When Groucho died, the London papers really paid him his due. John thought it was terrible how Elvis's death overshadowed Groucho in his own county. He always told me, 'Just make sure no one more important dies the same week you do.' John hated celebrity and fame and all that fake shit. That's one of the things I loved about him."

"He sounds like a great guy," I said.

"Oh, he was, darling, he was."

I asked Elaine about her favorite role over the years.

Without hesitation, she said, "Feste in Shakespeare's *Twelfth Night*. He was a clown—he drank and made people laugh. He was all comedy, and I am too. He has a great line, which I always thought was a perfect description of me, 'God give them wisdom that have it; and those that are fools, let them use their talents.' If that isn't how I made my way through life, I don't know what is."

* * *

The next morning, I got up early to make my exit. Typically, I would step quietly into Elaine's bedroom to wake her caretaker so that he or she could deactivate the alarm system and let me out. This morning, I tiptoed into the bedroom and tapped her male caretaker who was sleeping beside Elaine on the bed on the foot. He woke up and whispered that Elaine was awake.

"Her eyes are closed, but she's been awake for a while."

I approached Elaine on her side of the bed and gently called her name. She opened her eyes and said, "Good morning, John."

"Elaine, I'm heading out. I didn't want to wake you, but I'm glad you're awake so I can say goodbye."

"When you coming back?" she said.

"Not sure, but as soon as I can."

"Come anytime, you know that, anytime, darling."

I leaned in close and kissed her cheek. "I do. Keep eating, will you?" I said.

"I will if you will—have a milkshake now and then, why don't you?"

"I will. I love you, Elaine," I told her.

She grabbed my face and looked me in the eye and said, "I love you too. Now have a safe drive and call me when you get home so I won't worry."

I made my exit and sat in my car in front of the Dakota right across from her first-floor bedroom windows. Her first-floor bedroom glowed with the blue glow of some old movie playing on her television. I thought to myself that this might be the last time I would see Elaine. I thought back about this incredible journey I had taken with her and about all the ways she had influenced me.

With both gratitude and sadness, I drove away.

CHAPTER 17

Over the next two weeks, Elaine continued to lose weight, becoming more frail and weak. Her caretakers attended to her needs, and neighbors and friends were stopping by sensing that her time was coming to an end.

Chiemi Karasawa was with her for a few days, spending time, holding her hand, and talking with her. Elaine's breathing became labored and irregular. As it often does in the final stages of life, the breathing can be very deceptive. Those who were with Elaine reported that long pauses would pass between breaths to the point that they weren't sure if she had stopped breathing for good. But even through her last night, she kept on, without pain or fight.

On the morning of Thursday, July 17, Chiemi had to leave early to catch a flight back to New York. A few hours later, with her caretakers and a neighbor at her bedside, Elaine died.

News of her passing was picked up on most print and broadcast venues from New York to Hollywood. Her death was noted on the nightly news broadcasts of the three major networks and the cable stations.

The following day, the marquee lights on Broadway were dimmed as the New York theater community saluted Elaine with their highest honor.

Elaine's funeral was held in Chicago. It was a private ceremony for family and friends. Fitting for Elaine, the minister who presided included Broadway show tunes in the celebration and asked those in attendance to honor Elaine with something everyone agreed was her favorite sound: a round of applause.

As she had directed, she was buried next to John. Her portion of their shared tombstone listed her name and her birth and death dates. Underneath her name was her chosen counterpoint to the Groucho Marx quote "Hello, I must be going," which was, simply, "Later."

Oddly enough, two days later, James Garner died. And within three more weeks, both Lauren Bacall and Robin Williams passed away. Within the next month, Joan Rivers died. Each of them got a tribute cover on *People* magazine.

As Elaine predicted, she didn't.

1

About the Author

John Bell is an artist and arts administrator who has been providing leadership for undergraduate and graduate programs in dance, musical theater, opera, theater, and film for over three decades. He currently serves as the head of the division of performing arts at DeSales University. Prior appointments have included the University of Michigan-Flint, James Madison University, and the University of Central Florida. As a director, choreographer, actor, or conductor, professional credits include the Michigan Opera, Meadowbrook Theatre, Michigan Shakespeare Festival, Blue Ridge Theatre Festival, Virginia Opera, Orlando Theatre Project, and Orlando Shakespeare Theatre.

He has directed over one hundred productions, and his production of *M. Butterfly* garnered national recognition for his direction, choreography, and stage combat in the Kennedy Center / American College Theatre Festival. He served a professional internship on the world premiere of *Into the Woods* at the Tony Award–winning Old Globe Theatre. He coauthored *Music Theory for Musical Theatre (Scarecrow)* and contributed to *Playing with Theory (Palgrave)*. For more than a decade, he was a frequent contributor and guest editor for *The Sondheim Review* and *Everything Sondheim*. A composer and librettist, his musical *Rivers Run Deep* has been produced regionally, and his latest musical, *Making Home*, has been workshopped in New York.

CPSIA information can be obtained
at www.ICGtesting.com
Printed in the USA
LVHW041528081219
639814LV00005B/76/P

9 781644 627167